WRITING SUBURBAN CITIZENSHIP

Writing, Culture, and Community Practices Series
Steve Parks and Eileen Schell, *Series Editors*

Syracuse University Press is pleased to announce the launch of a new series, Writing, Culture, and Community Practices, with the publication of *Writing Suburban Citizenship: Place-Conscious Education and the Conundrum of Suburbia*. The series is distinguished by works that move between disciplinary identity and community practices to address how literacies and writing projects empower a population and promote social change.

WRITING SUBURBAN CITIZENSHIP

Place-Conscious Education and the Conundrum of Suburbia

EDITED BY ROBERT E. BROOKE

SU

Syracuse University Press

Syracuse, New York 13244-5290

First Edition 2015

15 16 17 18 19 20 6 5 4 3 2 1

∞ The paper used in this publication meets the minimum requirements of the American National Standard for Information Sciences—Permanence of Paper for Printed Library Materials, ANSI Z39.48-1992.

For a listing of books published and distributed by Syracuse University Press, visit www.SyracuseUniversityPress.syr.edu.

ISBN: 978-0-8156-3427-0 (cloth)
978-0-8156-3416-4 (paperback)
978-0-8156-5353-0 (e-book)

Library of Congress Cataloging-in-Publication Data

Available from the publisher upon request.

Manufactured in the United States of America

This book is dedicated to our colleagues in the Nebraska Writing Project and the National Writing Project: teacher-leaders are change agents, the last best hope for educational reform.

Contents

PART TWO

Writing from the Commonwealth

Claiming Local Place as a Cultural and Economic System

Illustrations

Figures

Tables

WRITING SUBURBAN CITIZENSHIP

Suburban Life and Place-Conscious Education

The Problem of Local Citizenship

ROBERT E. BROOKE

> The complexity of our present trouble suggests as never before that we need to change our present concept of education. Education is not properly an industry, and its proper use is not to serve industries, either by job-training or by industry-subsidized research. Its proper use is to enable citizens to live lives that are economically, politically, socially and culturally responsible.
>
> —Wendell Berry (2003a, 21)[1]

This book presents a challenge to American education. If education as a whole is to help create the citizenry necessary for the challenges of the century we've recently begun, then education needs to help students become more effective citizens. Citizenship, as we understand it, means more than just voting in (and kvetching about) presidential elections. We have in mind a more robust kind of citizenship, tied to the participatory traditions of our country, where active citizens take part in fostering and monitoring local communities, where citizens are witnesses and advocates for their region in national and international policy discussions. To create such a participatory citizenship, American education will have to immerse itself

1. Copyright © 2014 by Wendell Berry, from Citizenship Papers. Reprinted by permission of Counterpoint.

more effectively in the local communities where citizenship can be practiced and grown.

The authors of this book advocate for place-conscious education as the main way to create such participatory citizens. As teachers in the National Writing Project (NWP) have argued (Berdan et al. 2006; Brooke 2003; Robbins and Dyer 2005), children and young adults learn best when they actively connect their schoolwork to local concerns, when, that is, their schoolwork *matters* to them and to the community around them. At the college and university level, this same attention to community engagement is central to teachers committed to public rhetoric (Ackerman and Coogan 2010; Flower 2008; Rose and Weiser 2010; N. Welch 2008). In our *Rural Voices*, Nebraska Writing Project (NeWP) teachers summarized a main element of place-conscious education as follows: "Place conscious education centers schooling in a deep understanding of local place, spiraling outward to include more distant knowledge in all areas of the curriculum. While all people are certainly citizens of the world, place-conscious educators believe people learn to be active citizens by engaging with local issues, which they can actually affect and which directly influence the quality of life in their community" (Brooke 2003, 13).

Further, this book defines a particular kind of place as the crucial arena for place-conscious education: the suburban classroom. If the 2010 US Census and the geographers who study it are correct, more Americans now live in suburban spaces than anywhere else. In fact, in demographic terms the past century might well be named the century of suburban expansion (Beauregard 2006), a century in which Americans migrated to suburbs from small rural communities and from traditional urban centers in greater and greater numbers, creating what Robert Lang (2003) calls the edgeless cityscapes of today. Since the end of World War II, the constant population rise in this country has been in suburban living. It is in suburbia that most American youth are educated. It is in suburbia where the dominant modes of citizenship for the next century will be created.

And suburbia, as a location for place-conscious life and learning, is a particularly vexed space. The structures of suburbia (political, demographical, and architectural) make it hard to see connections between the suburban home and the region's peoples, environments, and history.

As geographer Jon Teaford (2008) points out, the cultural "myths" of the suburbs make suburbia itself hard to see. Contrary to the media's image of suburbia as a rich, white, prefabricated cul-de-sac of sameness (think *The Stepford Wives* or *The Swimmer*, the suburban image most denounced by critics like James Kunstler [1993, 2001] or Philip Langdon [1994]), there are so many kinds of suburbs, and so many different kinds of people living there, that generalizations rarely capture the full story. Instead, geographers point out three ongoing tensions or issues that illuminate suburbia.

Diversity and housing. With more than half of our nation living in suburbia, suburbia *as a whole* is remarkably diverse. As Teaford points out, there's a suburb for everybody. "There are straight suburbs and gay suburbs. There are suburbs for seniors and others for horses. Some suburbs are predominantly African American, others are overwhelmingly Hispanic, and still others are exclusively Anglo. . . . Nothing about suburbia precludes any form of endeavor or way of life. And as America becomes more suburban, the suburbs will continue to reflect the rich diversity of the nation" (2008, 218).

Yet *within* any single suburb, the residents are likely to be similar in lifestyle, class, and often ethnicity. To maintain this local similarity, the issue of housing—especially the percentage and definition of low-cost housing in any new development—remains the flash point and mechanism for self-selection of suburban residents. As Teaford puts it, "Municipalities make vigorous use of the zoning powers, excluding uses and people deemed detrimental to home values. . . . Though the nation has long given lip service to the ideal of equal opportunity, exclusionary zoning thwarts the efforts of some Americans to realize their desired place in suburbia" (159–60). Suburban life, thus, is routinely suspended between the astounding diversity of the region and the insularity of like-minded in the specific suburb.

Freedom/self-determination and responsibility. Geographers routinely point to suburban policy debates as test cases for contrasting American ideals of individual freedom and civic responsibility. As Goddard (2012, 164) points out, an acreage owner in an independent suburban community is curiously akin to Jefferson's ideal of the independent yeoman farmer, seeking life, liberty, and the pursuit of happiness alongside a spirited defense of individual property rights. At the same time, geographers such as Beauregard denounce the historical reality of white flight from urban civic responsibility as a "national shame." He writes, "The flight to the suburbs produced a moral divide. It created a spatial separation between one group of people—white, relatively affluent—and another, mostly non-white and poor. The separation that enabled suburbanites to avoid urban problems and people unlike themselves reflected and exacerbated a moral disregard for the needs of those in the cities and a political reluctance to support a collective response" (2006, 188). Suburban communities—especially those areas incorporated as separate municipalities—are routinely suspended between the protection of individual rights to property and self-determination versus the wider metropolitan region's needs for integrated approaches to decisions. The current and ongoing debates over Regional Competitive Acts, Metropolitan Compacts, School District Consolidation Agreements, and Smart Growth initiatives all point to this thorny issue (Lucy and Phillips 2000).

Landscape and ecology. "Suburbia was always meant to be green," writes Joel Garreau (1991, 399). But the specific nature of suburbia's green space remains an enduring issue. The relationship between the *imagined or iconic* green space of the suburban community, on the one hand, and the *actual geographic land*, on the other, continues to vex suburban living. This relationship is key to understanding the issue of suburban sprawl (Lindstrom and Bartling 2003) and the accelerating pace of suburban development of once agricultural or "undeveloped" land. Goddard (2012) describes how suburban living has, since the 1940s, been an imagined "country" space. Savage and Lapping (2003) describe how the influx of urban commuters to nearby rural communities changes the very idea of what life there is supposed to be. The New Urbanist movement in community planning (Duany, Plater-Zyberk, and Speck 2000) is centered on the idea of returning to the walkable neighborhood as the ideal place of human living. The issue of what the landscape is, what we imagine it to be, and what is actually sustainable given the physical realities of water, land, and resources continues to define the suburban experience.

Place-conscious education, of course, is centered in the complex tensions that suburban living is both shaped by and obscures. The issues of diversity, civic responsibility, and actual landscape are exactly the issues for local understanding and action that place-conscious education seeks to engage. To become active local citizens, young people must learn to see these three issues and understand how they impact local living. If place-conscious education, and the kind of active citizenry it seeks to create, is to have any force in American consciousness, then place-conscious education must take root in suburbia.

"The question can be validly raised," wrote poet and activist Adrienne Rich almost thirty years ago in another context (1972, 68), "Is this existing public educational system, school, or university the place where such a relationship to language can be developed? Aren't those structures already too determined, haven't they too great a stake in keeping things as they are? My response would be, yes, but *this is where the students are.*" In our era, more than three decades after Rich's words, "where the students are" has changed, but her principle endures. What does it mean, for educators interested in place-conscious citizenship, that "where most of our students are" is suburbia—and what does it mean that suburbia is where most of us are too? These are the questions we will explore in this book.

Suburbia as Geographical and Psychological Space: A Brief History

What exactly is a suburb, and what is it like to live there? These are crucial questions for educators, if, as contemporary geographers argue, more than half of the school-age children in the United States now live in suburbia. They are especially vexing questions because the term *suburb* is not precise. Officially, the 2010 US Census does not use "suburb" as a category: Census director Robert Groves argues that the term has "many potential definitions . . . best suited for different uses" and hence is imprecise (2011, n.p.).

In the geographic literature, the term *suburbs* applies to communities that surround and extend from a given metropolis, but the concept is complicated because the array of such communities includes very different kinds of civic bodies. Geographers identify at least the following four kinds of "suburbs":

- traditional suburban housing developments, tacked on to the existing city, either inside or outside that city-county boundary, primarily residential in character (Beauregard 2006). These suburbs are often loosely categorized as "first-tier" or "inner" suburbs, as opposed to "outer" or "metropolitan fringe" or "exurban" suburbs—categories that suggest an ongoing process of new suburbs creating rings of development around old ones. A crucial contemporary issue is the ongoing decline of "inner" suburbs, now long since city locked by more recent construction. Many of the nation's most ghettoized communities are "inner" suburbs (Lucy and Phillips 2000).
- edge or edgeless cities, full-fledged urban areas of recent origin (thirty years ago the new urban area was rural) that now meet residents' needs for jobs, shopping, and entertainment. These new communities might be organized around new civic hubs (the edge cities of Garreau 1991) or around uncentered sprawls of office development (the edgeless cities of Lang 2003). In both cases, claims Teaford, commercially "the edge" has become "more significant than the core" (2008, 92).
- micropolises and bedroom communities, or previously rural communities outlying a metropolitan center and presently buffered from them by some open country, in the process of being colonized by the larger metropolitan center. Officially, the 2010 Census requires an urban center of ten thousand for a county to be categorized as micropolitan (fifty thousand is required for metropolitan). Yet geographers interested in "suburban sprawl" are especially concerned with this changing boundary between rural and suburban and the changing nature of small rural communities in the "exurban" shadow of nearby micropolitan or metropolitan areas (Savage and Lapping 2003).
- Relovilles and Penurbia, or planned/gated communities for the affluent, located in the "penumbric shadow" of the metropolis's expanding exurban rim. Kilborn (2009) defines Relovilles as communities

> designed for mobile workers of large corporations drawing annual incomes between one and two hundred thousand dollars, who expect to stay in any given community only two to four years and need new, resalable housing. Goddard defines Penurbia as the affluent exurban country estates loosely connected to major metropolitan areas, a space that "looks like the country but thinks like the city. Or rather, it looks like the city thinks the country should look" (2012, 2).

While all four forms of suburbia are distinct, all share a common population history. Historically, the development of suburbia has followed a relatively consistent path, as metropolitan scholars Beauregard (2006) and Teaford (2006, 2008) both explain. Although urban expansion has of course been a feature of the American landscape since the arrival of the European Americans, the development of traditional suburbia can be dated to the period 1945–70. In this quarter century, traditional suburbs were built and settled around virtually all cities, with corresponding population drifts away from the urban cores of those cities and away from the rural areas of most states. This demographic shift in our nation came about because of the increased national industrial economy following World War II, the rise of the automobile as a cheap and individual form of transportation, and the corresponding availability of the "American Dream" of single-family dwellings and community self-determination.

Prior to 1945, as Teaford (2006, 2008) points out, the downtown of any major city centered urban life. People of all classes worked and shopped and were entertained downtown, used public transportation to reach and leave downtown, and lived within access of downtown. Although cities certainly were segregated into neighborhoods by race, class, and ethnicity, the primacy of the downtown area for jobs, shopping, and entertainment meant that daily life routinely involved contact with cultural and ethnic pluralism. Living in an American city, thus, meant living with an awareness of the cultural, racial, and ethnic diversity of that region, with all the corresponding tensions brought about by living in such close quarters. Teaford suggests that part of the motivation behind the explosion of suburbs after 1945 was a release from these tensions.

Between 1945 and the 1970s, the traditional suburbs that sprang up around American cities allowed most urban workers to move their families into lives of greater homogeneity. The country's economic prosperity allowed individual workers to afford the main elements of the American Dream of the 1950s: a single-family dwelling and a car. Suburban planners and housing developers catered to this new affluence by creating new subdivisions and suburbs with largely prefabricated houses of similar design and expense. The traditional suburbs hence allowed the urban population to segregate itself by class, based on the cost of those houses in a given area. In a traditional suburb, shopping, schooling, and entertainment all were within biking distance of the new residence. Whereas the family's wage earner might still drive the new freeway system to the office or factory, the family's life could become much more insular. Teaford provides some compelling evidence of the segregating impact of the initial suburban development period, from the planned race-segregated suburbs surrounding Los Angeles to the planned "retirees only, no children allowed" communities of Sun City, Arizona. Although suburbia as a whole has always been remarkably diverse, with settlements catering to the "richly contrasting mosaic that corresponds to the diversity of contemporary American life," (2006, 43), the specific suburban community is likely to be planned (and chosen by residents) to reflect a lifestyle island. Teaford (2008) points out that there is now a suburb for everybody. Those individuals valuing ethnic diversity might seek out the suburbs that are the most ethnically diverse cities in the United States (Aurora, Colorado, and Bellevue, Washington, as of the time of his writing); those persons wanting a community limited to seniors, or equestrians, or gays, or high net-worth individuals, will also find a place limited to those demographics.

The flip side of the suburban explosion, of course, was the depopulation of other areas, both urban and rural. In urban centers during this quarter century, urban neighborhoods became abandoned by the white-collar families moving to the suburbs, giving rise to the so-called ghettos. In rural areas depopulation occurred as families and young people moved to the suburbs for work. As Wendell Berry points out in his aptly titled *The Unsettling of America* (1977), the combination of national agricultural policies that had created the Dust Bowl of the 1930s alongside the new urban prosperity of the late-1940s postwar boom made it increasingly difficult to sustain rural life. He views the quarter century of suburban explosion as the last step in a century-long process of enforced "unsettling" of the American rural landscape. Berry's ideas are currently being reinterpreted by scholars of suburban sprawl (Lindstrom and Bartling 2003) and Penurbia (Goddard 2012), who point out that new suburban developments often sought to re-create an imaginary kind of "country living" just outside the existing metropolitan rim. Goddard (2012) analyzes the marketing of "country living" from 1945 to today as the iconic American ideal in mainstream magazines *Town and Country*, *Mother Earth*, *Good Housekeeping*, and *Country Living*. For Goddard, this idea of "Penurbia"—a pastoral space on the periphery of metropolis while still in the "penumbric shadow" of metropolitan cultural light—connects directly to the accelerating pace of suburban sprawl. (He cites the American Farmland Trust's 2012 rate of agricultural to suburban land development of "2 acres per minute" [2], and the *New York Times Almanac* estimate that "nearly one-quarter of Americans lived on farms in 1940; only one in fifty did in 2010" [4].) So Berry's historic depopulation of rural areas clearly went hand in hand with a new suburban reimagining of "country" life.

Summing up the period from 1945 to the 1970s, geographer Robert Beauregard claims that the rise of the suburbs produced a troubling long-term shift in American consciousness:

> Once the industrial cities began to seem obsolete and no longer offered opportunities for wealth and fame, Americans forgot about them. Only unavoidable pleas for help or the possibility that their problems would overflow into the suburbs elicited assistance. For Americans, history is the past, and the past is that which has been discarded. The history of the country is a record of what has been achieved and thus of places and institutions that have served their purpose and are now no longer needed. This is how the industrial cities were treated after World War II. (2006, 194)

Calling this shift in American consciousness "a combination of historical amnesia and chauvinism," Beauregard suggests that the rise of the suburbs meant that Americans "turned away from a robust and compassionate public culture" (196). He sees both the country's enduring political divisions during the civil rights era of the late 1960s and early 1970s and the urban crisis of the mid-1970s and early-1980s economic downturn as emerging from the "amnesia and chauvinism" of the rise to suburbia. When the national economy dipped in the mid-1970s, bringing with it a slowdown in the housing boom and widespread financial troubles in many industrial cities, the limitations of the move to suburbia became nationally apparent.

Of course, suburbanization has not ceased since the mid-1970s economic downturn. Instead, claim contemporary geographers, it has changed its form. As Joel Garreau (1991) has pointed out, what has happened since the late 1970s is that suburbs have ceased to be subservient to any preexisting urban core. The very word *suburb* no longer captures the geographic reality: whereas during the 1945–70 explosion a traditional "suburb" may have been a community that existed "sub-" or under the city it surrounded, in the metropolitan landscape post-1975 there is no actual center around which to revolve. Teaford goes even farther: "Suburbia's multitudinous communities have rendered the older notion of the city largely obsolete and have created the amorphous metropolitan regions of today where there is no single focus for the lives of residents throughout the area. They are not *sub*ordinate to the urb; but they are *sub*versive to the whole concept of the urb" (2008, xii; emphasis in the original).

Instead, our major metropolitan areas have evolved into centerless conglomerates of "Edge Cities" stretching across vast amounts of previously rural or residential territory. People living in these Edge Cities work, sleep, shop, and entertain themselves wholly within that civic space, not needing in any way the once center city to which they are sometimes attached. Garreau's examples of Edge Cities included the Eastern Seaboard cities stretching from New Jersey to Boston, the Western Seaboard of Southern California, and the conglomerates of new cities around Atlanta, Phoenix, Dallas–Fort Worth, and Washington, DC. By 1991 Garreau identified more than two hundred "Edge Cities" that should be classified under his now famous five-part definition: a city with at least five million square feet of leasable office space; six hundred thousand square feet of retail space; a population that increases at 9:00 a.m. on workdays; a clear local awareness of the city as a destination itself for jobs, shopping, and entertainment; and a recent history (the city did not exist as an urban center thirty years ago).

Peter Kilborn (2009) provides an intriguing update of the Edge City idea. As Kilborn points out, up until (and perhaps past) the home mortgage crisis of 2007, the development of newer and more affluent Edge Cities has been a constant feature of the new globalization of American business. With the development of global technology and large multinational corporations that sustain it, a growing number of American professional workers have become "relos." Kilborn defines relos as "corporate relocatees or career transferees" who move every few years as they shift companies or positions within companies and are relocated to new parts of the United States or abroad. As an upwardly mobile professional class, relos are "economically homogenous, with mid-career incomes of $100,000–$200,000," and are predominately white and midwestern in origin (though Asian Americans outnumber African Americans and Hispanic Americans, counter to the nation's overall demographics). Relovilles, or edgeless cities that cater to the new confluence of corporate and mobile professionals, are built on the cheap land outside existing metropolitan centers. Kilborn lists the top twenty-five Relovilles just after his title page, and his list includes several of the Edge Cities identified by Garreau (1991) and studied by Teaford (2006): Alpharetta, Georgia; Plano, Texas; and Woodbury, Minnesota. What's striking about the $250,000–$400,000 multibedroom homes in these new communities is that they are built to be resold. With the average relo expecting to be relocated again within two to five years, resale value is key.

In short, the history of suburban development since 1945 suggests some enduring themes for suburban living, whether in the traditional suburbs that sprang up after World War II or in the Edge Cities, Relovilles, and exurban Penurbia of today. Suburban living in all four forms is:

- tied to mobility and our financial ability to migrate
- based in the American Dream of self-determined single-family housing, located in diverse communities of others who are "like us"

- dominated by the "new"—new construction, new communities, and so on
- historically naive and disconnected, that is, not linked to the cultural history of the region's traditional urban centers or to the natural and agricultural history of the land on which the suburban development now rests

For the young people who grow up in any form of suburbia, the dominant message is of migration in service of career. As Kilborn explains, citing an interview with anthropologist Bradd Shore, career migration and relocation have now become the defining characteristics of the 70 percent of the population that make up the middle class:

> Bradd Shore segments the classes by their attachment to hometowns and their predisposition to move. As we toured the Relovilles north of Atlanta, Shore said a town's upper class—its entrenched doctors, lawyers, accountants, its leading stockbrokers, insurance agents, and business owners—has the means to either move out or stick around and prepare their own children to succeed them. By contrast, Shore said, many who land in the working class—as farmhands, grocery store cashiers, mill workers, and school janitors—are too rooted or ill-equipped to go. They might not have a parent to open doors, the skills for a better job somewhere else, or even the funds for the trip there for an interview. Or maybe they don't want to shed their only real wealth: their extended families, churches, ethnic ties, and shared interests and rituals. The remaining middle class, in Shore's view, amounts to about 70 percent of the population. Its kids have neither the choices of the rich nor the immobility of the poor. They are congenital itinerants whose families raise them to chase the American Dream wherever it leads, much as their forefathers did in chasing it west. Like the pioneers, the middle class equates wealth with perseverance and mobility. "You define yourself as belonging to the middle class through various kinds of mobility," Shore said. (2009, 87)

According to Shore's analysis, contemporary class consciousness is deeply tied to careerist mobility in the pursuit of individual wealth. The suburban life experience is a huge part of this class consciousness. Whereas both the very rich and the working poor are integrated into regional place, the mobile middle class is not, and the trappings of suburbia help obscure any connection that might be there. If the subdivision you grow up in did not exist thirty years ago, if your family has moved to similar (or slightly more affluent) subdivisions already at least once during your childhood years, and if you have been raised and taught to believe that you will need to move yourself to where the best job is in order to make a career of your own, then it becomes exceedingly difficult to imagine your region as something important in its own right.

Embedded in this view of the transitory suburban home, of course, are the psychological effects that so excite suburban geographers. Over and over in the literature, three main negative consequences are identified:

- *Suburbia, while overall diverse, is locally segregationist.* Although suburbia as a whole is extremely diverse, because individual suburbs separate the populace into isolated "like" groups, suburban living makes it harder to engage fully with social issues that cut across race, class, and cultural lines.
- *Suburbia is ahistorical.* Because the built environment of suburbia is so recent, it is harder for suburban dwellers to develop, understand, and act from any deep sense of regional history.
- *Suburbia is unsustainable.* Because the transitory nature of suburban living always requires newer, more modern suburbs, suburban development of all forms places unrealistic and unsustainable demands on the region's ecosystem while eliding the cost of such development.

Each criticism is psychologically complex because, as the critics point out, the felt experience of suburban living is in conflict with the geographical and demographical reality of the region. Let's examine the conflicted experience in each of these three widespread criticisms.

Segregation. The segregation criticism of suburban living is probably the clearest example of the conflicted nature of such experience. Put simply, while the *psychological effect* of suburban living may be a kind of segregation, the *physical reality* of most regions now works toward cultural pluralism. Hence, suburban experience tends to place additional psychological demands on its residents to make sense of the difference between their lived experience and their wider understanding of their region (and, for the high-income relos, of increasing corporate globalization).

Writing of the rise of traditional suburbs between 1950 and 1970, Beauregard summarizes the logical progression toward a segregationist mind-set:

> The embrace of suburbia meant the rejection of an urbanity that had nurtured the coexistence of diverse peoples and life experiences from the early nineteenth century to the mid-twentieth century. The resultant pluralism had been central to the nation's identity. An urbanization that rejected density and social diversity impaired the moral ties that might have enabled the country to "save" its cities. First, commitment eroded as households fled to the suburbs and the sprawling Sunbelt cities. Then, attachment diminished as the suburbs became self-sufficient. Finally, empathy waned as race and crime came to symbolize the central cities. A sense of national belonging was severely compromised. (2006, 173)

For Beauregard, the psychological effect of moving to (and living in) a suburb, surrounded by similar houses with similar families in them, was a gradual eroding of the cultural and ethnic pluralism that had been central to the national identity. Commitment to, attachment to, and empathy for that national pluralism eroded the longer Americans lived in segregated suburban enclaves. As what he calls "parasitic urbanization" (where a suburb needed the metropolitan center for employment and industry) gave way to Edge City autonomy, this lack of commitment, attachment, and empathy increased. The reality of ethnic and cultural diversity in the region, of course, never went away: the physical structure of suburban isolation just made it psychologically harder to see.

Yet, in direct contradiction to the isolating effects of suburban enclaves set apart by race and class, the demographic reality has been that, since 1950, every region of our country has increased in cultural diversity—including the array of suburbs within each region. As Teaford points out in his chapter on "boomburbs" circa 2001, many of the sprawling edgeless cities had become home to an increasing array of new immigrant Americans. According to Teaford, life in the boomburbs circa 2000 was exceeding different from the simple isolationism of the "parasitic" suburb of 1960. On the one hand, cultural plurality existed right in the boomburb. On the other hand, the charters of neighborhood home owners' associations, the emergence of gated communities, and the physical layout of freeways and major strip malls separating neighborhoods with real barriers caused suburban isolation to remain a felt reality. With more than seven million American households in gated communities by 2001, "the walls provided needed edges in the edgeless city, boundaries that distinguished neighbors from intruders, the privileged from the poor, and the protected from the vulnerable" (2006, 244–45).

In short, in most forms of suburban living, segregation is a mind-set but not a reality, a function of the carefully constructed nature of suburban space. The layout of suburbs, Edge Cities, and Relovilles, along with the neighborhood associations within them, allows for an implied "concept of community where some belonged and some did not" (ibid.), even while the overall demographics of the city or region may show large increases in immigrant population and cultural diversity.

History. Another psychological effect of living in transitory, recent, and replaceable space is a shift in our sense of history. History, says Garreau, is the Edge City's problem because "it has none" (1991, 9), emphasizing the recent built landscape of malls, tech parks, housing subdivisions, schools, and corporate offices that make up an Edge City. To live in such a space is to be reminded, hourly, of the newness of things. Of course, in the same bifurcated consciousness we saw in suburban segregation, the psychological newness of a twenty-five-year-old Edge City is located in a physical regional history that goes much further back—psychology is again at odds with physical reality.

Rural theorist Wendell Berry argues that such a lack of history is merely a symptom of a much deeper problem. He writes, "One of the primary results—and one of the primary needs—of industrialism is the separation of people and places and products from their histories. To the extent that we participate in the industrial economy, we do not know the histories of our meals or our habitats or of our families. This is an economy, and in fact a culture, of the one-night stand" (2003a, 113). For Berry, the migratory nature of suburban living depends on an almost absolute and widespread ignorance of history—not just history in the cultural literacy sense, as in the media questionnaires about American presidents that show up around Independence Day, but the history of all aspects of our lives. In Berry's phrase, "people, places, and products" all have become separated from their histories in the contemporary industrialized world. The corporate manager and family now in a Reloville outside Atlanta may have lived in Hong Kong, Colorado, New Jersey, and Texas in the past decade, and within Reloville culture what that manager "does" is much more important than where the family comes from. Similarly, because the family will live in Alpharetta for only four to eight years, there is not much point in learning Georgia history or even choosing to live in a subdivision based on "authentic" southern architecture (if one could be found). And, for Berry most damning, the products consumed by a contemporary migratory family are equally migratory and history-less. The family most likely does not know where the beef comes from that is served in the local strip mall, where the wood came from that frames their current two-year-old home, or even who made the furniture for the family's new den (or how those workers were trained, by whom, and where). As Berry sums it up, "The global economy institutionalizes a global ignorance, in which producers and consumers cannot know or care about one another, and in which the history of all products will be lost" (121).

Peter Kilborn, a much less polemical and prophetic writer than Wendell Berry, offers strong evidence for the psychological reality of the historical ignorance of transitory relos. Citing his interviews with pastors, mayors, and elected officials of many of today's major Relovilles, Kilborn (2009) points to a number of salient trends: the lack of attendance at school events, including athletics; the choice to donate to civic causes somewhere else (such as where parents or grandparents live) rather than in the local community; the difficulty of getting residents to volunteer for any forms of community service; and the desire for housing and churches and shopping venues that are similar to the ones in other Relovilles rather than anything specific to the region. In short, while the large estates of these communities may make a Reloville a nice place to live, rarely are they felt to be a "real" place to live.

Unsustainable. Directly tied to the criticism of historical ignorance is the criticism of unsustainable resource exploitation. Put simply, it takes a large amount of resources to transform a landscape of agricultural fields, trees, and open spaces to a built landscape of malls, subdivisions, schools, churches, and office complexes. The debate over whether that allocation of resources is worthwhile is ongoing. Critics of suburban experience all across the nation claim the pace of resource consumption is unsustainable (that is, we will run out of resources before we run out of places someone wants to build). Joel Garreau calls the debate over development "the new civil war" in our country (1991, 401). This "new civil war" is complicated because the strong arguments for sustainable "Smart Growth" conflict directly with deeply held beliefs about individual property rights. The two ideologies remain in daily combat wherever local zoning ordinances, right to sell property, and differing ideas of development come into contact.

At issue is the actual land that goes under the bulldozer in the development of suburban sprawl. As Savage and Lapping point out, the land that is to be developed is not empty: "Sprawl occurs not on a tabula rasa landscape but rather on a peopled and working rural landscape. Sprawl is an amazingly disruptive force that triggers conflict and rearranges the rural and village geography, economy, and society in the most profound ways" (2003, 5). The "working rural landscape" into which suburban development moves is a complex mix of agriculture, small rural communities, and any abutting areas of natural preserves left near urban areas in the continental United States. How we conceive of this landscape—as a regional resource shared in certain ways commonly, as individuals' property to do with as they see fit—is a core issue.

The basic assertion of the Smart Growth advocates is that suburban (and urban) development is possible in a sustainable way, if planned with a sense of the needs of the entire region. (See the active Smart Growth Network list of more than forty organizational partners [2013]. See also the "Canons of Sustainable Architecture and Urbanism" on the Congress for New Urbanism website.) Teaford summarizes: "The basic principles of smart growth are the creation of compact, dense, walkable, mixed-use communities; preservation of open space and farmland; promotion of public transit with a resulting decline in the use of the automobile; and provision of a range of housing options including affordable units. Dedicated to curbing sprawl and getting people out of their automobiles, smart growth proponents envision a world where Americans will waste less land and walk more" (2008, 197). The explicit target of the Smart Growth advocates is unrestrained suburban sprawl. In contrast to the unsustainable development of new suburbs in exurban areas, they advocate careful regional planning of "human scale" communities. The key premises of this movement reach across all forms of suburbia, addressing the potential revitalization of declining "inner" suburbs as well as the planned construction of New Urbanist communities, such as Kentlands, Maryland, or Celebration, Florida.

In contrast, the opponents of Smart Growth planning across the country argue that the regional zoning instructions necessary to enforce these ideas place too great a burden on individual property owners. This point was the core issue behind Oregon's Measure 37 of 2004 (and the revision, via Measure 49, in 2007). That proposition required adequate state compensation to the landowner if regional zoning would not allow development. If individual landowners could not sell exurban land to developers, the advocates argued, then their personal property rights were in jeopardy. By contrast, the penurban residents of Loudoun County, Virginia, studied by Goddard (2012) organized against planned development because they wanted to preserve the larger estates from planned higher-density housing developments. They also argued "personal property rights" in the face of regional planning.

In short, the debates surrounding suburban sprawl and sustainability point out enduring psychological effects of suburban living. The city's edge, the exurban arena where rural and metropolitan collide, is home to both ideological and ideational battles over the nature of country and the nature of property.

Basics of Place-Conscious Education

As this brief history of suburbia and its criticisms indicates, the physical and psychological experience of suburban living works against the development of robust citizenship as we define it in this book. To be able to live lives that are "economically, politically, socially and culturally responsible," as Wendell Berry states in the epigraph to this chapter, young citizens will need to imagine themselves in a different relationship to local place. Rather than seeing place as a transitory place you are currently passing through ("Now we're in Omaha, but Dad says we might be moving to Chicago next year") or an abstract, distant point of origin ("Our family's originally from Nebraska and before that eastern Russia"), robust citizens will need to see the local place as a particular rich mix of cultural heritage, natural resources and wonders, opportunities, and challenges. Place-conscious education takes up this task.

> Place-based education is the process of using the local community and environment as a starting point to teach concepts in language arts, mathematics, social studies, science, and other subjects across the curriculum. Emphasizing hands-on, real-world learning experiences, this approach to education increases academic achievement, helps students develop stronger ties to their community, enhances students' appreciation for the natural world, and creates a heightened commitment to serving as active, contributing citizens. Community vitality and environmental quality are improved through the active engagement of local citizens, community organizations, and environmental resources in the life of the school. (Sobel 2004, 7)

In his short, oft-cited manual for "place-based education," David Sobel suggests that the most successful and enduring communities are based on a "three-legged stool" of academic achievement, social capital, and environmental quality. Schools, he points out, do not exist apart from the community that sends its children there. Neither do schools exist apart from the physical landscape in which that community is located. Although it is possible to narrow attention to just one of these items, it is counterproductive to do so. He writes:

> While we all started out thinking that our focus was on school improvements and academic achievement, we have come to realize that our focus is equally on creating vital communities and preserving the quality of the environment. We are now aware that there is a dynamic tension

> between these three elements—that together they form a three-legged stool that will not stand if any one of the legs is missing. Try to improve a school without actively engaging the community, and your efforts won't garner the budget support and human capital necessary for success. Emphasize community development without the involvement of the school and you won't have the youthful energy that makes projects work. Build thriving local economies with little concern for the environment and you'll find businesses will have trouble attracting workers because people aren't willing to raise children amidst deteriorated air and water. (2004, 36)

Sobel's vision, in short, is for a deeply considered collaboration between schools and local place. His vision of healthy communities requires the mutual support of education, community vitality, and environmental vitality. With all three in place, a community will continue to thrive. With any one missing, that same community may well be at risk.

Within Sobel's vision of the "three-legged stool" of vital communities, education itself has an important role: helping students understand their role in the local community and environment. As other critics have pointed out (Brooke 2006; Zencey 1996), this role involves a significant redirection for American education, for the dominant educational model is toward portable, contextless information processing that leads our best and brightest students to imagine themselves as "rootless" or "migratory" intellectuals. If students are educated to see themselves as part of an abstract "ivory tower" committed to the study of a specific discipline, or to see themselves as developing globally marketable personal skills that they can use anywhere the best jobs are offered, then these students find little reason for imagining their lives as rooted in specific regions and communities. Although the dominant migratory model of education may have served the interests of American expansion and multinational economic development in the last century, this same model of education has exacerbated the decline of many American communities and regions because it leads students away from developing clear ideas of local citizenship. To embrace the goal of helping students understand their role in local community and environment, thus, would be to redirect education from inculcating rootless migration to developing committed local citizenship.

In the past decade this new role for education has been adopted and refined by many practitioners of place-conscious education, in a variety of rural and urban contexts. The task of this book is to consider how place-conscious education might be connected more directly to the particular context of suburban classrooms—a demographic area where place-conscious education has largely been absent. To prepare for the task of extending place-conscious work to suburban contexts, I would like to summarize the main ideas from the existing place-conscious scholarship. I will organize this summary around the current division in the scholarship between rural place-conscious work and urban place-conscious work. I will then take up suburban place-conscious possibilities.

Rural place-conscious education. David Sobel's (2004) "Place-Based Education Evaluation Cooperative" in New England is just one of many rural programs to see place-conscious education as a necessary focus for rural schools. Since the mid-1990s, the Rural School and Community Trust (n.d.) has been promoting place-conscious education as an important component of revitalizing rural America. To combat the ongoing "brain drain" depopulation of rural America, many schools across the country are now working with place-conscious principles. These educators are guided by a core set of educational concepts. Paul Theobald's (1997) concept of "intradependence" suggests that teaching how we "exist by virtue of the necessary relations *within a place*" might redirect American focus on "independence" as individual rights and self-determination and "interdependence" as the increasing rhetoric of global interaction. To have curriculum "spiral out" from the local to the examination of how national and international forces connect with the local (instead of the other way around) would help students imagine the way their lives, and their communities, are centered in and affected by the content studied in school—a far cry from falsely believing, in the words of Lisa Knopp (1996), that "all real life happened elsewhere." Toni Haas and Paul Nachtigal (1998) of the Rural School and Community Trust offer a prophetic list of the goals for place-conscious education, rhetorically crafted as a set of "five senses" to enhance the physical senses so often relied on in language-arts education.

Haas and Nachtigal imagine five different senses that might enable rural people to live well:

1. a sense of place, or living well ecologically
2. a sense of civic involvement, or living well politically
3. a sense of worth, or living well economically
4. a sense of connection, or living well spiritually
5. a sense of belonging, or living well in community

Our work in Nebraska with the National Writing Project's Rural Voices, Country Schools program fits solidly in this tradition of place-conscious rural education. In our book *Rural Voices* (Brooke 2003), teachers from the Nebraska Writing Project described place-conscious units devoted to understanding local culture, heritage, and history through interviews, oral history, and cross-generational partnerships as well as place-conscious units devoted to social action on specific community issues, such as preserving a rural school in the face of consolidation or career development in the region. We defined three principles guiding all such work:

1. Place-conscious education requires "active students" directly involved in defining and acting on the local issues they see as important.
2. Place-conscious education centers schooling in "a deep understanding of local place, spiraling out" to make connections across content areas.
3. Place-conscious education aims for a "specific kind of citizenry," active, engaged citizens who "know enough about their natural and cultural region to fashion lives that enhance the communities located there." (Brooke 2003, 13)

In the decade following our involvement with Rural Voices, Country Schools, we have used these principles (and the many examples of place-conscious units developed from them) as core components of our Rural Institute program—a three-week intensive workshop, based on the National Writing Project model, that helps rural teachers design their own place-conscious units from their knowledge and engagement with their communities. Rural Institute programs like ours have developed as well throughout the National Writing Project's Rural Sites Network and are aided by online introductions to place-conscious education offered by the Rural School and Community Trust. While all of these programs are complex and multifaceted, most are guided by a rich sense of inquiry into and care for the local region. Understanding that region as a natural, cultural, and historical area with particular opportunities and particular needs is what leads place-conscious rural teachers and their students to define the specific issues they choose to act on.

Urban place-conscious education. Whereas rural place-conscious educators use concepts of region as the guiding ideas for their work, urban place-conscious educators tend to employ concepts of social difference and social action as their guiding concepts. As described above, rural place-conscious education emerges from a nexus of ideas that explain and emphasize issues facing rural America. If you live in a small community located near productive agriculture and among an aging populace facing depopulation as the ongoing "brain drain" leads young people to migrate out of the region, then the idea of your surrounding region as something of value to be understood, preserved, and protected clearly has importance. Hence, concepts like Sobel's three-legged stool of academics, cultural capital, and environmentalism, or Theobald's "intradependence," or the new agrarianism promoted by Wendell Berry make a whole lot of sense. By contrast, if you live in a major urban center that has been through cycles of ghettoization and gentrification, where the "natural" landscape is mostly obscured by layers of "built" cityscape, where the community's boundaries are hard to discern and the community bears witness to the waves of immigration and emigration by a variety of cultural, national, and ethnic groups, then social difference and social action make more sense as concepts to guide your engagement with place.

In urban settings educators interested in connections with local communities, history, diversity, and public policies are likely to describe their work using a different array of terms. Along with "place-based" or "place-conscious" education (Powell and Tassoni 2009; McComiskey and Ryan 2003), urban educators are also likely to describe their work as civic engagement (Ackerman and Coogan 2010), public engagement (Rose and Weiser 2010), public writing (N. Welch 2008), and community engagement (Flower 2008). Within university composition and rhetoric programs, this array of terms is often located within the field's "public turn" (Mathieu 2005): the shift away from university academic discourses narrowly defined to the "public work of rhetoric" in shaping local policy in the full range of public discussions. Linda Flower (2008, 3), whose Community Literacy Center in Pittsburgh is often regarded as a model program for public engagement, summarizes this emerging field:

> For many educators, this search for both a new rhetoric and relationships that are more diverse has led outside the classroom. Here students no longer study public discourse or community writing from arm's length but become writers and researchers with those groups (Adler-Kassner, Crooks, & Watters 1997; Deans 2000). Researchers may draw their subjects into a partnership that goes public in policy discussions and statements (Higgins and Brush 2006). In community-based service learning projects, one uses the role of student, mentor, teachers, researcher, or activist to move beyond the academy and form working relationships across differences of race, class, culture, gender, age, status, or discourse. Many of these community projects then seize the power of publication, art, or multimedia to gain a hearing (Cushman 2006; Flower 2003; Heath and McLaughlin 1993; Heath and Smyth 1999; Hull and James 2007; Robinson 1990; Rousculp 2006).

For Flower and other practitioners of urban civic and public engagement, this process of encountering difference in the multiplicity of urban peoples, inquiring into the complex histories of those differences, and moving to intervention through community dialogue is, finally, a model for social action. Her "intercultural inquiry practice" (Flower, Long, and Higgins 2000; Flower 2008), for instance, brings students and representatives of the Pittsburgh community together to inquire into a local issue important to them all, leading often to shared social action. Similarly, Thomas Deans's service-learning model (2000) asks students to write "for, about, and with" their community, noting the different social action implied by each preposition. David Seitz's work ethnographies (2004) immerse students in the study of workplaces and their cultural histories, aiming at personal and social reconsideration. Nedra Reynolds (2004) invites students to adopt critical geography's metaphors of "mapping" and "dwelling" in their urban environments as a means of identifying, understanding, and acting amid the cultural differences they are exposed to by every journey through their city. Nancy Welch (2008) urges educators to teach urban students how to create public space for discourse, rather than merely relying on the preexisting (and to her mind often ineffectual) officially sanctioned public forums.

Within the National Writing Project, urban place-conscious education has been explicitly linked to social action. In the award-winning 2006 volume *Writing for a Change*, Berdan and her eleven urban colleagues (often coauthoring with their students) describe "social action" projects their classes developed, adopting processes from the Centre for Social Action in England. All of these projects involved students encountering, inquiring into, and intervening in the very local issues of differences in their school and community. Similarly, in the rich and exceptionally well-designed "Keeping and Conserving American Communities" program of the Kennesaw Mountain Writing Project outside Atlanta (2005), Sarah Robbins and Mimi Dyer use a cultural history approach to urban place-conscious education, offering five "national themes" that influence civic understanding and citizenship across America, along with five specific "local applications" to the Atlanta area.

National Themes

1A) Reclaiming Displaced Heritage
2A) Educating for Citizenship
3A) Cultivating Homelands
4A) Building Cities
5A) Shifting Landscapes, Converging People

Local Georgia Applications

1B) Re-examining the Cherokee removal
2B) Uplifting a "new" South after the Civil War

3B) Farming Georgia in the 20th Century
4B) Re-imagining Atlanta as cultured, corporate center
5B) Re-configuring 21st Century Suburbia

Teachers working with Keeping and Conserving American Communities worked in cross-grade clusters on one of these themes over a three-year period, designing with their students walking tours, dramatic presentations, museum displays, and other public writings. To live well in an urban center like Greater Atlanta, Robbins and Dyer argue, young citizens need to be able to understand the cultural differences around them through rich inquiry grounded in cultural history, and they need to learn how to intervene in their complex civic culture.

In sum, place-conscious education of various kinds has allowed rural and urban teachers to connect their classrooms to their communities and regions in powerful ways. Though rural educators have emphasized the root problem of sustainability (keeping and preserving vanishing landscapes and ways of life) and urban educators have emphasized the root problem of social action in the encounter with difference, both settings have led to direct connections between classrooms and community. Place-conscious education in both settings may also offer the possibility of new kinds of citizenship to develop, and perhaps in the long term new kinds of civic vitality.

But what about teachers and students in suburban settings? If the core problems of sustainability and difference situate place-conscious education forcefully in rural and urban settings, what core problems and experiences might situate place-conscious education for the simple majority of Americans now living in the suburbs, in the edgeless cityscapes and built environments?

Watershed and Commonwealth: How to Belong in Suburban Places

What are the crucial place-conscious issues for the suburban majority? If the brief history of suburbia in this chapter can be a guide, the central issue for suburban residents may well be the overwhelming feeling of disconnection that goes along with the migratory landscape. In the transitory world of today's Edge Cities and Relovilles, the largest felt issue may well be how to belong, and what to belong to, and maybe even where that belonging might take place. Belonging, as a deeply felt sense of continuity and community, is the emotion today's relos identified as missing in their interviews with Peter Kilborn (2009). Belonging to someplace, something, and someone likewise stands behind Joel Garreau's plea for the Edge City to work out the new meaning of the old words "community, civilization, and soul" in our new relationship to land (1991, 371).

Obviously, the question of "how to belong" is not limited to suburban dwellers. As noted above, Toni Haas and Paul Nachtigal identify belonging as one of the "five senses" crucial to effective place-conscious living. In the Nebraska Writing Project's 2003 *Rural Voices*, we elaborated on this sense of belonging:

> *A sense of belonging, or living well in community.* "Community," Haas and Nachtigal write, "is how we together create a story about our place" (1998, p.26). This final aspect of living well involved the collective meaning in which one locates one's life, along of continuum of heritage to imagined future that one shares with others. Developing a sense of belonging is, in part, understanding and internalizing the heritage, values, and history of a community, but it is equally developing vision and efficacy. Students need to understand who their community is and why it is that way—they need a healthy, historical, and contemporary sense of celebration and critique of local culture. At the same time, they need to be able to act effectively in and with the community—identifying current strengths and problems, negotiating satisfactorily with community members who hold different opinions, challenging local and external definitions of community that would restrict and stagnate. (Brooke 2003, 12)

Belonging, as we developed the concept, depends on knowledge and vision. To belong to a community, an individual needs to understand the "heritage, values, and history" that have brought that community into being. At the same time, commitment to a community relies on a vision for its future, for a healthy sense of what the community can become.

But the issue of belonging, while shared across the contexts served by place-conscious educators, may be especially important for suburbia.

Both aspects of belonging—a robust sense of history and a vision for the future—are routinely presented as missing in the contemporary suburban landscape, according to the scholars. Heritage, values, and history, if present in the single-family dwellings of suburbia, are brought there from somewhere else in the multigenerational family memory. And it is hard to have a vision for the future if you imagine yourself living somewhere else by the time the next decade rolls around. In short, the main issue for suburban place-conscious education would seem to be raising the question of belonging. What forms of historical knowledge and visionary imagination can help suburban students belong in their transitory place?

In this book we suggest that we can help suburban students find ways to belong by focusing their attention on the "watershed" and the "commonwealth," that is, on the two large-scale units of interdependence in which any community exists. Roughly speaking, a "watershed" is an ecological entity: a network of mutually interdependent natural systems that work together around a particular river system. A "commonwealth" is a cultural entity: a network of mutually interdependent cultural systems that work together within a particular political entity. To understand yourself (and your community) as part of a watershed and commonwealth, thus, is to see yourself (and your community) as enmeshed in a certain set of ecological and cultural relations.

We borrow the terms *watershed* and *commonwealth* from Wendell Berry's short essay of that name. Berry points out that any region is at once an ecological and cultural system and that viewing the region as a system carries with it a certain set of responsibilities. Writing of watersheds, Berry asserts:

> People who live at the lower ends of watersheds cannot be isolationists—or not for long. Pretty soon they will notice that water flows, and that will set them to thinking about the people upstream who either do or do not send down their silt and pollutants and garbage. Thinking about the people upstream ought to cause further thinking about the people downstream. Such pondering on the facts of gravity and the fluidity of water shows us that the golden rule speaks to a condition of

> absolute interdependency and obligation. People who live on rivers—or, in fact, anywhere in a watershed—might rephrase the rule in this way: Do unto those downstream as you would have those upstream do unto you. (2003a, 135)

Berry's rephrasing of the golden rule ("Do to those downstream as you want those above you to do to you") shifts the old biblical maxim from reciprocity to system. Instead of merely treating others as you want to be treated, Berry asks us to recognize our place within a mutually interdependent system of relations. Wherever you are in the watershed, your quality of life depends on those upstream. Although you cannot affect those people directly by how you live, your actions will determine the quality of life of those people downstream. We are part of an ecological system, and a complicated system at that, in which the ethics of others determines our life quality, even while our ethics affects still others.

Berry is quick to point out, however, that any given watershed is not only a physical or natural entity. Because of the human habitation within that watershed, because of the economic and cultural relations to the watershed that human habitation has developed, any given place is also a "commonwealth": "I have begun speaking of the river both because it is itself a common wealth, and because it instructs us so unsparingly about the condition and the requirements of living in a common wealth. We have come to think of the word 'commonwealth' as merely synonymous with 'state' or 'political body.' I am attempting here to use the term in its literal sense, unfortunately obsolete, of the general welfare, the public good, the wealth that can only be held in common" (135–36).

The "wealth held in common" in any region, of course, is more than simply the natural resources of the region (though natural resources are part of a region's common wealth). To see a region's wealth as only the exploitable natural resource (such as, say, coal in Berry's home state of Kentucky) is to miss the wider wealth of "general welfare, public good," that is held in common. "When your community loses a school, a church, a doctor, a grocery or hardware store, a restaurant, or a garage, what does that cost you and your community? . . . The point is obvious: In a national and increasingly international industrial economy, the land-dependent people who do the actual work of production are served last; their places and communities are served not at all" (138).

For Berry, a "common wealth" is the sum total of the heritage, values, and history of a given region, the ways of life that are part of the general welfare of the place. Like the physical watershed itself, these aspects of wealth held in common are part of a larger system of interdependencies. Hence, the life choices of work economics are involved in the same complicated ethics as the river itself—not simply "reciprocal economics, a game of tit for tat," but the more complicated system of responsibilities where those individuals downstream are always affected by the ones upstream.

To see watershed and commonwealth, in Berry's vision, is to focus on belonging and responsibility. The knowledge needed, he claims, is knowledge of interdependencies: How does a watershed work? How does what happens upstream affect lives downstream, and what would make the whole system healthy? Similarly, what is the local commonwealth, the cultural and natural elements of the general welfare, and how does our work contribute to that commonwealth? Contrary to the "reciprocal economics" suggested by the "increasingly international industrial economy" where trade is oversimplified to mean the exchange of product for wage, or labor for wage, Berry suggests we develop knowledge about the more complicated economics of watershed and common wealth, for a wider sense of how the whole system works, and what our place in that system might be. He writes: "I am interested in preserving the common wealth—the land and the people—of Kentucky. I don't see how this can be done if we Kentuckians don't develop strong, stable, land-and-people-conserving local economies, making the most of local investment, local labor, local loyalty, local diversity, and local caretaking. I think that real jobs—that is to say vocations, callings, lives of work, and working lives—are offered and preserved only by such economies" (140).

In Berry's view, preserving the common wealth—land and people, or watershed and commonwealth—will come about when individuals in his region choose working lives that are aware of the systemic relations in which their localities are involved. His spiritual terms for these life choices (*vocations, callings*) suggest the deep sense of belonging that can come from seeing the wider systemic relations.

Seeing wider systematic relations, of course, involves the development of vision. A sense of belonging emerges from a developed vision of your place in the world. *Vision* here means two distinct things. First, vision means seeing what is around you clearly, that is, being able to describe what actually is going on now, here, in this place, in its relation to other places—a sense of vision related to understanding the present as it has been shaped by the past. Second, vision means having a vision for the future, that is, a critical, informed idea of what your place can become and how it can contribute.

In this book we suggest that developing vision of the wider systemic relationships of watershed and commonwealth is crucial for suburban students. Such vision can enable them to address the central question of belonging found in so many critiques of suburban life. All three of the consistent critiques described earlier in this chapter stem from difficulties with vision, with the distance between the psychological effects of living in suburban spaces and the physical realities of the region. The alternative to the issues of segregation, historical naïveté, and unsustainable exploitation is a clearer vision of what is really in the region, why, and how that knowledge might lead to a vision for the future.

Vision, in short, leads to understanding. At the same time, understanding the connections of the home suburb to the watershed and commonwealth of the region is the route to the new kind of citizenry called for by place-conscious education—a citizenry not merely absorbed into the unsustainable migratory lifestyle of today's edgeless cities, but also able to address the "contemporary civil war" of land use and the "pluralistic national identity" of an increasingly multicultural America.

The teachers who have contributed to this book have chosen to focus on watershed or commonwealth issues in their particular kind of suburbia. Like most regions in our nation, the Great Plains of eastern Nebraska are a mix of all the forms of suburbia identified by contemporary geographers.

Traditional suburbs. Ralston, Nebraska, where Jeff Lacey and Daniel Boster teach, is a traditional suburb south of Omaha, now landlocked by further development since 1975.

Edge and edgeless cities. Papillion–La Vista, Nebraska, where Mary Birky Collier teaches, fits the general profile of Edge Cities. Both communities are large relatively recently built landscapes that serve as "single end destinations" for most residents. Papillion–La Vista now boasts the third-largest school district in the entire state of Nebraska.

Exurban areas and micropolises. Henderson and Aurora, Nebraska, where Sharon Bishop and Cathie English both taught, are communities of fewer than 10,000 in driving distance of the major metropolitan area of Lincoln-Omaha and in the "penumbric shadow" of the smaller urban area of Grand Island–Hastings. Fremont, Nebraska, where Susan Martens lived while in Nebraska, is, at 30,000 people, too large to be considered a micropolis anymore, though much of its population boom in the past ten years has been from families where the wage earner commutes to the Omaha metro area, forty miles away.

College campuses: New Urban Penurbia. The University of Nebraska–Lincoln (UNL) campus, where Aubrey Streit Krug, Bernice Olivas, and I all teach and Susan Martens taught, is, like many state college campuses in our nation, the result of human-scale New Urban planning, an architecture and landscape crafted to seem gloriously "countrified" to the walkers and bikers who move between the buildings (each state of the art the decade of construction). UNL's grounds are part of the Nebraska Statewide Arboretum (2013), whose website splash page boasts "Sustainable Landscapes for Healthy Homes and Communities." At a little more than 250,000 people, Lincoln (where the university is located) is just a little smaller than many of the suburbs studied by Beauregard (2006) and Teaford (2008). (Compare Aurora, Colorado, at more than 300,000, or Plano, Texas, at 270,000.) One of the standing jokes in the region is that Lincoln, although the state's capital city, is really a suburb of Omaha—since the edges of the two urban areas are now separated by a thinning agricultural corridor of fewer than twenty miles. Given Lang's (2003) idea of edgeless cities sprawling region-wide with no definable real center or at best competing centers, it is increasingly easy to see the entire eastern Nebraska region in which we all teach as part of just such an emerging network of all the forms of suburbia, swirling together in a vast melting pot of regional suburban stew.

From these various suburban spaces, these teachers, all experienced Teacher Consultants for the Nebraska Writing Project, have been exploring place-conscious education with their students. Although all the teachers are involved in several place-conscious programs in their schools, for this book we have chosen to highlight a set of programs related to the "watershed" and "commonwealth" issues in our region. Collectively, we hope our work in the suburban spaces of eastern Nebraska may inspire other teachers to develop place-conscious programs appropriate to the watershed and commonwealth of their regions.

In the watershed section of this book, we will feature four projects. University teacher Susan Martens describes writing marathons as a pedagogical activity that requires writers to pay close attention to local place through writing, walking, and sharing in direct contact with the local landscape. Secondary teacher Sharon Bishop engages her students in a deep investigation of water in our region, literally making the physical relations of our watershed the subject of study for Henderson's tenth graders. Borrowing ideas and methodology from the Aldo Leopold Institute, secondary teacher Jeff Lacey describes his Ralston Almanac project, where secondary students learn to look closely at the natural environment of their suburban space. Finally, university teacher Aubrey Streit Krug explores her semester-long first-year writing course focused on connecting local environments to global ecologies.

In the commonwealth section of this book, we will also feature four projects. First, secondary teacher Mary Birky Collier will describe her multiyear exploration of place-conscious literature study in Advanced Placement (AP) literature classes, in a unit that challenges her students to first represent and then act in their community of Papillion–La Vista. Secondary teacher Daniel Boster describes an activist writing project in which high school students in Ralston engaged in reforming their school's fourth grade "Discovery of America" unit and convinced the curriculum director to allow them to teach the "real history" of Columbus. Drawing on the work ethnographies of urban place-conscious teachers, dual-enrollment teacher Cathie English presents a secondary/college unit that uses community interviews to explore the multigenerational history of work. Finally, university teacher Bernice Olivas describes her place-conscious approach to Native American literature, a multicultural elective course routinely selected by mostly white suburban students.

All of these projects help suburban teachers and students envision their place more completely. If, as we argue here, such envisioning is key to addressing the particular issues of suburban disconnection, then we can hope that projects such as the ones we describe, adapted to the particular region housing any suburban space, can help young citizens develop the necessary knowledge and vision for the future all of us will face.

PART ONE

Writing from the Watershed

Claiming Local Place as Natural and Geographic Space

Introduction

ROBERT E. BROOKE

The first part of our book explores our place-conscious approach to the watersheds in which suburban schools are located. In Wendell Berry's distinction between watersheds and commonwealths, watersheds are conceived as the physical environments to which the place is connected. The metaphor of the actual watershed, the network of rivers, lakes, and waterways that provide the region's all-important water, here serves to mark all the ways the physical realities of the place are connected. For us, the goal of place-conscious watershed education is to develop an understanding of these physical relationships so that young citizens can imagine themselves as belonging to the place and acting productively within it.

Because suburbia, in all its forms, is such a constructed environment, the actual physical realities of the region are frequently hard to see. As Thomas Hothem argues in his ecocomposition approach to teaching writing in suburbia, one reason for focusing attention on suburbia is that, for residents, the suburbs seem so normal that they remain unseen. Citing Derek Owens's definition of ecocomposition as "the study of one's immediate and future environs . . . so that students might explore how their identities have been composed by such places and vice versa" (2001, 6), Hothem writes: "The fact that many college students hail from such an eminently legible, formative environment confirms its ripeness for ecocompositional inquiry. It is a decidedly ordinary, familiar landscape—to some a 'placeless' or 'in-between place' that students . . . often find 'mundane and difficult to grasp because we are so used to ignoring [it].' Yet this is all the more reason to study it: in reexamining the suburban experience and the normalcy it has come to represent, students can refine their sense of place and reevaluate the language in which they express it" (2009, 37). Hence, guiding suburban students to give attention to the actual physical presence of their suburbs in relation to the actual physical region surrounding them is a primary task of place-conscious education.

Because suburban development routinely occurs on the edges of metropolitan areas, two key challenges to place-conscious awareness of watershed are sprawl and the penurban myth. As Teaford points out, the physical reality of sprawl is "at the heart of the debate over planning suburbia" (2008, 188), since unrestrained sprawl clearly threatens the nation's agriculture (191), natural environment (192), historic treasures and landmarks (193), and health (194). Lindstrom and Bartling (2003) emphasize that "while the surface appearance of sprawl may appear homogeneous . . . in reality the phenomena of suburban sprawl takes place in localities with distinctive ecologies, histories, and cultures" (xxvi). To understand suburbia's place in the region, thus, means becoming aware of the relations between the edge of the city and the region's exurban landscapes. The farms and ranches, the small towns within driving distance, the nature preserves, the region's historic battlefields, and the Natural Resource Districts responsible for the quality of water, air, and land are all in the "penumbric shadow" of the suburban edge.

The "penumbric shadow," of course, is Joseph Goddard's metaphor for the iconic and mythic form of "country" living that he believes has motivated the constant push toward the suburban edge since *Town and Country* started publication in 1846. As Goddard points out, the idea of "country" living imagined by suburban development is often directly at odds with agriculture; the political independence, organization, and continuity of rural communities; and the sustainable upkeep of natural resources. "Penurbanites longed to move to the countryside, partly because of the stories they created out of their cultural heritage. These cultural ideas originated from the city, meaning that the places that migrants created were not country as it was, but country as they imagined it and wanted it to be" (2012, 19). For Goddard, the penurban myths affecting the use of suburban and exurban country include a full array of distinct positions, from equestrian estate holders to voluntary simplicists to community agriculturists. He would see the New Urban "human scale" communities as a full-fledged participant in the penurban impulse.

In short, understanding the challenges of sprawl and the penurban myths of "the country" is part of the work of place-conscious suburban education. To see the watershed in which a suburban community is located means seeing the physical landscape and cityscape of the particular suburb, as well as seeing the regional relationships between that built environment and the urban and rural contexts surrounding it.

Further, in exploring the regional relationships between the different social groups that have a stake in the environment of a particular suburb, place-conscious watershed education connects directly with community literacy work. In addition to drawing on geographers' concepts of sprawl and penurbia, our watershed work also relies heavily on Linda Flower's concepts of community literacy as a process of public inquiry and rhetorical action. We are guided by Flower's cogent definition of community literacy as a "rhetorical practice for inquiry and social change" that arises from "an intercultural dialogue *with others* on issues that *they* identify as sites of struggle" (2008, 16, 19). Once the local environment shifts, in student consciousness, from an unexamined "given" in their world to a "public site" full of competing understandings over the best uses of land, air, water, flora, and fauna, then the exploration of a suburb's physical location becomes an inquiry into the local public sphere.

For Flower, productive participation in the public sphere involves four traits:

1. It is open to discovery.
2. It accepts discursive conflict.
3. It reaches for resolution, not consensus.
4. It requires rhetorical competence. (34–35)

In our communities (and region), watershed work directly engages young people in all four kinds of participation in the public sphere. Anyone investigating the watershed needs to be open to discovery, because the watershed is a public issue affecting a variety of different interest groups seeking both to persuade each other and to affect public policy and behavior. In Flower's image, the local public sphere is a space of discursive conflict, where "a network of multiple publics" tries to "elbow their way into other publics," circulating "good arguments" and "intensively performative acts of poetic world making" in the attempt "to realize a vision of the world through address" (37). The resulting context is, for Flower, an opportunity for community literacy exploration in and beyond the classroom—that is, for sustained inquiry into the issue, guided by our knowledge and practices as literacy educators, leading to an awareness of the particular "relationship among strangers" (37) that makes up public rhetoric. In Flower's discussion of community literacy, the scaffolded space of the classroom or community center can thus become a "counterpublic" space—a "safe house" where individuals can develop ideas, identities, arguments, and plan actions. Such a space "builds identities and arguments" and "transforms public interaction" (39). Flower writes: "Intercultural inquiry and collaborative problem-solving calls for a hybrid discourse and for rhetorical competencies that are rarely developed in public schools, college composition classes, political debates, or community organizing. So for community literacy, 'going public' does not simply mean publicizing positions and arguments but nurturing and structuring a way to become a diverse, deliberative local public" (40).

Key to Flower's conception of going public through local inquiry is her concept of rhetorical agency and the rhetoric of engagement. Flower identifies four interrelated forms of rhetorical agency, each potentially important in engaging with the local public sphere:

1. *Speaking up*, or giving voice to a personal or group position that would otherwise go unheard;
2. *Speaking against*, or engaging in critique of positions, proposals, and arguments advanced by others;
3. *Speaking with*, or working to articulate ally relationships with groups, positions, and persons different from one's own; and
4. *Speaking for*, or stating commitments for projects, positions, principles, or visions for the future. (78–81)

All four of these forms of rhetorical agency involve complex negotiations between learners and the various publics and counterpublics of the local public sphere. In most any engagement with local watershed inquiry, learners become involved in one or more of these forms of agency.

The four writers in part 1 of our book all take up these issues of understanding the local community in relation to the watershed surrounding it. University teacher Susan Martens describes the use of writing marathons to immerse students in the physical realities of their place, guiding them to see and notice what is there and to move them toward bearing witness for their place. Secondary teacher Sharon Bishop shares a unit focused specifically on the rivers and water system of our region—a complex issue for her exurban community, currently in the penumbric shadow of the state's eastern metropolitan areas. Jeff Lacey's students at Ralston Secondary Schools immerse themselves in deep study of and action for the city's park, in relation to the region's ecology. Finally, university teacher Aubrey Streit Krug considers a local-global connections approach to the work of inquiry and argument in first-year composition. All of these writers strive for ways to make the local watershed of eastern Nebraska visible and important to the various kinds of suburban students in their classrooms.

Move the Writer, Move the Pen, Move the Mind, Change the World

Writing Marathons for Place-Conscious Teaching in Suburbia

SUSAN MARTENS

A writing marathon is a thing of pedagogical beauty: elegant, simple, and powerful. It involves small groups of writers moving together through a landscape, writing and sharing along the way for a class period, an afternoon, a day, or longer. Since first developed in the Southeastern Louisiana Writing Project (SLWP) in the early 1990s, writing marathons have taken root and spread across the country because of the many benefits they yield for participants. First of all, they bring students and teachers together in writing communities. Second, they move writers out into the world to experience the food, the art, the sounds, the weather, and all the rich sensory input that makes up a place. Most important, they allow writers to focus attention, raise awareness, and make connections to people, locations, and ideas they encounter through the experience of exploring, writing, and sharing in places beyond classroom walls.

Marathons are powerful techniques for raising place consciousness and practicing place-conscious education. Like most of the other teaching and learning activities described in this book, marathons can be used in urban and rural as well as suburban teaching contexts, in landscapes that range from the mountains of Montana to the streets of Philadelphia. Marathons are especially useful, however, for teachers and students living and working in suburban environments. James Howard Kunstler insists that children are the "biggest losers" when it comes to the social costs of the suburbs (1993, 115)—an environment he calls "a landscape of scary places, the geography of nowhere, that has ceased to be credible human habitat" (15). Although suburbs have often been praised as wonderful places for kids to grow up, Kunstler claims that young people experience the isolation and homogeneity of suburbs most acutely of all because they cannot drive themselves around or venture beyond their home neighborhoods without hazard (115).

Although Kunstler's dim portrait of suburbia may be extreme, for suburban teachers the writing marathon may be an even more important tool in place-conscious teaching than it is for teachers in other types of settings. The reflective exploring, writing, and sharing excursions that constitute writing marathons, undertaken in small groups as part of a writing community, help participants feel less isolated as they discover a deeper sense of place. Marathons can connect suburban writers to nearby urban and rural places draining into their social and cultural watersheds, attune them to ecologically significant and vulnerable areas within their environmental watersheds, open up the academic and personal watershed spaces of suburban college campuses, and even help writers resee and revalue the suburbs themselves, each of which Thomas Hothem reminds us "is historically unique," and therefore "a potential watershed for purposeful critical inquiry" (2009, 39).

This chapter explains how writing marathons help suburban students and teachers become more thoughtful and engaged citizen-writers. In the first half, I provide a brief history of writing marathons' origin within the National Writing Project and of my own experience facilitating them. I also explain what marathons actually do, through examples of marathon writing from suburban teachers and students in several contexts. In the second half of the chapter, I suggest theoretical frameworks for understanding how writing marathons work and where they can lead us as place-conscious suburban citizens by identifying two sets of interrelated marathon processes. These processes support the two kinds of vision Robert Brooke identifies in this volume's introduction that are central to developing a sense of belonging in suburban communities, both "seeing what's around you clearly" and "having a vision for the future of what your place can become."

The first set of marathon processes I discuss involves several that support developing Brooke's first kind of vision—seeing "what is actually going on" in a given place—and includes the physical and sensory actions of *walking*, *sensing*, *noticing*, *writing*, and *telling* with the intellectual actions of *mapping* and *connecting*. These processes immerse writers in their physical surrounding in a way that helps them see landscapes and relationships that might otherwise remain invisible, particularly the regional relationships between environments and the urban, rural, suburban, and exurban contexts within which they exist and change. The processes in the second set I discuss support the development of Brooke's second kind of vision—a vision for the future of a place and how an individual's actions can shape that future—and include the emotional and social actions of *honoring*, *claiming*, *questioning*, and *dwelling*. Through these processes, writers participate in and contribute to their communities through celebration, critique, inquiry, invitation, and bearing witness through writing. Engaging in the public rhetoric of the writing marathon in these ways helps suburban teachers and students cultivate a sense of community. On marathons they learn "how to belong" by telling the stories of places they see more clearly and by lending their voices to the changes they imagine as possible.

To help readers understand what a writing marathon is like, this chapter is framed by vignettes from four different stops during a single Nebraska Writing Project marathon in a historic district in Omaha. This gathering of eighteen writers was mostly composed of suburban teachers from the Omaha suburbs of Ralston and Papillion–La Vista, from micropolises and bedroom communities ringing Omaha, and from the University of Nebraska–Lincoln (itself a kind of suburb, as I discuss below). This marathon's location—Omaha's Old Market—is one significant to suburban place-conscious educators in the region. The only historic Omaha neighborhood to survive the controversial 1989 demolition of the city's famous Jobbers Canyon (a century-old wholesale warehousing and distribution, or "jobbing," district), today the Old Market is a gentrified but thriving "mixed use" neighborhood, home to upscale and trendy retail shops, ethnic restaurants, art galleries, professional offices, and loft apartments. It illustrates exactly the kind of urban rehabilitation efforts that Jon Teaford documents in *The Metropolitan Revolution: The Rise of Post-urban America*. Teaford explains that the target audience for such centers of "reconstructed urban heritage" was always the tourists and suburbanites attracted to their perceived charm and authenticity that "did not exist just down the suburban streets where most Americans lived" (2006, 183).

Thus, such spaces are ideal for sparking the kinds of reflective inquiry that place-based educators hope to engender. While lovely, walkable, and filled with charming eateries, shops, and galleries, redevelopments like the Old Market are still inherently suburban in that they are designed to attract suburbanites escaping their bland landscapes for more "authentic" and "urban" culture and experiences. The growing popularity of such developments in cities across the country raises the question of authenticity, one Sharon Zukin (2010) takes up in her compelling study of newly hip neighborhoods in New York City such as Williamsburg in Brooklyn. When suburbanites crave connection with the urban centers that form part of their cultural watersheds, the flavor of "urban" they seek tells a great deal about the competing motivations in their quest to belong. Often, they go to places with reasonably accessible parking and artsy food, music, and shopping where the city's historical heart overlaps with the suburban fantasy of the city's urban heart.

What Writing Marathons Are

9:45 a.m. The Starting Line: Délice European Bakery and Café in Omaha's Old Market

Sitting alone at a long table set for twenty-four, I'm anxious. Again. Even the perfect chocolate croissant—ritual writing food à la Natalie Goldberg—gives me little comfort in this cozy café where I am usually so relaxed. I'm about to launch my seventh writing marathon for the Nebraska Writing Project. You'd think I'd be an old hand at this by now, but as always, I worry. What if no one comes? What if someone gets left out during group formation? What if, this time, it doesn't "work"?

I watch the Old Market's mixed crowd of hipsters, tourists, artists, and yuppies pass by the café windows, scanning them for familiar teacher faces and waving them in. Eventually, the table fills in a gentle flurry of introductions, latte getting, and pastry selection. Gearing up for my big welcome and pep talk, I realize that the café is loud. Louder than I expected, and certainly too loud for the standard orientation talk. Quickly, I recruit seasoned marathoners to explain the basics to newbies within earshot. Negotiations ensue regarding possible itineraries. One group wants to observe a giant construction zone nearby. Another wants to see the glass installation at the Bemis Center for Contemporary Art. A "family" group forms with two of our NeWP teachers and their combined four children. I find some kindred souls willing to indulge my desire to write at Mr. Toad's Library and Pub. And then . . . we're off. Notebooks and coffee in hand, small bands of writers trail out onto the cobblestones. Each group will follow its own path, make its own discoveries, and establish its own writing groove. Now it's out of my hands.

What were originally called "New Orleans writing marathons"—now usually called, simply, "writing marathons"—have been practiced by teachers and writers in the NWP since their emergence in 1994. According to their creator, SLWP director Richard Louth (2011), they evolved from an activity in one of the SLWP's Summer Institutes that was itself based on the writing-marathon technique described in Natalie Goldberg's *Writing Down the Bones*:

> So for the first session, we all write for ten minutes and then go around the room and read what we've written with no comments by anyone. . . . A pause naturally happens after each reader, but we do not say, "That was great" or even, "I know what you mean." There is no good or bad, no praise or criticism. We read what we have written and go on to the next person. . . . What usually happens is you stop thinking: you write; you become less and less self-conscious. Everyone is in the same boat, and because no comments are made, you feel freer and freer to write anything you want. (1986, 150)

Louth adapted this technique for a writing activity he organized during a writing teachers conference in New Orleans. He knew that the teachers would be tired of sitting through workshops and anxious to get out into the French Quarter, so he decided to take the marathon to the streets. As the story goes, he meticulously worked out writing groups and itineraries on note cards and then, at the last minute, decided to scrap the plan entirely. He gave participants a map, a list of interesting writing sites, Goldberg's advice about responding, and then let everyone determine their own groups and paths.

He explains, "Miraculously, everyone returned, and when they did, they were somehow different. An excitement filled the room, a common bond that came from this strange experience" (2011, 3). After that first experiment, Louth began incorporating marathons into SLWP's Summer Institutes. He has since launched countless other writing marathons at NWP SLWP events, and the activity has spread widely to dozens of NWP sites, classrooms, and writing groups across the country.

I went on my first writing marathon in July 2006 during the NWP's Writing and Technology Professional Writing Retreat in Nebraska City. The retreat took place at Arbor Day Farm's Lied Lodge and Conference Center, a lovely complex with lighted paths and orchards that perfectly embodies the kind of suburban pastoral ideal that Joseph Goddard (2012) calls "Penurbia," particularly as it is situated within the intersection of Omaha's and Lincoln's twin "penumbric shadows." One of the retreat facilitators, Dakota Writing Project director Michelle Rogge Gannon, used a writing marathon to help retreat participants jump-start their writing and help group members get to know one another. She armed us with sturdy notebooks, urged us to apply sunscreen and bug spray, gave a basic orientation pep talk, and turned us loose on the conference center's beautiful grounds.

On that very first writing marathon, I was amazed by the liberating power of this in-the-moment writing *in place*. My writer mind went crazy at first, rebelling against the professional writing task that was my ultimate goal. But eventually, I found that the simple act of writing in the inspiring setting, in the supportive company of other writers, set up a powerfully meditative framework that opened up veins of creative energy I had never accessed before. At each writing stop, I began by paying attention to my surroundings, noticing what I was noticing through the meditative act of writing, allowing sensory observations to carry my thoughts outward, and finally reflecting back on how all of these layers might be connected.

After my initiation into writing marathons, I wanted to explore their pedagogical and professional development possibilities further with the teachers of the Nebraska Writing Project. In October 2006 I launched a pilot writing marathon in Lincoln's historic Haymarket district. Eleven teachers came that day, split into two groups. When we reconvened two and a half hours later, we swapped tales, read bits from our notebooks, and talked about how we might share the marathon with other teachers and use it in our classrooms. Everyone agreed that the NeWP needed another one soon.

Based on the success of the pilot marathon, I began organizing seasonal marathons for the NeWP and annual marathons for our Summer Invitational Institutes for teachers and for our Advisory Board retreats. As word about writing marathons spread among our teachers, both attendance and requests for future marathons increased. I have since conducted dozens of writing marathons with high school and college students in my own classrooms, and I have worked with many people across the country who have done the same. I have watched them work and analyzed how and why they work, especially within the context of suburban place-conscious teaching.

What Writing Marathons Do

10:45 a.m. First Writing Stop: The Passageway

My writing group enters the light-filled four-story courtyard, agrees to meet on the stone steps opposite at 11:10, then spreads out to write. We see members of another group on benches and steps, already writing. I climb up to the mostly abandoned office level and make my little camp. I write very little, managing only "The textures of the brick walls, terra cotta planters, and climbing tendrils of vines sing to my senses. Vague incense wafts up from the New Age shop two floors below. Brooding 'emo' kids move slyly through the shadows while snow sprinkles softly on the plastic skylight above."

After our designated fifteen minutes, I move toward the rendezvous point, wondering if this marathon will fizzle. A few of our group members read, and I am inspired by their sparkling insight and keen observation. Then a teacher friend from my school, Stephany, starts to read. It's her first marathon, and I am especially anxious for her to have a good experience. As I listen, she connects this place to a story about her husband who is having knee surgery soon. A simple procedure, but one that leads her to contemplate his advancing age. She's worried about his health. Her voice breaks, and she pauses. I reach out and touch her arm with encouragement. She apologizes, but everyone in the group affirms that there is no need.

She finishes and sighs with a great sense of relief. Lisa, who is also on her first writing marathon, says, "I don't know you very well, but I'd like to give you a hug." There is a magic here on this stone landing, in the middle of this very public place. Five writers are standing together, reading and sharing and nodding. I relax, ashamed that I ever had any doubts about this marathon. Something about the process has helped Stephany connect this beautiful, historic place to her life with her husband. Something made her decide to bravely read it aloud to us, her fellow writers. And all of a sudden, we are all empowered and freed by her choice.

In this section, I provide an overview of what writing marathons do to help suburban teachers and students "learn to belong" by presenting them as a pedagogical platform for participating in Flower's (2008, 81) four forms of rhetorical agency. Marathons invite writers to *speak up*, *speak against*, *speak for*, and *speak with* people and places by shifting people from their "normal" roles as suburban teachers and students to the roles of writers, shifting the focus of the connections they make to specific observations while writing in local places outside of the classroom, and providing opportunities for writers to share those connections as acts of community building both within and beyond the marathon itself.

First of all, marathons help teachers and students shift out of their everyday roles and take on the roles of writers. Claiming this identity is pivotal for many marathon participants. Emphasizing the importance of claiming a writer's identity, marathons usually begin with a teacher or facilitator asking participants to turn to one another and say, "I am a writer." Louth explains that "thinking of yourself as a writer not only affects you but also others, and [can] open many doors" (2011, 4). For students, embracing their identities as writers can be the most powerful benefit of the writing marathon by far. Often, learning to *speak up* through their writers' voices is the shift that opens the door for learning many other things about writing and place—for *speaking against*, *for*, and *with* their places and communities.

For NWP Teacher Consultants, renewing their sense of themselves as writers is vital to restoring their enthusiasm for teaching writing and connecting with students as fellow writers. The following two poems were written by NeWP Teacher Consultant Mary Birky Collier, whose excellent work on place-conscious teaching in suburban Papillion–La Vista, Nebraska, appears in this collection. She composed them while she observed a construction site during the same Old Market marathon that generated this chapter's vignettes. The poems illustrate how writers can draw strength and inspiration from the act of seeing through writers' eyes:

"Urban Renewal"

The pain
Jagged edges expose
Innards of history
The crane operator pummels, pulverizes
The wrecking ball of renewal

"Thawing"

Before I write, I need to thaw
My hands stiff from the cold,
Absorb the warmth
Until the blood moves, then flows,
Then runs hotly through veins.
Before I write, I need to thaw
My mind—stiff from the week's
To-do lists, alarms clocks, job demands,
Absorb and look deeply

Until the ordinary moves,
Then extraordinary flowing beneath
The surface,
Words, suddenly, hot in my veins

Mary's poems capture the wonderful mirrored movement of the writer's body in space as well as the writer's mind. They also clearly represent a writer *speaking against* urban renewal and against the constraints of a demanding teaching job. Her first piece speaks up to bear witness to the "wrecking ball of renewal" tearing open the old building and exposing the "innards of history." The second piece, "Thawing," presents a more gentle vision of renewal on a smaller scale—the blood rushing back into her cold hands. She tells us that her mind, like her hands, has grown stiff with the mundane details of life, and she speaks against "To-do lists, alarm clocks, job demands." But then her writer's eyes "absorb and look deeply," prompted by the shift in perspective when "the ordinary moves," and her mind is "warmed" by "extraordinary flowing" of words "hot in my veins." The juxtaposition of these two pieces illustrates the complicated notion of "renewal" for cities as well as for writers. More important, Mary's writing illustrates the invigorating effect of moving through a landscape and experiencing it with a writer's eye, ear, and mind. Her piece *speaks for* the benefits of writing teachers writing in place, for the renewal that comes from the writing marathon itself.

Students, like writing teachers, draw energy and inspiration from writing marathons while they also discover new ways of connecting to their local place. Organizing such outings within the confines of secondary school rules and schedules presents some challenges for teachers, certainly more so than for college-level teachers. However, it was well worth the effort for my high school freshmen in Arlington, Nebraska, as an invention activity in their unit on personal essay writing.

A school with a K–12 enrollment of six hundred students, Arlington is classified as rural, but it shares many characteristics of traditional suburbs, serving as a bedroom community for people who mostly work in Omaha (thirty miles away), its suburbs, and its satellite micropolises. I persuaded my freshmen to bring their lunches out onto the football field one afternoon and wrote with them as they arranged themselves on the bleachers, sprawled out on the forty-yard line, and propped themselves up against goal posts. One student, Molly Miller, began by describing the place with strong sensory imagery. Her writing then shifted toward observation of her fellow writers and their engagement with the landscape. She wrote:

> I can smell a storm coming. The moist, humid air feels cool and wonderful against my skin. A bird twitters and flies overhead. Its beautiful sound deeply contrasts with the quiet zooming of cars on the highways and the clanking of the nearby flagpole as its strings and wires dance in the breeze. . . . The blades of grass vibrate before me like ocean waves just beginning. As I turn slightly, I see a napkin sitting in the grass. I think it's evil to ruin the beauty of nature with litter and trash. As I ponder the intent of the people guilty of littering the earth, I realize the wind has grown stronger. I can hear it whistling now, almost howling. I decide that I should pick up the napkin before it is taken somewhere else where it could possibly do more damage.
>
> The wind just grabbed my classmate's lunch sack. As I watch her chase it down, it makes me laugh. It also makes me glad. She could have just let it fly and add to the trashy landscape. I'm glad not everyone is evil and uncaring.

Molly's writing suggests her emerging environmentalist sensibilities and also illustrates the specific observations of local place writers often make on marathons. She notices the storm-rich air, the way birdsong interacts with the sounds of traffic, a clanging flagpole, and the blades of grass vibrating "like ocean waves." Her observation of a discarded napkin, then of her classmate running after a lunch sack taken by the wind, leads her to commend the girl for not contributing to "the trashy landscape" of her suburban place. Like many marathon writings, Molly's focuses on mundane details, observed through a writer's eye, then interprets those details in a way that leads her readers toward some consideration of their significance. In Molly's case, she *speaks against* littering, but she also *speaks for* her friend's effort to resist the tendency for people to be "evil and uncaring."

Interactions like Mary's and Molly's, between writers and the places where they write, sometimes lead marathon participants to unexpected and moving revelations about the connections between landscapes and their lives. When these connections are then shared with group members and with other audiences, marathon writers employ a rhetoric of engagement by participating in acts of community building. This result is my third answer to the question, "What do writing marathons do?"

I have been fortunate to experience many marathons where such place-based community building occurred in my own groups. One vivid example occurred on a NeWP marathon in Lincoln's Haymarket district—a neighborhood very similar to Omaha's Old Market, with an urban revitalization ethic designed to draw visitors from Lincoln's many middle-class suburbs. I was in a group with NeWP technology liaison Jeff Grinvalds, who teaches high school English in the suburban Omaha district of Westside. We were writing in the Great Plains Art Museum, at an exhibit called "Last Day on the Farm" that featured artworks about people forced to leave their farms. Viewing these paintings and reading the stories behind them led Jeff to write about his father, who left the family farm in Latvia when he was drafted into the German army before he came to the United States. While writing about this connection, Jeff became so moved that he stopped in the middle of it to phone his father and ask him what it was like that day, leaving his home, his family, and his culture behind. Jeff wrote, "When I look at this painting of a stoic barn and silent house, all that I see is my father's last day on his farm outside of Smiltene, Latvia. In 1943, he was fifteen—drafted into a war that was not his to fight. Did he kiss his mother goodbye? Was his father proud to see his son leave the family farm forever?"

His Last Day on the Farm

Those ice blue eyes reflecting the northern sunlight,
green pastures radiate
a barn, ancient, standing on stones pried from the Latvian soil.
His home, white, humble,
a silent river whispering next to fields of grain.
Chickens peck at the ground,

a single horse neighs,
while two somber milk cows low in the distance.
He walks down the road toward a fate—a destiny
that he could not possibly fathom. At just fifteen.
Saying goodbye to not only his mother,
his father, brother and sister,
but everything that he has ever known,
always knowing one thing for certain.
He was never going to be a farmer.

When Jeff shared this piece in the museum, the depth of feeling in his writing moved us, his writing group, deeply. He told us the story of his family, told to him through his own father's voice and memory, triggered by the paintings of artists who were telling their own stories of loss and longing. Although his narrative and poem were highly personalized, featuring people and places unknown to the rest of us, his connection to the artwork led us all to more deeply consider our own stories of family, farms, and lost landscapes alongside the ones depicted by the artists. Together, we bore witness to the layers of interconnection among the places of the gallery where we had stopped to write, the places depicted in the artwork, and the places called forth in our writing and our minds.

Jeff was *speaking up*, certainly, by sharing his family story, but he was also *speaking with* the artists—and with the Great Plains Art Museum staff who composed the exhibit—by *speaking against* the loss of heritage, of family, and of landscape. By sharing such a personal story and such a strong reaction to the artwork, Jeff was also *speaking for* the power of visual and verbal rhetoric to address issues of social justice, participating in and advocating for Flower's "rhetoric of engagement" (2008, 75).

Transformational experiences like this one—where writers not only discover their voice but also discover their capacity to use that voice to *speak up*, *against*, *for*, and *with* their places and communities—are common on writing marathons. They clearly answer Wendell Berry's call for teachers and academics to overcome the limitations of overspecialization through engagement with local landscape. Berry says, "They will have to get out of their 'fields,' so to speak, and into the watershed, the ecosystem, and the community; and they will have to be actuated by affection" (2003b, 39). Marathons help writers get out of their fields and into the landscapes well, and they definitely actuate affection. But how?

How Writing Marathons Work: Walking, Sensing, Noticing, Writing, Telling, Mapping, and Connecting

11:30 a.m. Second Writing Stop: La Buvette Wine and Grocery

Emboldened by our first round of sharing, we enter one of Dan's favorite spots. He warns us that the rude wait staff is part of the place's European character, but we find the place strangely accommodating of our writing group. Some order coffee or tea, but I go for the cheese plate, starving now since failing to finish my precious chocolate croissant. Jeff goes off to a table by himself. Sipping espresso in the corner, his poetic profile sends my pen flying to my notebook. I write, "The magic of good food in a good place with good people. . . . Pepper, cracked fresh, wakes up my tongue. Musky stilton, fresh tomato, briny olives. These colors and textures stand up straight against the cloudy, chilly morning. So much depends on the crusty baguette topped with cheese globs beside the racks of wine." A little indulgent, I admit, but at least I am feeling the place, tasting the food, experiencing this familiar corner of the city through a writer's eyes. The group is comfortable now, humming along in the writing zone.

In this section, I seek to answer the question of *how* writing marathons work by examining several independent processes within any given marathon. As illustrated in the diagram below, these are *walking, sensing, noticing, writing, telling, mapping,* and *connecting.* These processes create an experience of interactive engagement between the writers as a group, between the writers and the places in which they write, and within the minds of the writers as the marathon unfolds. Each process interacts with every other process, though not necessarily in sequence. Each one contributes to the cumulative effect of connecting people, places, thoughts, and experiences in ways that cultivate writers' clear vision of suburban places and their relationship to those places.

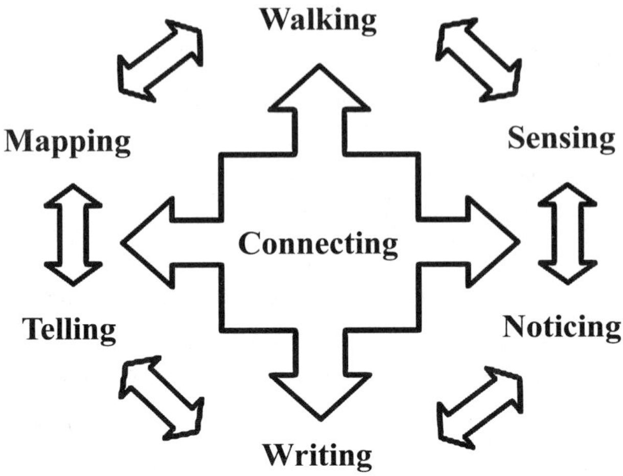

Figure 1. How and why writing marathons work.

Most traditional writing marathons start with *walking*. The group decides upon a general direction or goal and sets out down the street, across the campus, or through the woods, interacting along the way with each other and with the landscape. The walking aspect of the writing marathon provides the most basic physical access for all of the other processes on the diagram (as well as for the *dwelling*, *claiming*, *honoring*, *questioning*, and *acting* I will take up in the next section). The writing marathon's emphasis on walking relates strongly to Nedra Reynolds's identification of walking as a rhetorical practice. She says, "Learning to see takes place at the street level, through walking. While other ways of moving through the world might also teach us to see, only walking embraces so many senses and has the 'hands on' (or feet first) materiality of place" (2004, 69).

Walking is also an important part of the methodology behind a type of cultural geography approach that Reynolds calls "streetwork" (115). She explains that streetwork is a kind of fieldwork that focuses on an active street scene rather than the traditional "field" of research. It places emphasis on observations of the environmental, historical, and cultural aspects of a place, and of students' and others' experiences of that place, in order to understand how a sense of place is constructed. Reynolds notes that the principle behind streetwork is that a shift in perspective can help jolt students out of their familiar patterns of seeing and allow them to see in new ways (115). Likewise, one of the principles behind a writing marathon is to help inspire good writing by giving writers an opportunity to see new places or even familiar places in a new way. As Louth explains, "The important thing is for the setting to shake one up a bit—to be unfamiliar—and sometimes that happens not because it is a new place but simply because it is being seen through new eyes, a writer's eyes" (2011, 8).

This idea of disrupting routines also underscores the important connection between walking and the next two processes in the diagram, *sensing* and *noticing*. Certainly, it is possible for people to go tramping through a place without much awareness. In a writing marathon, however, the senses are finely tuned and open. As writers, we are actively looking for inspiration. We are also looking, listening, and extending our other senses in search of the elusive "sense of place." Yi-Fu Tuan, who claims in *Space and Place: The Perspective of Experience* that his own purpose was to "increase the burden of awareness" (1977, 202), writes convincingly of the powerful potential available to human beings when they employ their full range of perceptive attention, of simply noticing. He asserts that "an object or place achieves concrete reality when our experience of it is total, that is, through all of the senses as well as with an active and reflective mind" (18). In a process similar to some meditation techniques, marathon writers often take this power of perception even further in *noticing what they are noticing*—a process that manifests in writing marathons very concretely through the *writing*.

Another vital process central to the writing marathon experience is the *telling*, a process where the function of the small group really shows its power. At each stop, writers in a group gather to read what they have written. Often, they also gather for a "read-around" at the end with all of the other groups who have participated in the marathon. Writers publicly read their writing to an immediate human audience. They engage in the telling and hearing of stories, in the bearing witness—aloud and in the company of others—to what each place has meant, in that moment, to each writer or what issues the experience of place has led each writer to publicly name. Each of the examples above—Mary's critique of urban renewal, Molly's environmentalist stand, and Jeff's story of his father's last day on the farm—is an example of this telling process at work.

The last process I identify in the diagram is *mapping*. Strongly related to her conception of walking, Reynolds's (2004) notion of mapping is one that offers both material and metaphorical connections to writing marathons and can lead writers toward greater place consciousness. Maps are rhetorical texts constructed with audience, purpose, and context that can be useful, satisfying tools. Most marathons begin with some kind of map, often marked with the launch location, or "starting line," and with the final gathering and reading location, the "finish line." One layer of mapping occurs as a writer physically moves through the lines and figures indicated on the map, rendering them real and allowing writers to claim them through experiential knowing. More important, this experiential knowledge includes critical things that maps do not show: the shortcuts, the construction zones, the lack of sidewalks on a busy street, and which spots or neighborhoods most epitomize the character of a particular place.

As writers explore an area, they layer onto the physical map another much more detailed mental map, making sense of their experiences spatially but also temporally (that is, "We left the farmer's market around noon"), sensually ("The smell of the waffle cones brought us to this ice cream shop"), and personally ("On this corner Lisa read the sad piece about her daughter"). Such layers of interactions with the landscape in this way yield rich, multilayered physical, mental, and social maps that honor places through detail and memory. Particularly in suburban spaces, mapping place on a writing marathon can help writers defamiliarize themselves with landscapes that may have grown "placeless" or invisible to them over time and imbue them with new meaning by new mapping of memories and associations, as happened to Stephany in the vignette from the Old Market marathon.

As Reynolds points out, "mapping" is also used as a metaphor for charting, understanding, exploring, or organizing. Metaphorical mapping of this kind certainly figures into writing marathons. In one sense, individual writers may find themselves in "uncharted territory," following their own walking and writing paths into realizations about their communities or their families, as Jeff and Molly did. Writers may also map new mental pathways, connecting people, places, or ideas that were not previously connected in their minds, such as the concepts of writing and thawing in Mary's example.

Here is another example of the mapping process at work, one from a student in a college composition course I taught with a place-based frame. With its manicured lawns, tasteful landscaping, and sprawling parking lots, our University of Nebraska–Lincoln campus (like most campuses) really does feel like a suburban neighborhood, especially when we give ourselves permission to walk through and to really stop and notice things, as writers do on writing marathons. Like the Lied Conference Center mentioned above, it embodies the suburban pastoral ideal of Goddard's (2012) "Penurbia." In addition, there is a very suburban sense of alienation, of not knowing one's disciplinary "neighbors" in a campus community where colleges and departments sometimes feel like gated communities, walled off from others in their "big box" buildings.

My college composition students almost universally note this feeling on marathons, especially when we push ourselves to explore buildings we are unfamiliar with, as we did on the marathon featured below. In it Molly Rangel maps out the contrast in the funding of campus facilities as she finds them represented in the decor of several nearby campus buildings. She suggests a link between the rich furnishings of the computer engineering building and the popular university football program, exploring both the symbolism of the luxury study desks from which she writes and the value of spending time in more rustic campus spaces:

> The Engineering Building is a new building attached to the football stadium, which if you know anything about the University of Nebraska, our "gods" live there. So I was not shocked to find a modern cathedral of a building attached, though I'm still not sure if I covet the building or loathe it.
>
> I now know why I have to sit down with caution, in fear of getting splinters in Oldfather Hall. It is because the Engineering Building has plush black leather chairs, with proper space to write and even a cup holder. Because in the Engineering Building your coffee is far too

> special for the floor. They also have large, rectangular windows that allow for looking out into the edge of campus, unlike so many other buildings that seem to be going for the dungeon feel. Though I have to say, as I walk around the perfectly kept building, I feel as though I have magically transitioned from campus into a Holiday Inn or Hilton. So maybe there is something to be said for having lived my college years in buildings with dusty air from chalk boards and faded walls that remind me of the esteem and age of my campus. Or maybe I should just figure a way to sneak one of the leather space chairs out of this building and into Oldfather or Andrews Hall.

Although it illustrates both the physical and the metaphorical mapping processes at work in writing marathons, Molly's writing also represents engaged public rhetoric. Read aloud in the public space of the computer engineering building itself, then read aloud again back in our classroom, her piece bears witness to the story of an uncharted campus space (at least to most of us in the class) and helped initiate a class inquiry for us about decisions regarding the funding of campus facilities. The question underscored many of our subsequent discussions about our campus community, particularly when another group on a later marathon shared writing from their stop in the plush football players' lounge. *Speaking up* for herself as a paying student, *speaking against* perceived inequalities in facilities funding, *speaking for* "buildings with dusty air," Molly was also *speaking with* the other writers in her marathon group who shared similar impressions of the computer engineering building's symbolic "deck chairs."

This example of classroom inquiry also clearly underscores the primacy of the process at the center of my diagram, *connecting*. Through this process writers synthesize their experiences and come to a greater understanding of themselves as writers within the places where they write. In all of my marathon experiences, the phenomenon of connecting dominates all other processes—connecting movement with writing, connecting places with memories, connecting thought with feeling, and connecting people with each other.

To help illustrate how these processes of walking, sensing, noticing, writing, telling, mapping, and connecting work together in a writing marathon, here is another example of student writing from a marathon. Beth Buehler composed this short piece in another one of my college composition classes, on a marathon stop next to an old campus tree. In her writing Beth reflects on the age of the tree, the campus, her four years as an undergraduate, and her place within the grand scheme of place and history:

> I'm sitting in the shade of a tree. There is a monument in front of it, reading, "This Austrian Pine is dedicated to Willa Cather, Class of 1895." Even sitting on this edge of campus by the older buildings such as Architecture Hall and Brace Labs, it's hard for me to fathom that students have been sitting where I'm sitting now for over 110 years. It makes me think on how much history our university has—how there will be students sitting in this very same spot for another 110 years. I'm part of a cycle, and this is my turn to sit here, but I'm a senior. I'm leaving this place.
>
> I have four years of memories here, added to the countless other students who have sat here. What mark will I leave here? Only the people I have touched. Looking at the tree from 1895, I'm feeling very much like Whitman's blades of grass. Here today, gone tomorrow.
>
> The trees are in full bloom. Students are laying all over—on the grass in the shade of trees, on benches. A light breeze flows, ruffling my notebook pages. Even from my spot in front of this tree, I can see the Sheldon, Ferguson, the Lied, Westbrook, and into downtown. It seems to me that this is the perfect spot for a picnic, or to come just to read a good book.

Beth's writing includes *sensing* and *noticing* brought about by the *walking* to this final stop by the Cather tree on her group's route through the campus. She documents, in writing, her awareness of the blooming trees, students studying on the grass, the wind ruffling her notebook pages, and the shape of campus buildings. She shared this writing aloud with other members of her group, *telling* her own experience of place and listening to others' stories.

The Cather tree was the group's final stop, one that facilitated the processes of *mapping* and *connecting* reflected in this excerpt. Beth's writing moves from an observation of the tree and its memorial plaque to a sense of herself as a participant within the storied landscape of the campus, illustrating that sense of connection so common on writing marathons. There is a clear mapping of the tree's relationship to other campus structures and a mapping of its place in time. Beth even references Walt Whitman's *Leaves of Grass*, echoing "Song of Myself" as she notes, "I'm part of a cycle, and this is my turn to sit here." She expresses an awareness that the campus existed before she arrived and would continue after she leaves, and she wonders whether she leaves any kind of "mark."

I was not with Beth's group during their writing marathon, nor did I give her class any particular directions about what to write about. I did, however, ask students to use the marathon as a chance to really observe their campus in relationship to the themes of "place," "tribe," and "community" we had been using to study writing all semester. Along with the other writers featured in this chapter, Beth's experience points toward the possibilities for writing marathons to help writers honor, claim, question, dwell within, and act on behalf of the places they write about.

Where Writing Marathons Can Lead Us: Dwelling, Claiming, Honoring, Questioning, and Acting

12:30 p.m. Third Writing Stop: Mr. Toad's Library and Pub

This place is an Old Market institution. It's mostly deserted at this hour, so we can all spread out in the dim but cozy booths while admiring the towering bookshelves and stained-glass windows. Writing on the wobbliest of tables, I feel I could stay here forever. I write, "Outside the window, Ollie the Trolley goes by, mostly empty. This is not the Old Market at its liveliest, but it suits writers just fine. We are accustomed to the loneliness and the quiet. Perhaps it is the Guinness, but I feel my heart expand as I write in this precious pub. Writing in public, out in the elements, takes us out of ourselves. It makes us look with fresh eyes, not just at our surroundings, but at ourselves within our surroundings."

This diagram, like the one above, identifies a set of interrelated processes that I will discuss in this section—ways that writing marathons lead

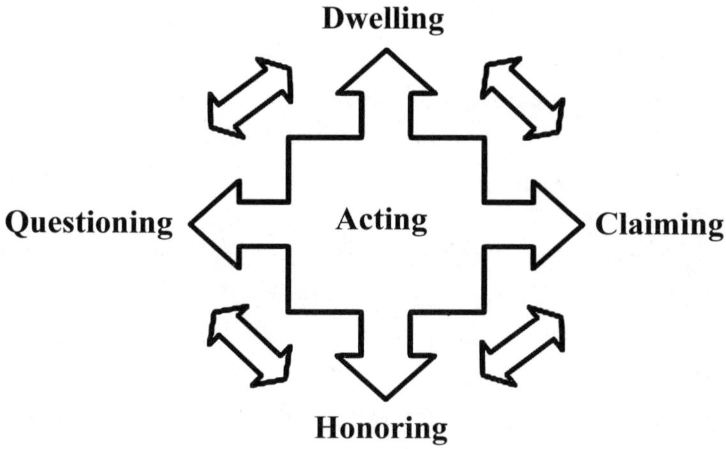

Figure 2. How writing marathons support place-conscious citizenship.

participants toward place-conscious suburban citizenship by cultivating the second type of vision Brooke explains in our introduction. This vision leads writers to imagine the future of a given place and their role in shaping it by cultivating a deeper sense of belonging to, understanding, appreciating, and engaging the range of suburban spaces where we live and work. Writers who feel themselves as part of a place—as engaged, conscious participants within it—can discover ways to improve that place through honoring it, claiming it, questioning it, dwelling within it, and acting on its behalf.

In *Geographies of Writing: Inhabiting Places and Encountering Difference*, Nedra Reynolds explores how the physical and metaphorical processes of walking and mapping can lead writers toward a kind of interaction with place she calls *dwelling*. She explains, "Learning to dwell doesn't necessarily mean 'loving' a place and settling in happily for years at a time; it means paying attention to place, not just to the borders that surround it, and building thirdspaces. Learning to dwell means tapping into the circulation of practices that don't show up on a map or a photograph of a village" (2004, 143). Experiential, place-based practices "in the field" can help students "learn to dwell" in their own places, she says, helping them overcome their prejudice about places deemed "other" and "be 'moved'—persuaded—to encounter difference, to walk beyond the city walls" (175).

The real-world experiences of place that form the backbone of the writing marathon can also help writers encounter difference, go beyond the walls of their classrooms and beyond the boundaries of their familiar neighborhoods to "learn to dwell." One primary way that marathon writing functions in this way is by providing opportunities for writers to bear witness to what they see, hear, and experience in their communities. Doing so purposefully and honestly, marathon writers often seek and represent the "situated knowledge" of others—a rhetorical practice that Flower insists is vital to building the community literacy needed for effective community advocacy (2008, 82). As she explains, "Rhetoric places its bets on the power of transformative knowledge, on knowing that how we represent and re-represent our shared reality can change that reality" (151). Marathon writers who record what they witness use their rhetorical skills to document and showcase realities that other people may not take the time to notice. In the marathon writings above, for example, we see writers bearing witness to urban renewal, environmental responsibility, and the loss of rural lifeways as depicted through artwork.

Strongly related to dwelling is the marathon process of *claiming*. Walking, sitting, and writing in public places on a marathon constitute acts of claiming, with marathon participants creating spaces akin to Nancy Welch's (2008) concept of a "living room," where "ordinary people make rhetorical space" through occupying and speaking in public space during actions such as sit-ins and strikes. In marathons with my college composition classes, for example, I often ask students to explore and write in buildings that they have never entered before or that they do not know very well. Writing in unfamiliar campus places, such as in the computer-engineering building example, helps students claim their campus in new ways, opening up physical and rhetorical spaces where they often say that, previously, they felt they did not belong.

Another way marathon writers claim places and expand a sense of belonging, both for themselves and for others, is through invitation. In my college composition classes, I encourage students to share their favorite campus nooks or to show marathon groups members around places they might not otherwise see. These "show-and-tell" marathon stops have led students to invite classmates into places such as fraternity houses, athletic facilities, the architecture print lab, hidden dormitory elevators, and music practice rooms. Once, for instance, a group of four athletes invited me to come on a marathon with them to see the Student Life Complex that houses their study rooms, dining hall, and training facilities. Leading me confidently beyond the little sign that said, "Athletes only beyond this point," these students not only claimed their own space in a new way by inviting me to write with them there, but helped me see the complex as part of my own campus community.

By inviting me into their space, the student-athletes were also celebrating one of their most cherished places and *honoring* it through writing. Honoring local place is another powerful marathon process that helps raise place consciousness, one that place-based educators have hailed as crucial to creating the awareness and affection for place that lay the groundwork for engaged citizenship. As Lane-Zucker explains, "The solutions to many of our ecological problems lie in an approach that celebrates, empowers, and nurtures the cultural, artistic, historical and spiritual resources of each local community and region and champions their ability to bring those resources to bear on the healing of nature and community" (2004, i–ii).

Derek Owens also calls for celebration—for honoring local place—as an antidote to the suburban malaise that particularly afflicts freshmen composition classes. He says, "Educators have a responsibility to help students resist the cynicism and hyperboredom of contemporary consumer culture by discovering the kind of self-worth that comes from being amazed at one's local worlds" (2001, 69). Writing marathons honor such "local worlds" by celebrating them through writing, whether they are bedroom communities, micropolises, traditional suburbs, or the Penurbias of college campuses. Beth's writing about the 110-year-old Willa Cather tree is one example of this kind of honoring, as are the many details I have included in the vignettes from Omaha's Old Market, from the hanging gardens of the Passageway to the stained-glass windows of Mr. Toad's Library and Pub. Such celebratory writing furthermore constitutes what Jennifer Sinor calls "an ethical act" that helps save the places we write about. She explains, "To belong to a place and to write about that connection means that one more place might escape damage, whether because you become invested in saving that place or because you convince others to save it" (2011, 9).

Yet another place-conscious process common to the marathon experience is *questioning*, an aspect that drives productive inquiry for writers and leads to close readings of places and communities. As an expression of place consciousness, critique is a vital companion skill to the processes of celebration and honoring. Brooke explains that, along with the ability to know and celebrate local places, "we want students to be able to critique their localities, identifying and confronting the social, political, economic, and environmental practices that can make local life unsustainable" (2003, 63).

Flower's conception of inquiry illuminates how question-based marathon writing can lead to place-conscious citizenship. She explains, "Inquiry starts in a sense of felt difficulty—of wondering, questioning, being perplexed—that leads to posing the problem . . . or explor[ing] the dissonance between the reality you see and what others assert it is or should be" (2008, 230). On marathons participants often respond to "a felt sense of difficulty" by posing questions that serve to name problems and confront conflicts. Several of the excerpts from writing marathons featured in this chapter have also hinged on questions that help writers draw connections between personal experiences and political issues. They ask questions like the following: Why do people litter? What happens to family farms when all of the children leave? What mark will I leave on this campus?

Ultimately, marathons spark processes that lead writers toward *acting* in ways designed to improve their communities. These actions lead to even deeper connections, strengthening the sense of belonging that makes people want to understand, celebrate, and improve places where they live and work through many different forms of advocacy. Ecocritic Alan Thein Durning even suggests that affection for local place might be the *only* way to overcome the despair and hopelessness some feel about environmental issues such as climate change. He says, "The only cures possible may be local and motivated by a sentiment—the love of home—that global thinkers have often regarded as divisive or provincial. Thus, it may be possible to diagnose global problems globally, but impossible to solve them globally. There may not be any ways to save the world that are not, first and foremost, ways for people to save their own places" (1999, 261).

Although marathons often do spark projects that involve traditional forms of advocacy, such as public blogs, radio shows, Web stories, and community networking events, they also do significant work in cultivating what we are calling in this volume a *preadvocacy stance*—a frame of mind characterized by an understanding of the independencies at the heart of our conception of "place" and by an openness to engagement—that lays the foundation for future action. Place-conscious educators must recognize the value of the preadvocacy stance in its own right, knowing that it is a crucial starting point in opening the door to future learning and action. Nancy Welch explains that "though we can't call a strike or launch a social movement from a classroom, we can teach and learn the attitudes, relationships, and practices that are the preconditions for imagining oneself and others as participants in social policy making and agents of social change" (2008, 15).

Paramount to this preadvocacy stance is the "vision of belonging" that Brooke and others in this collection discuss as central to our argument for place-conscious teaching in suburbia. It is the same sentiment that Hothem underscores as the vital teaching benefit arising from the intersection of ecocomposition and suburban place studies. He explains, "However it is understood, ecocomposition should inspire students to imagine their world as a text and themselves as its authors, so that they build a kind of rhetorical home in their immediate surroundings and cultural contexts" (2009, 55).

My college composition students often complain about feeling lost and alone, especially the ones who move to our large university from small towns and close-knit suburban communities. They complain that they feel disconnected, especially as they struggle to settle into dormitory life, manage the frequent uprooting in both housing and majors, and navigate the constant rush of classes, exams, events, and social media environments.

Writing marathons provide a "rhetorical home," opening up physical and rhetorical spaces where they can actually look around the campus, notice what it has to offer, hear others' observations alongside their own, and feel more connected to both the class and their campus community. Likewise, marathons create rhetorical homes for suburban elementary and secondary students as well as for their teachers, helping draw students' attention to where they are by having them *write where they are*—not just in the classroom but out in the world where they can participate in their suburban landscapes as well as in the urban and rural places that feed into the watersheds that connect them.

The more marathons I attend and facilitate, and the more I participate in the collaborative place-based inquiry that marathons sponsor, the more I notice how much the suburban experience is shaping our perceptions of place, our preferences about where we choose to spend time and money, and even the spaces themselves. As many of us note throughout this collection, rural and urban spaces are being reconfigured through the suburban aesthetic—by residents, consumers, and developers both reinventing the flawed original suburban design and creating and supporting "escapes" from suburbia. With thoughtful framing and planning by teachers and organizers, marathons can help people resee their landscapes through this suburban place-conscious lens. The reflective walking, mapping, exploring, writing, and sharing on marathons—the moving of writers, pens, and minds—give us the vision both to resee natural and cultural watersheds feeding our local places and to imagine our role in creating better futures within them.

1:45 p.m. The Finish Line: Soul Desires Bookstore

The generous bookstore staff members are letting us invade for a read-around. They shift displays, tables, and chairs to accommodate the writing groups as each one arrives. We go around the circle, each person reading a short piece from his or her notebook. Dan delights everyone with poems imagined as the thoughts of people walking through the Passageway. Robert reads an eloquent essay that explores his study of place-conscious education in suburbia. Several people read pieces composed in the public library, a stop that led some writers to address Omaha's issues of homelessness and poverty. The stars of the reading, though, are the kids from the family group, bravely sharing writing as thoughtful and observant as any adult in the room. The youngest among us, Jeff's daughter, Maija, shyly declines to read when it is her turn but then at the end asks if she can read after all. Her hopeful young voice is the perfect ending to a remarkable day.

Water for a Dry Land

An Environmental Unit in a Secondary English Class

SHARON BISHOP

> If there is magic on this planet, it is contained in water.
> —Loren Eiseley (1957)[1]

It is late March 2008 in Nebraska. Winter is ending, and there are a few hints of spring in the air. One of the harbingers of spring on the central plains is the presence of migratory waterfowl. Central Nebraska is home to the Rainwater Basin and the Platte River, and both figure prominently in the cycles of snow geese, sandhill cranes, and other species of waterfowl. The geese and other ducks are familiar features to my students. Their honks and calls fill up the sky, and many people here hunt during the appropriate seasons. Still, not all of my students can name these birds. For many, they are just a kind of "white noise" of spring, making no real impact on their daily lives.

I have seen change during the almost three decades I have taught in Henderson, Nebraska, a small community located an hour's drive west of the urban center of Lincoln, in what Joseph Goddard (2012) calls the

1. Excerpt from *The Immense Journey: An Imaginative Naturalist Explores the Mysteries of Man and Nature*, by Loren Eiseley, copyright © 1946, 1950, 1951, 1953, 1955, 1956, 1957, by Loren Eiseley. Used by permission of Random House, an imprint and division of Penguin Random House, LLC. All rights reserved.

"penurban shadow." Because of the shift from smaller family farms to larger ones, our student population has undergone a steady decrease. Even though half of the students in this class live on farms, they are not the farms of their grandparents, where cows and chickens were staples, requiring "farm kids" to be present for morning and evening chores. The farms of my students are run by expensive farm machinery, and the farm families live in modern houses that have all of the same amenities as the homes of their classmates who live in town. Satellite dishes and the latest technology in computers and iPods connect them to the same wider world as students who live in the large metropolitan areas to the east. They dress like students across the United States and listen to the same music and view the same movies and television shows. Hip-hop culture occasionally invades their language, and I smile when I hear them ask, "Waz up?"

A decade ago decreasing school populations brought about a consolidation with a nearby small town, creating Heartland Community Schools: Henderson/Bradshaw. Now our students come from a larger geographic area, and the cohesive community that once made place-conscious work easier here has disappeared. The population of this community has changed as well. Because we live on the Interstate 80 corridor, many parents drive to larger towns within the area for work. My students have grown up with the interstate; they routinely drive to nearby towns for shopping and entertainment and "hanging out at the mall." We are only fifteen minutes from a Super Walmart and a Starbucks. And we are very mobile, making driving an absolute necessity for living here. We jump in cars and drive to one town to the south because there is a good Italian restaurant there. A smaller town to the east has built a large community hall that serves as a site for wedding receptions and other activities. Dinner and a movie at the larger county seat fifteen minutes away are a given. Trips to Omaha for concerts and to Lincoln for college and professional sporting events are routine. The small towns of Nebraska are less and less the center of social life. In short, my merged communities are part of the "rural dimension" of suburban sprawl that Lydia Savage and Mark Lapping identify. They write: "Sprawl impacts rural communities in many and significant ways. It is a process and a force that alters in permanent ways how rural people live and work, how they sustain their families and social and cultural networks, how they construct their communities and decision-making processes, and how they define their spatial and cognitive realities" (2003, 5). Many of my students see themselves as citizens of a local region rather than one town. An unfortunate result of this attitude is that they feel less connected to one specific place, and as the median age of the communities of our merged school district continues to creep upward, young people do not entertain the possibility of returning here to live after postsecondary education.

The Platte River Watershed, Sandhill Cranes, and Public Engagement

My present students live in two small towns, and as they drive to school, they pass fields of corn and soybeans that reflect a rural economy. Yet they are less and less knowledgeable about the natural history of the area. If they do live on a farm, their view of the land is one of financial provider; the land is there to produce crops. Because irrigation from an underground aquifer is the foundation of agriculture here, any discussions about the future of that water supply are met with skepticism. And even though a thirty-acre native preserved prairie is only a few miles from our school, students cannot name the native grasses or even recognize it as the natural ecosystem of our place. For most, if they are familiar with the place at all, it is dismissed as "some kind of pasture."

Despite these changes, I continue to teach a sophomore English class called Nebraska Literature and Composition: A Sense of Place. Throughout the school year, my sophomores have been immersed in the process of learning a Sense of Place. We have visited this native prairie, read the literature of Nebraska authors whose works reflect the settlement period of our state, and learned of the state's involvement in World War II. Students have interviewed community elders and have used the stories of their own lives and families to write poetry and prose of place.

Now it is March, and they know the tradition: a trip to the Platte River valley, where one of our main purposes will be to view the sandhill cranes. These birds are far enough removed from the school where I teach to be more of a rarity than the ducks and geese that fly over daily. This field trip is a collaborative project with the biology teacher. In biology class the teacher gives them necessary background information on these birds before we actually set out for the Platte River valley, where we hope to see the cranes. In English class we read a small novel by a naturalist who teaches at the University of Nebraska (Johnsgard 1986). Students learn that these birds have been coming to the Platte River valley for thousands of years and that it is a vital stop in the migratory flight north to the tundra, where a mated pair will lay two eggs. Because the Platte is a prairie river, it is shallow, and, in its natural state, before it was dammed and diverted for human use, it was free from vegetation that could have shielded predators such as foxes; the cranes were safe on the old Platte River. The Platte also provides needed nourishment that the cranes will require for the long flight north. The birds will stay in the area for almost two months, providing a "spectacle of nature" that draws tourists from all over the world (National Audubon Society 2013). However, civilization has narrowed the river to an eighty-mile stretch, and it is here, along the wet meadows and at bridges, that tourists line up to see and hear the cranes come into the river each evening to roost or to leave it at dawn to go to the fallow fields and wet meadows to feed. But the Platte River that we view this spring of 2008 shows the effects of several years of drought in the state. Where there should be water, there are sand bars and large islands overgrown with shrubs and vegetation. Without the intervention of humans who quite literally mow the river, the cranes would be forced to crowd into ever increasingly smaller spaces on the Platte.

What would the loss of this natural habitat mean for the cranes? Before we go on the field trip, my students examine this question from a variety of perspectives: some point out the loss of millions of dollars from tourism to the state; for some, the loss would be meaningless—the cranes do not impact their lives; for others, the loss of the cranes would be a calamity, a signal that humans have once again displaced a part of the natural world. Eventually, we arrive at the view that if the cranes are gone, then so is the Platte River. Does it matter? Because the Platte does not flow in our immediate area, we begin a search for the Platte's importance to the state of Nebraska and to our own lives.

This search turns into a study of water: water for our communities that make up our consolidated school district, water for the corn and soybean fields that are the foundation for the agri-based industry that forms an economic base for the area, and water for the state of Nebraska—for industry, municipalities, and recreation. All of my students live in modern homes, and like the rest of the civilized world, they take water for granted. It is there when the tap is turned on; it is there when the center pivots are turned on for the first time to water the fields. They expect that water will always be an available and safe commodity for them. Interestingly, just as we begin this study in 2008, the town of Henderson has invested time and money in two water projects. Because of high nitrate content in the town's drinking water, two new wells have been dug outside of the city limits. Then a crew is brought into town for a task that will take several weeks—to clean and paint the inside of the water tower. This means that the tower will need to be drained. Official letters are sent from city hall requesting that all citizens living in town use water carefully. It is an unofficial kind of rationing, for no one will enforce this request, but it will be several weeks before the tower is again functioning at full capacity.

All these different positions on water lend some authenticity to our study in my 2007–8 sophomore English class. In our community (and region), water policy is what Linda Flower calls a "public" issue, affecting a variety of different interest groups seeking both to persuade each other and to affect public policy and behavior. My goals for the water unit are similar—I want my students to understand something of the diversity of positions on water in the regional community and begin the work of becoming a thoughtful, "deliberative" local public. After all, as Linda Flower observes, students in a writing class are not "a professional decision-making body or a political action group." Still, as does Flower, I want what she calls "the fruits of inquiry" to follow them after they have left my classroom (2008, 59). For this transformation to happen, Nancy Welch notes that teachers who attempt to have their writing students write for "the public" must help their students discover that the voices of ordinary citizens, even teenagers, matter (2008, 43). Nothing is more central to place-conscious education than this idea of involving students in the past, present, and future of their place, particularly students who live in the exurban communities increasingly impacted by suburbia.

Writing a Sense of Place

The Nebraska Language Arts Standards state that:

> LA 12.2 Students will learn and apply writing skills and strategies to communicate.
>
> LA 12.2.1 Writing Process: Students will apply the writing process to plan, draft, revise, edit and publish writing using correct spelling, grammar, punctuation, and other standard conventions appropriate for grade level.
>
> LA 12.2.2 Writing Genres: Students will write for a variety of purposes and audiences in multiple genres. (Nebraska State Board of Education 2008–9)

Sophomores write for a variety of purposes and in a variety of genres throughout the school year, but for the purposes of this chapter I will use student quotes from two main sources: reflective journals and nature poetry. I believe these two genres match what the National Writing Project defines as the reason for writing in *Because Writing Matters*: writing is "a means of inquiry and expression" (2003, 3). The work of this class means several visits to "outdoor classrooms" such as a preserved prairie and the Platte River, the National Audubon Society's Rowe Sanctuary, as well as traditional museums at the Nebraska State Historical Society and more interactive museums such as Stuhr Museum (n.d.) and the Great Platte River Road Archway Monument (n.d.). While students are at these places, I ask them to take notes. When they have returned, I ask them to write reflective journals about our visits to these sites. They are always asked to include how these visits helped them, or perhaps did not, to learn what we call a Sense of Place, the main theme that is embedded in all of the work that we do. These journals are invaluable to me as a teacher. They give me insight into what the students experienced on these trips. They are also invaluable to the students because they ask them to engage with the place we are studying, to reflect and to analyze. Students also write reflections after conducting the community interviews that are part of this water unit.

Students also write poetry, and much of it is generated from our field trips. As a class built around the work of Nebraska literature, we are fortunate to have many poets, and we read the poetry of those individuals who write about nature such as Twyla Hansen (2003) and Don Welch (1992). Welch often writes about the Platte River, and both write about the sandhill cranes.

Mary Pipher, in *Writing to Change the World*, observes that poetry is "every civilization's record of itself" (2007, 213) and that poets write for a variety of reasons: "to create beauty, tell the truth, . . . call attention to that which is fragile, and encourage us to be mindful" (217). And she quotes Wallace Stegner, who includes poetry as part of knowing a sense of place; he writes, "No place is a place until it has had a poet" (205). Writing some nature poetry after the field trip to the Platte River valley is a given, an assignment. The sandhill cranes provide wonderful poetry moments as students are drawn into this spectacle of nature. Still, I was surprised when I read the poetry that emanated from this water unit. Much of the poetry contained a definite environmental message, even though I had not explicitly assigned that task. The examples that I cite in the rest of this chapter offer an example that our work on the water unit has begun to influence their thinking.

These genres of writing replace a more traditional research paper. Flower encourages the use of other forms of written communication that reflect personal views and "unresolved questions, or perspectives not well captured by formal prose." The use of student photography, journal reflections, and nature poetry may also help to create what Flower calls "a local public dialogue" with the student writers (2008, 232).

History of Water Use in Nebraska

The unit begins with some historical background. A long article in Kuzelka and Flowerday's *Flat Water: A History of Nebraska and Its Water* is the first reading assignment. This article, "Land and Water in 19th-Century Nebraska" by historian Dr. Robert Manley, brings some new information to my students. They learn that the earliest towns in Nebraska were not built around the railroads, as history has taught them, but built on or near a water source, a river or a large stream. Power from mills constructed on these rivers and streams was an important part of commerce. Students also learn that many bridges were built over the Platte and other important rivers but were periodically wiped out by floods and spring ice. These facts paint a new picture of early Nebraska settlement for them. Manley's article also points out that a discussion of irrigation for the semiarid western part of the state began early. Most of my students who are familiar with local history know only about the use of deep well irrigation here in the late 1930s and 1940s. But Manley points out that drought in 1890 motivated farmers to find ways to water their crops or give up their homesteads. Manley notes, "By the end of the 19th century, Nebraskans began to realize that water was a valuable resource. They also understood that irrigation was practical and, in some parts, essential" (1993, 29). The efforts of many changed the face of Nebraska, and irrigation is now an accepted fact of life for much of rural Nebraska. Even those students who do not live or work on farms are accustomed to daily drives past summer fields that are watered by the latest technology, the center pivots that are a part of the agricultural landscape of modern Nebraska.

Although this history is specific to Nebraska, it echoes the history of our continent. According to the Watershed Information Network/Environmental Protection Agency, "A watershed is an area of land that drains into a lake or river. . . . We all live in a watershed. Watersheds are the places we call home, where we work and where we play. Everyone relies on water and other natural resources to exist. What you and others do to the land impacts the quality and quantity of water and our other natural resources. . . . Everything that is done in a watershed affects the watershed's system" (2013, n.p.).

Scott Russell Sanders even suggests that perhaps our geographical boundaries should have been drawn along the boundaries of watersheds. "A true map of our continent would show a pattern of curving watersheds stitched together along high ridges, like a paisley fabric." The Ohio River, so important in his life, "stretches into fourteen states, including ones as far afield as New York, Maryland, and Alabama, draining an area that is roughly the size of France" (1994, 62). The natural world pays no attention to the artificial boundaries that man has carved on to the nation.

When European immigrants began settling these watershed areas, they altered the natural environment by cutting down forests; by building industry, towns, and cities; and through mining and agriculture. A study of water in one's place might well begin with a study of the watershed of that place and the ways that human settlement has altered that watershed. It is clear to me that this unit for my Nebraska students must focus first on the Platte River and its importance as a watershed to our state. Because the Platte does not seem to be an immediate part of our place, I begin with the sandhill cranes, for whom the Platte is essential.

At this point, early in the unit, my students are not asking many questions about water. It is still a taken-for-granted resource to them. They do express surprise at the fact that early settlers used mills for hydropower and that irrigation was a part of the history of the late nineteenth century, but that *history* belongs to a long-ago past. In one class discussion, I tell them about a television documentary I have just seen about the dropping water levels of Lake Powell and the drastic effects it would have on large metropolitan areas in Nevada and Southern California. They express concern, but it does not affect them in any way that seems important to them now. We discuss the famines and droughts in parts of Africa. One student is honest when she says that she knows she *should* care but that she really does not. It is not unusual for sophomores to withhold concern for abstract ideas in places that are far away. It is clear that, to interest them in this unit of water, I must begin with the local—or at least Nebraska.

Historical Perspective on Place-Conscious Education

Some of the theory behind what is now called place-conscious education, as summarized by Robert Brooke in the introduction of this volume, is derived from the work of educator John Dewey. In his book *Experience and Education*, Dewey advocates for what he calls a "progressive education," one that does not depend solely on a textbook and a teacher to instruct students. Dewey advocates for "learning through experience," and for him this kind of learning is superior because it prepares students for the future, "a society where change is the rule, not the exception" (1963 [1938], 19).

Dewey makes it clear that it is the job of the teacher or the educational institution (or both) to provide experiences that are educational and not just fun, but these experiences must provide what he calls an "agreeableness" for the students. "Everything depends upon the *quality* of the experience which is had" (27). In addition to this "agreeableness," the experience must also have what Dewey calls an "experiential continuum" (28). The experience should be part of the educational and intellectual growth of the participating students. "Growth, or growing as developing, not only physically but intellectually and morally, is one exemplification of the principle of continuity" (36). The quality of an experience affects the outcomes of future experiences, and it is the job of the educator to provide positive experiences for students. In thinking about the experiences that he or she provides for students, the teacher is to remember that "all human experience is ultimately social; that it involves contact and communication" (38). Dewey notes that it is again the job of the educator to know what places and conditions could provide these experiences. The traditional educational system, according to Dewey, did not ask that "the teacher become intimately acquainted with the conditions of the local community, physical, historical, economic, occupational, etc., in order to utilize them as educational resources" (40). But Dewey, who is providing an early definition of place-conscious education, notes that his ideas of a progressive education based on experience must follow this concept. As this experience continues, it means that "the future has to be taken into account at every stage" (47). But this kind of learning does not ignore the past; indeed, as Dewey notes, "It can expand into the future only as it is enlarged to take in the past" (77). I believe that this water unit, as well as other units that my sophomores have already participated in, reflects many of these ideas of John Dewey.

Dewey's ideas were in many ways integrated into the Foxfire approach to place-based learning. In the late 1990s I was fortunate to be included in some training by Foxfire (Starnes, Carone, and Paris 1999), which had its origin in rural Georgia. As Foxfire continued to train Georgia's and adjacent states' teachers, the philosophy enlarged to include urban and suburban settings. Foxfire advocated that place-based work should extend beyond the classroom, into the community. This outreach can take many forms, of course, but one that I was already doing involved the idea of student work having "an audience beyond the classroom." Each year my sophomores made a booklet of poetry, prose, and photography of place. Because of the Foxfire training, I looked for other ways to include the community as an "audience" for student work. Each spring the music department in our school gave a community concert that showcased the work done by music students over the school year. Administrators encouraged other teachers to display their work on the night of that concert. I asked my students to choose their best work in writing and photography, and together we set up a display for that evening. Often, the biology teacher and I reserved space in the school for one evening to present the work (writing, photography, videos of science experiments conducted in the wetlands or on the prairie) done in our shared classrooms. The theme: "A Sense of Place, a Sense of Self."

For me, the water unit captures Dewey's emphasis on experience and Foxfire's emphasis on community involvement. I believe it is important to heed this call for local experience that matters to the community. After all, I had to remove a novel from the curriculum to make room for this unit.

Scott Russell Sanders, a proponent of knowing one's immediate place, writes movingly of his relationship to the rivers in Ohio. In *Staying Put*, Sanders writes about the importance of water on earth:

> Water is the medium of life. We are made of it, mostly. Our cells are tiny seas. Anyone who has held in the hand a freshly caught fish can see this streamlined shape as a bit of water with a temporary skin around it. So are we all. Near the river, you are reminded that water is the fundamental element on the surface of our planet; land is a latecomer and everywhere vulnerable. The mountains are hustling, grain by grain, toward the oceans. Near the river, you see water in its metamorphoses: as liquid, as fog and steam, as ice and snow, the endless cycling of stuff through its many forms. Near the river you are never far from awareness of time, vast and moody and inhuman. Is time an arrow or a loop? The river dissolves that puzzle, for it is both arrow and loop, a current that moves in a circle, from hills to sea and back through snow and rain to hills, and so down to again to the sea. Perhaps our lives are segments in such a larger circle. (1994, 90)

It is a field trip to the Platte River valley in March that "hooks" my sophomores on this unit—an experience that carries with it aspects of Dewey's agreeableness. We begin at the Great Platte River Road Archway Monument (2013), near Kearney. This unique museum shows the history of travel and eventual settlement along this natural corridor that followed the Platte River. Early trails, the Pony Express, the transcontinental railroad, the Lincoln Highway, and finally Interstate 80 all followed this important river. This experience shows students the importance of the river that we have just begun to learn about. In her reflective journal, Jennifer writes: "By going to the Arch and viewing all the ways the Platte River led and guided people makes me feel proud of the river and makes me hope that civilization won't cause too much damage to it."

We also visit the Murdoch Site, several acres that preserve some faint swales from the wagons that crossed the prairie many years ago (National Park Service 2013). The graves of some members of the Murdoch family are there, and the University of Nebraska has identified even earlier graves of Native peoples who followed the land bridge long before the white man found this natural way west. This spot overlooks the diminished Wood River that once provided enough energy for a sawmill owned by the Murdoch family, a mill used to cut planks from Iowa trees for the new Union Pacific Railroad that raced west to meet another railroad racing east to meet at Promontory Point, Utah. This place provides a history that is more "real" to some students than the wonderful displays at the Archway Monument. Students sit and write, and Brittany's reflections show the agreeableness of the experience: "A chill runs down my spine as I feel the sun beating down upon my back; the rustling of the grass blown by the wind echoes in my ears. To connect with the people who traveled through Nebraska through textbooks is one thing but to *see* the tracks of a covered wagon is a whole new feeling."

Our next stop is the Rowe Sanctuary, run by the National Audubon Society (2013). Large windows overlook the Platte River, and even though the cranes are not yet on the river, other waterfowl visit. A tour of the new building brings some points of conservation to the students: the structure is made of straw bales covered with stucco, and the beams are reclaimed trees from along another river in Nebraska, the Niobrara. Other wood has been rescued from an old rural schoolhouse; the toilets in the bathrooms conserve water. Somehow these kinds of lessons are always better accepted by students when they come from outside of the classroom. Jaylen notes that here at the Rowe Sanctuary, she expanded her sense of place: "The energy-saving and nature saving taught me a Sense of Place because Nebraska and the earth are where we live, and we need to save it. The staff at Rowe taught me that things we see every day can save money and still work effectively."

This excerpt from a poem written after the field trip shows that Connor has grasped an important ecological fact about the Platte River:

The Platte's channels choose
  where the water flows,
 but man controls
if and when it flows.

But it is a remark made by our guide that both motivates the students to invest in this water unit and provides, for me, a justification for a study of water. As we look out over the Platte River, our guide says, "The main issue of the twentieth century was oil—in the twenty-first century, *your* century, the issue will be *water*!" Heads nod, and most jot down this fact in their journals. We then walk, quietly, to a large blind that overlooks the Platte. The breeze rustles in the large cottonwood trees, and birdsong fills the air. In the distance a soft noise draws our attention. In the southern sky a large flock of cranes circles, but it is still too early for them to come into the river. To the students, we seem removed from the sounds and sights of the familiar world. They are quiet in the blind for a long time, looking out over the river, writing in journals, and soaking up a place that, to Connor, "showed with all of the senses how our world was before man remade it with technology." Then we are given a gift. A large flock of cranes heads for the river. Whispered hopes wish for them to land in front of us. But the birds are "playing," says our guide; they drift and spin on thermals of warm air, and we hear the soft sounds of their chatter. All of the facts that students have learned in both the English class and in biology are now made real to them: the cranes must have this protected portion of the river to survive. This long section from Carlin's journal reflects his reactions:

Cranes are not on this earth to feed us or provide us with our physical needs.

Cranes are here to be learned from and listened to—to teach us. The cranes, although they probably don't realize it, are a wealth of knowledge. They know how to survive, how to adapt, and how to keep living. Being in the blind with the stillness and silence all around us was my favorite part of the whole trip! I loved just listening to nature—not touching it, not changing it, just listening to it. It is very important, when listening to cranes, to realize that before us—before a lot, really, there were cranes crossing this hemisphere. . . . Why did the white man have to change everything? The lives of all creatures are something to be preserved, not taken away.

Abby's complete poem reveals her awareness of the plight of the Platte:

Necklace

The Platte is
a necklace of blue silver
laced with brown sandy beads
    covering the neck of Nebraska.
Slowly receding inward
like a necklace
stretched to its limits
the Platte, drier from irrigation,
is a mess of sandy beads
broken, cracked, and chipped.
Who will wear this necklace?

Kara's poem reflects the impact of our time in the blind on the river:

Tension on the Platte

The Platte moves slowly,
gentle currents like a light spring shower
shifting the water little by little.
The river is shallow,

the sandbars a drought-stricken desert
empty and desolate in the riverbed.
The air is chilly with spring,
light breezes hit the blind
whistling into the afternoon silence.
The blind creaks,
the air thick with freshness
floating through the open windows.
My mind spins,
a mystery
unfolding before my searching eyes.

Laini's two poems reveal Pipher's definition that poetry can "call attention to that which is fragile" (2007, 217):

Crane Cries

Try telling the children of tomorrow
the cranes are nothing. Let them hear
of your selfish and ignorant ways.
Show them how you have changed the land,
and tried to erase history. Cover their ears
as they desperately try to hear the cries of the cranes.
Take your plows to the fields and the dams to the river,
and as your pockets get heavier with money you made
from their land, try not to feel for the children
who never knew of the creatures you took from them.

Understanding the River

She was throwing knives with her words
into the back of the river she ignorantly depended on daily.
And as the river decreased
so did her respect for it,
looking at it as if it were the lifeline on a hand:
so wrinkled, so aged and unappealing to the eye.
She turned her cheek with disloyalty to the river

as it tried to tell her its tales.
But slowly
slowly she was forced to hear the stories.
It screamed a message
showing her that even old and fragile hands
have strength and greatness.
She began to remove the knives,
looking at the river with new eyes
the words from her tongue
reflecting her respect.

Expanding the Unit of Study to Community Inquiry

After this field trip, students are ready to study and learn about water. Because I believe, with Linda Flower, that community inquiry is a necessary part of learning and that the "safe collaborative space" of my classroom should aim to become a "demonstration of a public dialogue that uses difference as a resource for inquiry and decision making" (2008, 40–41), in the next part of this unit I invite my sophomores to become inquirers into the many approaches to water in our local community.

Because irrigation is such an important part of living here, I ask a former student who has farmed for almost twenty years to come and speak to both sections of the class. He prepares well and brings maps and diagrams of the Ogallala Aquifer and water tables. He draws diagrams of how wells are dug, bringing the water from the aquifer to the surface. With plastic glasses of water and drinking straws, students learn firsthand the principle behind siphon tubes, an early form of irrigation after the deep wells were dug here. This presentation is meaningful to the students for many reasons, I believe. To hear about this topic from someone from the community, a person who has been involved in farming for many years, makes the information "personal." It also honors the knowledge of a person who has lived in a place and learned to care about it and to care for it as he makes a living from it. I believe that the students are beginning to grasp Sanders's observation: "What matters is the durability of land and water, how they bear up under our use" (2004, 91).

Students next view a DVD of a 2007 production by NET Television, *The Price of Water* (updated 2012), that informs them of water use in the state by many stakeholders: farmers, people in towns and cities, and the natural world. This production not only adds to their knowledge of the history of water use in the state but also shows them several examples of how water is being sustained and preserved for the future.

Students then read two articles from the magazine *NEBRASKAland*, "Tapped Out" and "The Great Water Debate," both by Eric Fowler (2007a, 2007b). One of these articles introduces students to the litigation between Kansas and Nebraska over use of the Republican River. The articles and the DVD all make clear to them that water crosses state boundaries and that water can never be just a local issue. The connections beyond our immediate place begin to be clearer to the students.

Because interviewing local citizens is part of the work of this class, I then ask students to interview someone locally about some related issue of water. Some choose farmer grandparents, some members of Natural Resource Districts or someone who is part of agribusiness in the area, and some choose farmers. This activity requires students to write appropriate interview questions, to set up an interview time, and to conduct an interview. They are instructed to listen during the interview and write down notes later; they are not allowed to tape the session.

The following excerpts from reflective journals indicate to me that the students have collected a variety of opinions from people who are local experts, yet they are not the published writers found in our formal research, demonstrating what Flower (2008, 232) advocates, the use of multiple voices in the inquiry process:

> My interview was interesting because he [the man she interviewed] told me about the [new] drip system of irrigating, which makes me think that maybe we won't have gated pipe or even center pivots. It's interesting to think about how something like that can change how farmers do their business. So companies that sell drip systems will probably become successful just like the well diggers we read about. He talked about how he thinks people from this area would be some of the best people to represent Nebraska in Lincoln or Washington D.C. because they know

> what they're talking about. So maybe that will get some young people thinking about future careers. (Jennifer)

Katie interviews someone at city hall who shares new information with her. "I had no idea how much water Henderson actually uses! It's amazing . . . but I wonder how much is actually wasted? I learned that a water bill in Henderson averages around $32 a month and that 1,073,800 gallons of water are used every day! The water tower holds 200,000 gallons of water and it is supplied by 3 different wells outside of Henderson. Knowing this shows a Sense of Place by having a knowledge of what is used every day. It also shows me how we need to conserve water."

Connecting knowledge to the local helps Kara integrate all of the other information when she interviews a longtime agribusinessman: "I think that I learned more from my interview about irrigation and water in Nebraska because it wasn't just a bunch of numbers calculated by scientific research, but from somebody who works with it all of the time. He had a lot of information about the efficiency of modern irrigation and how things have changed over the years since his dad started Northern Pump."

The final part of the water unit involves some research. In pairs students choose topics relating to water use in Nebraska and conduct some research. Then each pair gives a class presentation with a goal of teaching their fellow students about this topic. (In some years but not this one, the students have presented the results of their research at a community meeting or to members of adult work groups, as I have reported in Bishop 2004.) Each presentation is to include a handout and some kind of visual aid. These topics range from the number of dams on the Platte River to the smaller Blue River in our own backyard. One pair shows the class maps of the water table and concludes that our area in York and Hamilton Counties has enough water for irrigation to continue, but that many parts of the state have restrictions on well drilling. An awareness of the plight of those individuals who live outside of our immediate area was, to me, an indication that, in the course of studying water, these students are now able to see water in its wider perspective.

Students finish the unit with a final reflection on water, stating what they have learned. These reflections show that attitudes change and new information is accumulated:

> Water to me is irrigating with my dad in the heat of the summer, riding up and down the rows on the back of his red four-wheeler. Water is fishing behind our house in the small dam and falling in when I was seven years old. Water is tubing at Harlan County Dam every summer and seeing who can hold on the longest. Water is the Blue River that is so famously told about in my grandpa's best scary stories. Water is irrigation run-off that makes the best mud sliding areas. Those are the things that show how water teaches me a Sense of Place. When we started doing this water unit, I couldn't quite understand how it was so important to me, but now I realize that, without water, I would have had a completely different childhood. Even though this may not be the most important reason to conserve water, it is still why water means so much to me. (Taylor)

Taylor already has a connection with this place, but Amy joins our class later when she moves here from a larger city. To her much of this information is completely new, and she lists what she has learned throughout this unit: "It seems I'm learning more and more the longer I stay here. I never thought of water being so important; I find out we have an aquifer—I never even knew the word existed! And I think I actually get it—that the Ogallala Aquifer connects to the rivers, and to irrigation. Water is really a major issue for this century. I learned about methods of irrigating and I also learned that some of our water is needed for endangered species."

Because of this study, Lance is now aware of the conflicts over water use from the Republican River, as this excerpt from his journal illustrates: "Last Sunday I rode my motorcycle down to Concordia, Kansas, and on the way we rode over the Republican River 4 different times. Every time I was more depressed because I saw hardly any water. On one place there was even an abandoned pickup in the middle of the river, on a sandbar." Without this study, I doubt that Lance would have been aware of this river and the changes he saw.

Teacher Reflections on the Water Unit

This unit has so many layers of complexity, it could easily have lasted for the whole school year. Many of those layers belong to other content areas such as science and geography. David Sobel advocates for making "ecological literacy a serious part of the school philosophy" (2004, 48). One of the principles for this literacy, according to Sobel, is to "engage the students in real-world projects in the local environment and the community" (53). Although this unit does not come close to complete ecological literacy, I believe that it is a start and that it fits into Sobel's goal for place-based education. It also fits in with John Dewey's principle of the continuity of experience. An important part of place-based work in my classroom has always been to offer students experiences that show them that people who live in a place care about it and care for it. We sometimes expect that students who live in a place know a great deal about it, which is not necessarily true. I think that the initial experience of a field trip to the Platte River to see the sandhill cranes spiraled out into broader learning that took into account some past history but also spun the students into the future—a future that they will be an integral part of. This growth reflects Dewey's ideas of making a study of the past part of a study of the future. One of the goals of place-conscious work is to create knowledgeable citizens for the future, and I think that these sophomores will be more aware of water issues that are a part of the present as well as the future. These two final journal entries sum up what these two students have learned in the course of the school year about this place:

> The water interview helped the most because I did not know much about the wells in this area before. These wells are the main reason my family lives here and they are what keeps us [the economy] going. (Crista)

> When you learn about water, most people could care less. That, as a matter of fact, used to be me! Now that I have more information and knowledge about water, I've begun to care more and to try to conserve water. This issue is huge and kind of scary because we can't live without water. (Sara)

In the preface to *Writing Nature*, editor Carolyn Ross writes of the urgency of educating young people about nature and the environment:

> We must reassess our individual and collective attitudes about our relationships to nature and come to understand the world in ecological

> terms in order to both know who we are and to resolve the many crucial environmental problems we now face. These problems will multiply and intensify as we enter the next millennium, and students currently in their teens and twenties will feel the full brunt of environmental concerns soon enough. We need citizens who understand both themselves and the environment, who grasp the personal and public dimensions of environmental issues, their context and complexity, and who can think critically and communicate clearly if we are to expect success in meeting the challenges ahead. (1995, viii)

The millennium that Ross refers to is here, and current issues such as the water shortage and rising gas and oil prices are indeed the subjects that our present students will be asked to deal with. Dewey's future where change is normal has arrived. The ultimate goal of place-conscious education is the development of good citizens who not only celebrate the past history of their places but will also be involved partners in meeting the challenges of the present and of the future.

Advice to Other Teachers

Replicating this water unit in other places is indeed possible. The beauty of place-conscious education is that it must fit the setting of the place where it is taught. This idea may seem to be overwhelming, but it also gives teachers a great deal of latitude in choosing what topics of place to consider. Water is universal. Suburban students see water used daily, on lawns and in swimming pools; they also probably see those large water tanks that supply the water to their homes. Often gaily decorated in some theme that fits the culture of the place, they may go unnoticed by students as places of water storage. All students have probably experienced some kind of recreation or tourism that involved water. Writing about that experience might be a first step into a study of water in your area. What streams and creeks may be present? What major rivers do these connect to? Scott Russell Sanders (1994) reminds us that we all live in a watershed—as modern citizens, we just are not aware of its presence. The website for Conservation International reminds us that "water shapes and nourishes life on earth . . . and the world's unique biodiversity and human communities both depend on clean water's availability." We cannot live without this resource that is now declining. "The global freshwater crisis is only going to get worse" (2013, n.p.). News reports reveal problems across the nation: Chesapeake Bay, the Everglades, Puget Sound, Lake Powell, the Great Lakes, and many others. There will be no shortage of materials that can be fitted to a local suburban area.

I, of course, chose material that fits Nebraska. Other teachers can search out essays, poetry, articles, and history readings for background research. Many writers such as John Steinbeck, Wallace Stegner, and Jim Harrison have written both fiction and nonfiction that address water. Search out the writers—the poets, the novelists, the essayists—in your region, and see what they have and are writing about water. I noted earlier in the chapter that I removed a novel from my curriculum to teach this water unit. Although I am an advocate for teaching literature in an English classroom, language-arts teachers are increasingly being asked to include other genres in the curriculum. This water unit offers opportunities to do just that. Because water can be a controversial topic, students are asked to analyze what they read and identify whose perspective is being addressed—or left out. There are many stakeholders in issues of water—agriculture, industry, municipalities, recreation, and energy—and suburban students need to be guided into these public discussions with all the care and guidance of place-conscious community literacy education.

I believe that the success of this water unit is a valuable component for my students who are asked to learn a Sense of Place. Paul Gruchow, a proponent of place-conscious work, notes that we now must apply some new principles to the way we judge our living spaces. "We will judge the strength of society as a whole by the health of its local communities. If gains in one place come at the expense of the viability of another place, we will count the cost too high" (1995, 143). A study of water is a perfect example of this principle.

The Leopold Education Project for Suburban High School English Students

Teaching about the Watershed in Ralston

JEFF LACEY

To begin, I should probably start with the photograph of the farm. The farm is in Wisconsin and was owned by Aldo Leopold. The photograph was taken in 1935, the year Leopold bought it. It is a black-and-white photo, and it is hazy, almost an inkblot. At left center of the photo is a haggard chicken coop, its boards flayed by heat and time. The chicken coop is surrounded by land that was, when the picture was taken, almost completely sand. The sky in the photo is slightly overexposed and is only a few shades lighter than the beach beneath it. The air seems bleached. It looks hot.

The man who owned the farm, Aldo Leopold, had many roles: a naturalist, a teacher, a writer, a scientist, a father and husband. The Aldo Leopold featured in this essay is Aldo Leopold the writer. He was prolific. He is considered one of the founding fathers of wildlife ecology, and the thesis he sets forth in the essay entitled "The Land Ethic" in his book *A Sand County Almanac* (1949) has become one of the most influential ideas in environmentalism.

The narrative that follows is the account of how I came to read and present his work in my suburban classroom. In 2007 I began the Ralston Almanac Project in my tenth grade English class at Ralston High School.

Instead of a shack and a farm, my students had Turtle Creek Park, a municipal green space close enough to walk out to and back from in our eighty-seven-minute English period. For Leopold, the difference in the contexts would not have mattered for the "conservation ethics" he promoted. He writes: "Like all real treasures of the mind perception can be split into infinitely small fractions without losing its quality. The weeds in a city lot convey the same lesson as the redwoods; the farmer may see in his cow-pasture what may not be vouchsafed to the scientist adventuring in the South Seas. Perception, in short, cannot be purchased with either learned degrees or dollars; it grows at home as well as abroad, and he who has a little may use it to as good advantage as he who has much" (1949, 174).

The Ralston Almanac Project has changed since 2007, both inside and outside the classroom—for example, one of the highlights of the project was the creation of Ralston High School's Conservation/Green Club by members of the 2008 class. Currently, I teach at both Ralston Middle School and Ralston High School, but the force of the project endures for teachers interested in connecting suburban students to the rich ecology of local place. In the students' engagement with their local park, they explored the "watershed" of southeastern Nebraska and some of the complexities of entering the contentions of "public space" surrounding that watershed.

As for the farm in the picture, Aldo Leopold brought it back to life.

If you go to the Leopold Education Project website (n.d.), the mission statement reads, "The Leopold Education Project (LEP) is an innovative, interdisciplinary, critical thinking, conservation and environmental education curriculum based on the classic writings of the renowned conservationist, Aldo Leopold. The Leopold Education Project teaches the public about humanity's ties to the natural environment in the effort to conserve and protect the earth's natural resources."

The above statement is followed by a quote from Leopold: "The problem, then, is how to bring about a striving for harmony with land among a people many of whom have forgotten there is any such thing as land, among whom education and culture have become almost synonymous with landlessness. This is the problem of conservation education" (1992, 418). I remember first reading these sentences. As a teacher, they were two home runs in a row. An interdisciplinary curriculum that inspires critical thinking? Yes. And landlessness? Yes. What an accurate description of what ailed my students.

A little about the idea of being landless: Ralston is a town of six thousand people landlocked by Omaha. It possesses its own city council, its own mayor, and its own parks and public works services. In many respects, Ralston is independent from Omaha, and this strong local control over its resources is a boon for its citizens. The school district is separate from Omaha as well, and the same advantages are afforded to it. After seven years of working at Ralston High School, I have noticed that there is a general enthusiasm and respectfulness toward teachers and the work of school, but there is also an attitude that nothing much happens in Ralston, or in Omaha, for that matter. Many of my students believe that this prairie city, far more suburban than urban, is, to misquote my college poetry teach Don Welch, the presence of absence more than anything. It lacks any unique features of its own. Additionally, as far as the land is concerned, Ralston was built on lots, not land. A sense of natural history is utterly absent from any idea of place the typical Ralston high school student might have.

During my first years of teaching at Ralston High School, I was also faced with societal problems as they manifested themselves in a suburban public school classroom, everything from unfunded mandates that ask teachers perpetually to do more with less to overscheduled students to violence. Ralston High School had two bomb threats in 2006–7. I had students miss several days of school after the Von Maur shootings in 2007.

In short, on many days, Ralston reminds me of the stereotypical suburban community critiqued by Richard Louv: "What will it be like for children to grow up in socially and environmentally controlled environments—condominiums and planned developments and covenant-controlled housing development surrounded with walls, gates, and surveillance systems, where covenants prevent families from planting gardens? One wonders how the children growing up in this culture of control will define freedom when they are adults" (2008, 127). Louv's point is that suburban and urban life, for students, is often so gated and controlled that it becomes hard to see the local landscape and hard to see how one's actions might have any consequences in that watershed. Louv's insight dovetails nicely with Derek Owens's core tenet of ecocomposition: "And of awareness, sustainability cannot exist without a developing awareness of the conditions and limitations of one's immediate environment" (2001, 36–37).

Consequently, the task I brought to the Leopold Education Project was how to guide my suburban students toward a closer examination of their local environment.

To set up the yearlong Ralston Almanac Project for my tenth grade English class, I have my students take a "test" meant to jar them into realizing how little they really know about the ecology of the place they live. Essentially, it asks them a series of questions on a PowerPoint presentation. The questions are composed to test their knowledge of local culture and of local ecology. "Where does your tap water come from?" and "Where does your tap water go?" are alongside questions such as "Who is the mayor of Ralston?" and "How many people live in Ralston proper?" I also use the test to introduce specific terms that they will work with. "Topic: Natural History. 'Ecologically, Ralston was built on a a) riparian corridor, b) tallgrass prairie, c) shortgrass prairie, d) forest." The test also presents them with photographs that ask them to identify trees in front of the school, common birds, and the like. This test is never graded; it is just used to begin the discussion about what they know about the land they live on.

I also have them answer essay questions that we then use to frame our discussion, the most important of which is "In your opinion, is knowledge about the natural world that directly surrounds you important? Does knowing how to build a campfire matter if you have a furnace? Does knowing the constellations matter if you have maps, GPS systems, phones, etc., and if you are smart enough to avoid getting lost in the woods? Use examples to support your answers."

This question has, so far, yielded two major responses in discussion sessions. First, several students always assume that understanding local ecology and being land wise in general would be good *in a disaster*. I call it the doomsday scenario, and then we joke a little, and then I ask them to play the odds and to not assume apocalypse. After this discussion, the class usually comes to the consensus that, while intimately understanding local ecology would be interesting, it does not approach necessity. To live without an understanding of your locale is in no way detrimental.

To live without understanding your locale is not detrimental: a central tenant of landlessness. Then I tell them that this idea is what we are going to examine.

I was first introduced to the Leopold Education Project at a one-day workshop. At the workshop I was given a wealth of materials from the project coordinator, Christine Jacobsen, but in order to make myself more of an expert, I needed to further immerse myself in the project. I applied for, and received, district money (around five hundred dollars total) to attend a four-day workshop in Biraboo, Wisconsin, at the Aldo Leopold Legacy Center. The workshop focused on the work of Aldo Leopold and how his ideas might be translated into schoolwork. I highly doubt the Ralston Almanac Project could have been as successful as it was without my having undergone this intensive instruction.

I attended the workshop in June 2007. The workshop was excellent, and the facility at which it was held, the Aldo Leopold Legacy Center, deserves an essay of its own. What I learned in those four days really helped me focus my own ideas about how the Leopold Education Project should look in my classroom. The workshop focused on how to make teaching practice correspond to Leopold's land ethic, as articulated in his writing: "All ethics so far evolved rest upon a single premise: that the individual is a member of a community of interdependent parts. His instincts prompt him to compete for his place in that community, but his ethics prompt him also to co-operate (perhaps in order that there may be a place to compete for). The land ethic simply enlarges the boundaries of the community to include soils, waters, plants, and animals, or collectively: the land" (1949, 203–4).

A few of the presenters whom I met were integral in crafting my version of the project. One of the people I met really helped me understand how this project could be used in an English classroom. Her name was

Lisa Eddy, and she ran a workshop called "Wandering, Wondering, and Writing: Place-Based Literature and Composition." She was an English teacher at Adrian High School in Michigan. I am radically indebted to her for my work.

Two other important individuals whom I met at the workshop were Dave Ellis and Chip McAllister. They cotaught a prairie science class at Fergus Falls Middle School in Minnesota, and their workshop, entitled "Teaching Outdoors Workshop," really helped me understand what fieldwork should look like. Their program involves fieldwork every day, and the entire sixth grade curriculum is fulfilled via the class, including reading and writing benchmarks. Of course, I had to extrapolate what I needed from their workshop, as they have a wetland prairie reserve a stone's throw from the door of their school. However, I was still able to see how the fieldwork should be structured and carried out. I am indebted to Dave and Chip for many of the practical details of the Ralston Almanac Project.

Several additional groups contributed to the development of the Ralston Almanac Project. There was, of course, the school district. A governmental organization, the Nebraska Natural Resources District (n.d.), introduced me to the concept thanks to their education program and also donated a class paperback set of *A Sand County Almanac*. Also involved were the Leopold Education Center (n.d.), a nonprofit group, as well as another nonprofit group called Pheasants Forever (n.d.), which is a nonprofit group dedicated to "the protection and enhancement of pheasant and other wildlife habitats throughout North America." Pheasants Forever has partnered with the Leopold Education Center in order to achieve common goals. Why do I mention this information? Because too often as a teacher, I feel that, as far as the classroom is concerned, no one not in education (with the exception of parents, and they only ephemerally) is concerned with what I am doing. Outside of education, there is no vested interest in meeting the specific challenges I am faced with. This project is by far a more collaborative effort than anything I have ever been involved with in my teaching career, and my conversations at the workshop (with hunters, with naturalists, with scientists) were incredibly enriching and important to me. There were resources, intellectual and otherwise, made available to me that I did not know even existed.

After the workshop in Wisconsin, I returned home, ready to develop the specifics of the unit I would be teaching in class. One of the great things about Aldo Leopold and the Leopold Education Project is that their work reminds you that, as a suburbanite, you do not live in an absence. The place you inhabit is a genuine place. The project is true to Leopold's edict that "perception can be split into infinitely small fractions without losing its quality. The weeds in a city lot convey the same lesson as the redwood." This bias is one that I had to overcome, but once I got used to thinking this way, the weeds in the city lot began to bloom for me.

In order to further engage my students in the Ralston Almanac Project, and in order to introduce them to *A Sand County Almanac* and Aldo Leopold, I spend some serious time telling them the story of how the book came to be. At its heart *A Sand County Almanac* is the story of a person and the land he owned and what he did with it. It is a story that anyone considering this project should probably know as well. It is a dramatic comedy, in that it is the tale of disaster avoided.

When Leopold bought the farm, he told his family that he had bought some land along the Wisconsin River, which was true. But the farm in the picture was not of the dells his family had dancing in their heads. There was no brilliant cabin set quietly upon a promontory with river and woodlands framed pristinely in the window. The farm was a combination of muddy, mosquito-conquered flood land that, as you moved away from the river, transitioned into the macerated plain of a glacial run, predominantly granite that had been over the course of millennia pulverized into sand.

Leopold purchased the farm from the state. It had been abandoned by the previous tenants after they farmed what little topsoil there was until it blew away. Then, to complete the ruining, they had set up shop as bootleggers in the farmhouse until it burned down. Leopold says of the farm: "My own farm was selected for its lack of goodness and its lack of highway; indeed my whole neighborhood lies in a backwash of the River Progress" (1949, 46–47).

Leopold and his family brought the place back to life. I mentioned a picture of the farm in the opening of this chapter: I use this picture to tell this story to my students, along with pictures of the farmland the way it looks presently. Now the chicken coop in the picture straddles a healthy pine forest and a strip of restored prairie. To its west lies what could rightfully be called young oak savanna. The coop, which at the time of the photograph was filled knee-high with cow and chicken manure, is now known as "the shack." It is visited regularly by ecologists, teachers, nature enthusiasts, writers, and environmentalists. It is a healthy place. I try to emphasize the heroic nature of this story to my students and the dramatic contrast between the old farm and the new farm.

"He was crazy," I remember a student named Vince saying. But nearly all were impressed by his dedication to the place, to what it became, and to the following that Aldo Leopold and *A Sand County Almanac* have built. Why did it happen?

Some of the central themes of this history were the themes that I started with when I undertook the Leopold Education Project with my students: the idea that you need to pay careful attention to a place in order to truly know it, the idea that there are different kinds of literature, and, most important, the idea that a place can be renewed and is even able to renew us. These ideas are what I was thinking of when I implemented the Leopold Education Project in my classroom.

After reading *A Sand County Almanac* closely, with emphasis on Leopold's main ideas and elements of his writing style, we embarked on what I dubbed the Ralston Almanac Project. I report here on the Ralston Almanac Project taught in the fall of 2007 to a tenth grade honors English class of twenty-seven students. Here is an excerpt from the assignment sheet for the Ralston Almanac Project:

> *Why*
>
> Consider your day: when you are on the circuit from home to school, and then to practice, or to work, and then finally home again, or out and off to be with friends; even if you are idle for an hour (or perhaps an entire day), are you really aware of where you are, and what is happening around you? Are you aware of the impact you are having on the place you occupy? Or are you, like many of us, just skimming the world's surface for the most part, like a long-legged flies skating across a pond's top?

> In other words, how connected are you to the place you inhabit?
>
> And what does it mean to be connected to a place, anyways?
>
> The project you are about to undertake asks you to find answers to these questions by testing a theory. The theory is Aldo Leopold's, and it is one you should be familiar with by now, because it is outlined and modeled in Aldo Leopold's book *Sand County Almanac.*
>
> This project asks to you to pay attention to the natural world around you in order to come closer to really knowing it. It asks you to work with the attention of a scientist, and the creativity of a writer (although, if you think about it, both disciplines require attention and creativity). It also requires that you consider your impact on the place you are in. Do you make it better, or worse, by being there?
>
> The name of this project is the Ralston Almanac.

The project was essentially a portfolio-based series of assignments that asked students to think about Ralston as not just a suburb of Omaha, but as a piece of land as well, as defined by Leopold: "soils, waters, plants, and animals, or collectively: the land" (1949, 204). The elements of the portfolio were two field journals, four site-analysis essays, a home-range site-analysis essay, a quote-response essay, a lyrical poem about a chosen site, and a foreword to the almanac.

Field Journals

One of the most critical and interesting pieces of this portfolio was the field journal. Essentially, field journals were diaries of observations made by students. Field journals included elements such as physical maps, sound maps, temperature recordings, cloud identifications, plant identifications, sketches, and various other structured observations. These journals were made of two pieces of white paper folded in half to form a booklet. I took my students about a block away from school to a site called Turtle Creek Park, a four-acre park with a creek running through it. (Site selection was critical: I could march them there and back in the span of one forty-five-minute class period, and it was a big enough space to set them each by themselves and still small enough to supervise with the help of a volunteer counselor or free-period teacher. By our last visit, I felt confident enough to accompany them to the park by myself.) About half the park is wooded. The other half is open lawn. You may not think that a park provides an enriching natural setting, but it was easily enough for them to go on. Leopold's reminder that even a field of weeds is enough to begin understanding a place was truly empowering in this case.

The students loved it, with several in the class even citing their fieldwork as the highlight of the class in the year-end evaluations. In my opinion, the success of the field journal experience rested on two things: the implementation of protocols and the fact that the observations were structured.

Protocols. Protocols are essentially guidelines for behavior in the field. I simply lifted many of them from Dave and Chip. I instructed the class on hand signals that I would use to coordinate movement (stop, go, look, listen, and so forth), which eliminated the need for anyone to speak, let alone yell, and which they got a kick out of using. I also equipped some of them with responsibilities, including jobs such as line leaders, field-guide librarians, and binocular managers. These jobs would be rotated from day to day. The most important protocol of our fieldwork was the edict "Leave no trace."

Structured observations. The entries in the field journals were not freewriting. The field journals asked students to make detailed descriptions of the natural phenomena they noticed. They were required to note colors, shapes, temperatures, textures, and sounds first. Things such as feelings and personal thoughts were given space in the journal, but were not the focus of the work. This structure served to imbue the fieldwork with the feeling of truly doing *work*.

One of the most important pieces of the field journals, and one I took from the Wisconsin workshop, was the importance of getting students to ask questions. I am not a social engineer. I did not want the project to be a spooning of platitudes that they would then regurgitate ("Nature is important," "Nature is beautiful"). But I did want them to start paying attention to and asking their own questions about the ecology of the place they live. I wanted their learning to be as inquiry based as possible.

The field journals were handed in with their portfolios, but the fieldwork did not end when the portfolio was turned in. In order to fully embrace the spirit of Aldo Leopold's idea that to know a place we must pay constant attention to it, we visited the park at various times throughout the year in order to do more journal work.

Site Analysis and Home-Range Essays

The fieldwork and field journals were essentially used as prewriting for what I called site-analysis essays, which were essays I asked the students to write about their observations. The purpose of their site-analysis essays was twofold. First, they were challenged to practice the fundamental writing skill of describing carefully the things they saw. The second was to think hard about style—particularly, Aldo Leopold's writing style. I asked them to think about how Leopold crafted his sentences and the rhythms of his prose and then challenged them to imitate it. Not only did this assignment reinforce the idea that a place a block away from their school, a place that one might consider relatively featureless, actually teemed with narratives, with intricacies, with beauty, but it required them to show their grasp of the literary techniques used in the central text.

A related assignment, the home-range essay, asked them to do the same things that we had done together, but at a site of their own choosing, preferably as close to their home as possible. This home-range essay, named after phrasing from *A Sand County Almanac*, I can attribute to Lisa Eddy's work.

The site-analysis essays were not only a chance to write vivid descriptions of the places they visited, but also a chance for students to ask questions about the things they observed and engage with the place by asking their own questions. Here is an example from a winter-visit site analysis by a student named Emily: "I see what looks like white mold growing on one tree trunk. It flakes off in random patches, and wraps itself around the whole base of the tree. What is it? I turn my eyes elsewhere. I look up into the tree branches and see four bird nests high in the branches. These I wouldn't have been able to spot through the leaves earlier this year. How many other nests were left to fend for themselves? Are nests re-used by the same birds, or are they 'for rent'? All these thoughts swirl in my head."

At their best, these site-analysis essays not only asked students to engage in writing concretely, but also became opportunities for them to articulate their own relationships with their place and to make personal discoveries. The following was written by James, who lived right behind the park we visited for the project: "Even though it was supposedly the same park, Turtle Creek Park in late fall resembles nothing of its summer brother. It was as if a tornado had torn through here, except for the vast scattering of leaves still on the ground. Living close to the park all my life had prepared me for this, but now I looked on it in a whole different 'light.' Paying careful attention changed what had always been familiar."

Here is a reflection written by a student named Ryan: "I find that as I observe the outside, I observe myself just as much, if not more, than I do my surroundings. I learn more about what gives me peace. I think that in that lies the true success of going out to observe the environment and the natural world. By observing your surroundings, you are observing yourself."

At the end of the project, I asked the students to reflect on their own learning and about what value the project had for them. Although not everyone experienced personal epiphanies like James's and Ryan's, 100 percent of them considered the site-analysis essays as a demanding but beneficial writing exercise, and 100 percent of them enjoyed the novelty of it.

Quote-Response Essay

I chose to include a quote-response essay for two reasons. The first was to introduce ideas from other writers regarding the central theme of local place and local ecology that we had not addressed in class, a kind of miniature "independent study" of other strains of nature writing. The second reason was that the curriculum at Ralston High School requires the continuation of a discussion about the techniques of writing literary analyses, so I used this essay as a chance to introduce that discussion to the class. Quotes students favored heavily were Emerson's idea that "nature hates calculators" as well as Byron's poetic explanation:

> There is a pleasure in the pathless woods,
> There is rapture in the lonely shore,
> There is society where no one intrudes,
> by the deep sea, and the music in its roar:
> I love man not the less, but nature more.

The school provided no anthology of nature writing for them, so students depended upon a combination of Web searches for nature quotes and a menu of quotes I provided for them.

Poem Assignment

I included a poem assignment that asked students to write twelve to twenty lines of poetry in reaction to something they saw at their site. I did so for variety, but I also used the introduction of the poem assignment to discuss assumptions the students carried about the term *nature writing.*

Here is a poem by Katie:

Struggles

A ladybug struggled
on a leaf.
The wind blew,
and the bug fell back
and had to regain distance;
Again and again
the wind blew,
Again and again the bug struggled upwards.
In the end,
It arrived at the top edge of the flower,
The beginning of it.
And only I saw.

As far as student responses to the Ralston Almanac Project, most of them said that they enjoyed the project. Many of them began thinking about

Ralston not only as a suburb but also as a place with an interesting ecology as well, even if only for a short time. But what did they learn?

From reading their reflective responses as well as their portfolios, I have discerned two tiers of student reactions to the central theories presented by the project and by Aldo Leopold's book *A Sand County Almanac*. The most important of these theories were the idea that the weeds in a vacant lot are just as ecologically vital and as important as a forest of redwoods and the claim that failing to know your locale is truly detrimental. In Leopold's words: "The 'key-log' which must be moved to release the evolutionary process for a [land] ethic is simply this: quit thinking about decent land-use as solely an economic problem. Examine each question in terms of what is ethically and esthetically right" (1949, 224). In their responses, an overwhelming majority of students acknowledged the former idea as a valid and real one.

A student named Zach wrote one of the clearest articulations of this acknowledgment: "This experience has taught me you don't have to be in a forest or a park to see nature. You can simply retreat to your own backyard. The creations in your backyard may not be as spectacular as other places, but it is still real nature. In addition to that, I really didn't even pay attention to the nature that surrounds my house before this project, but now I notice it. I learned that sitting and looking and listening carefully to the world around me makes a difference to what I think about." However, this tier of students did not necessarily accept the idea that it is vital to know about one's local place. A student named John said that this "gap of knowledge," as he described it, was not dangerous, "as long as you know it's there."

The second tier of students, and a much smaller tier, not only considered the weeds-redwoods concept a valuable one, but also took to heart the idea that learning about one's place (in this case, the ecology of a place) is important to both its health and their own. A student named Alan wrote, "The fact that you can find such a small delight in the leafy grass makes a trip to Oak Park all the more enjoyable. Going into nature, and discovering small wonders is a great way to get people interested in nature. Leopold's idea of getting people interested in what's around them may be the first step in making conservation a new trend."

Hopefully, exposure to Leopold's ideas will serve as a catalyst for their own ideas about the spaces they inhabit and what their roles are as citizens of those spaces, specifically as caretakers of the natural heritage of those spaces.

I have continued to develop ideas and practices from the Leopold Education Project since the 2007 class I showcase in this chapter. As the project has evolved, I have included not only investigations into the local watershed, but also investigations into the cultural elements of the place my students inhabit as well. For example, I have made connections with the leadership at the local history archives in Ralston and have developed a piece that asks students to explore not only their local environmental history, but their cultural history as well. Although the core of the project remains learning about their shared watershed, I have found that even small forays such as this one into the cultural aspects of local place have yielded profound insights. I have also explored this direction because, simply, the opportunity is there: the Ralston Archives museum is just down the street from the school and is a place a majority of Ralston students pass every day. Further, I have been careful to circumscribe the activities and projects that the students do at the archives with the original goals of the project: that is, gaining a better understanding of their local watershed. This circumscription is achieved by asking students to explore the histories of various geographical features of Ralston and then asking them to trace how they were (and are) used. Over time, students have researched topics such as the following:

- a green space that was once a field, and then a lake used to supply an icehouse for Omaha, and then a golf course, and now a hockey arena
- the more unusual species of mature trees around town, including fifty-foot catalpa trees and at least a half-dozen different species of oak
- the first modern owner of the land, a wealthy newspaperman, wanted to create an "English Hunting Ground" and so had thousands upon thousands of trees planted all across the prairie

- even the histories of specific city blocks and the histories of the houses on them

Another piece I have developed is a public presentation. One of the great flaws in the first version of this project was that, although students did go back into the field throughout the year to gain insight into their local habitats, the work did not make its way much further beyond the classroom. In other words, in 2007 I never asked them to engage the public. As I have worked with our suburban research team, however, I have become convinced that public engagement is both necessary (as most strongly argued in Flower 2008) and practically possible for secondary teachers such as myself (Linda Christensen's 2009 "Into the World" project is a clear example). In later versions, however, I assigned kiosk-type display-board final assignments that asked students to outline what they had discovered. These informative kiosks were put on display in the school library. Further, in keeping with Sarah Robbins and Mimi Dyer's (2005) suggestion that students should be asked to engage in cultural work as an essential part of their classroom literacy, I have even coordinated with motivated students who have created both cultural and environmental exhibits for the Ralston Archives as part of their service-learning graduation requirements. These projects have impacted not only their class grades but the community at large as well by making available carefully researched information about the local watershed. Many of these projects carried simple titles: "Where Does Ralston's Water Come From?"; "Before Ralston High School: What Was Here?"; "A Brief History of My Neighborhood"; "The Silver Maple: Ralston's Whirlibird Trees." This community engagement did not require a change of system. It only required working within the system to exploit opportunities where place-conscious education could be present.

Hopefully, this narrative has engendered ideas about place-conscious teaching that focuses on an intimate knowledge of local ecology. There is a line from the introduction to Joseph Goddard's *Being American on the Edge* that I connect to the goal of this project: "Penurban places are products of deep-seated mind-sets—imagined, washed over people's cultural retinas, and then thrown out across landscapes. . . . These places are difficult to pin down as they are as much about feeling as physicality" (2012, 2). Using this metaphor, I have come to understand that the goal of the project is to simply help students focus on their local place in the literal sense of the word, to unblur, if you will, some of the green spaces that they pass on their way to school. I encourage you to seek out the Leopold Education Project and to consider implementing your own version of it in the classroom.

Solving for Perennial Patterns in University Composition

Connecting Local and Global Arguments for Place-Conscious Citizenship

AUBREY STREIT KRUG

If the goal of place-conscious education is to use writing to produce suburban citizenship, then place-conscious educators must consider what is already being produced—and reproduced—in first-year writing classrooms that have a suburban context: an annual model of citizenship. Students are taught to participate in temporary, transitory relationships to suburban places that "naturally" happen to be blank slates. These constructed environments are emptied of history and diverse social and ecological communities. In the introduction to this book, an annual progression is defined as the "migratory" problem of suburban education. I am particularly concerned with the migratory reality of college spaces and first-year composition.

At the University of Nebraska–Lincoln where I teach, my composition students are new to me each semester. Few of them identify themselves as rural, and many of them do not see the city of Lincoln as a particularly urban place. These suburban students arrive at a campus that is part of the New Urban Penurbia (Goddard 2012). The familiar fountains, lawns, brick buildings, and green space meet their expectations for a "normal" university environment. They come to learn at a place that feels suburban in a city that continues to sprawl.

However, my students tend to be more concerned with how they are spending their time than with the place in which they are located. Because it is a required general education course, many of them tend to see composition as a short-term, semester-long task rather than as part of a multiyear, ongoing process of education. Some of them see their own writing work as a series of problems to be solved with specialized, expert solutions, and so they seek quick fixes to learn to write the "right" way in order to get a good grade and therefore someday a good job to pay off their student loans.

When students see the point of education as helping them to move on (and move up), it becomes natural and normal for writing and learning to be temporary and transactional. Similarly, the spread of suburban developments and the increasing expenses of higher education are culturally produced as natural and normal effects of progress. Meanwhile, material watersheds are made invisible, and damage to social and ecological communities is rendered as inevitable.

When young people are taught that their role in the community is to accept these systemic changes passively, they are being offered what I call an "annual model of citizenship," in which individuals prioritize their own short-term economic gains and mobility above their relationships and responsibilities to the social and environmental community of a place. My concept of "annual" references the agricultural economy of annual crops in Nebraska, as well as the annual turnover in my composition classrooms, where each semester I interact with a "new crop of students" in a place made to feel "placeless."

Does it have to be this way? Could it be different? Could teachers of writing make cultural processes and material watersheds visible so that students could make active, informed choices as place-conscious suburban citizens?

In this chapter I share the story of how I as a teacher tried to question the norms and denaturalize the nature of the annual systems that are taken for granted in suburban university composition classrooms. In particular, I explain a sequence of interconnected writing projects I developed for a general education course on writing, rhetoric, and argument at the University of Nebraska–Lincoln. These three assignments ask composition students to:

- explore a local argument on campus
- analyze an argument about a global issue
- make a public argument that traces cultural, economic, or ecological connections between local, bioregional, and global systems

Based on what my students taught me, I suggest composing place-conscious citizenship on a perennial model and teaching composition with a perennial pedagogy.

My concept of the perennial has its roots in the tallgrass prairie bioregion of the North American Great Plains where I live and work and specifically in the Land Institute's efforts to breed "perennial polycultures" in Kansas. As Wes Jackson explains, researchers there are using perennial tallgrass prairie plants to try to create agricultural systems that are longer lasting and more diverse than current annual monocultural systems, in which fields are typically plowed and planted in one kind of crop each year (2010, 146—76). The Land Institute is not so much re-creating the prairie, almost all of which has been lost, as it is using the prairie as a model for creating new resilient and relevant communities (which include soils, plants, humans, and other animals) in prairie places. This strategy of *re-placing*, or constructing a renewed sense of social and ecological community and place in a space that has been depleted of one, could be valuable as we look to re-place suburban watersheds and instill a sense of place consciousness in suburban students and teachers.

A perennial pedagogy could be based not upon passive and unquestioning belonging to a place or conditioned acceptance of it (that is, not upon inevitability), but rather an active and reflective sense of place (that is, upon possibility)—a sense of place that is both constructed and constructive with regard to how place is used to produce bodies, food, knowledge, culture, and citizenship. Building on Freire's idea of a problem-posing education (2000, 79–86), a perennial model suggests a first-year composition pedagogy that encourages students to think of their writing processes not as problems but as *patterns*—patterns that have been developed over time in relationship to other patterns in the world around them. The concept of "solving for pattern" comes from Wendell Berry (1981), who suggests that good farmers cannot do good work by simply solving local problems as they come up; instead, they must see how local problems are part of larger situations and solve for these larger patterns.

By solving for patterns, composition students and teachers can begin to consider why they have the models for writing, reading, and learning that they do. They can begin to perceive patterns in their cultural and material watersheds. Writing projects can then become locations for composition that help students identify, experiment with, respond to, and alter these patterns. As they build on each other and are revised over time, writing projects can become places in which knowledge is collaboratively produced by the student writer, teacher, and learning community, reaching outward into the larger watershed community.

In summary: in a perennial pedagogy, teachers and students together turn from a short-term problem-solving approach to composition toward a longer-term practice of solving for pattern through writing. This temporal turn also suggests a spatial one: namely, the use of writing to understand how local observations are implicated in larger-scale ecological and economic forces and discourses. Solving for perennial patterns—in this sense, the patterns that persist time after time, place after place—can help students perceive and make informed choices in response to the natural and cultural systems that structure their own learning and their rhetorical practices of writing, reading, thinking, and doing. And as I hope my narrative below demonstrates, solving for perennial patterns can help teachers analyze, reflect on, and develop their pedagogical choices over time and across places.

Exploring a Local Argument

To make these ideas of perennial pedagogy visible, I will report on the actual progression of two sections of English 151, Writing: Rhetoric as Argument, from the fall of 2012. In these courses, I explicitly tried to create and practice a perennial pedagogy. Like all sections of English 151, mine fulfilled a general education requirement at UNL and thus operated by a standard set of course objectives. Students were expected to write texts in a variety of forms, to identify their purposes and intended audiences, to conduct research, and to document their sources.

By design, I wanted to help students inquire into the suburban university as a place and to begin to "see" their material watershed. My research in ecocriticism has led me to understand how ecosystem issues are not just scientific problems; they are also cultural patterns. Whether (and how) people perceive their watershed is based upon writing, rhetoric, and arguments. Arguments influence beliefs, actions, and perspectives—they can conceal as well as reveal. Arguments can change who people think they are, what they want, and what they do. Arguments affect culture and alter nature. So for us to be active citizens and responsible human beings, we need to be able to recognize, understand, and evaluate the arguments around us. And we need to be able to make our own arguments informed and effective.

This argument at least is the one that I made at the beginning of the semester to my students, as I tried to convince them of the importance of our class. I also invited them to keep an open mind about the course and to see our shared work as a project of inquiry and discovery. Because I expected that some students would bring to class a mental model of making arguments as merely expressing opinions, I wanted to start the semester by considering how asking questions could precede, inform, even cross into the acts of generating claims and making a complex argument.

So the relationship between inquiry and argument was central to our first writing project (WP1), an essay that I called an exploratory argument. We started the unit by reading and inquiring into James Farrell's exploratory argument *The Nature of College: How a New Understanding of Campus Life Can Change the World*. Farrell is a college professor in Minnesota who has taught a class called Campus Ecology, in which he asks students to apply environmental ideas to their own lives and habitats. His book is based on this course and is marketed to college students. As the subtitle suggests, Farrell provides information that challenges students to see the material places or watersheds of higher educational institutions in a more critical, historical, and cultural context and to use that new perspective to make more knowledgeable choices within and beyond their learning environments.

Over the next several weeks, I asked students to draw comparisons and connections between their own lives at UNL and Farrell's chapters on water and waste, materialism, food, technology, and parties. Because we were the university students that Farrell is, in part, trying to influence, I suggested that looking around at our local place—the modern system of higher education that we were writing and learning within at UNL—would allow us to think about what his argument meant for us and begin to solve for patterns in our everyday experiences. This idea generated engaged discussion, though not on our local watershed and thus not in the way that I had planned. I expected our conversations to lead to explorations of the physical systems of UNL's watershed; I thought students would want to compare Farrell's points to the UNL food system, for instance, or that they might conduct research about waste or recycling on campus. When I took one section of my class on a writing marathon[1] to observe arguments in their local environment, I hoped they would return with observations about how things like campus green space, building architecture, and school-pride signage were part of a built local environment that argued for students to behave and think in certain ways. Instead, they returned with observations focused on social interactions between people and groups: conversations they overheard, postures they noticed, cultural cues given by who chose to sunbathe and who was covered up, and ways they felt others—both peers and authority figures—observing them.

Though I had planned for a more material focus, I might have predicted this social emphasis. Students perceived their watershed through the lens of the human community—which, given how invisible the watershed tends to be in typical suburban designs, is not too surprising. In general, they responded to Farrell's information about physical places and systems by questioning his representation of the values and norms of the human community that interacted with and constructed those places and systems. For instance, several of the more outspoken students in class expressed frustration or even anger at Farrell's critique of "them" and his implication that they were part of the average clueless college

1. To learn more about writing marathons, see Susan Martens's chapter in this volume.

student demographic he was describing. Overall, students were primarily interested in the multiple voices of the university community that, in my understanding, gave shape to different representations of the community's watershed.

As this pattern emerged in class discussion, it provided a good opportunity to explore deeper questions about what motivates our emotional responses to texts, as well as how this text might not offer a satisfactory solution to a singular problem. Instead, Farrell seems interested in identifying patterns and wants to invite readers into challenging conversations. Because he analyzes normative aspects of campus culture and ecology, Farrell's book necessarily uses generalizations about college students, and he is keen to invite students into "conversation" and "constructive dialogue" about this dynamic (2010, 3). At the end of the introduction, Farrell situates his own identity as a teacher and learner and links his own generation and other Americans with the culture of college students. Though "we are all in this together," he writes, "in all cases, you'll need to decide for yourself if you're a part of the 'we' I'm describing" (11).

Identifying this invitational rhetoric was crucial for me. I wanted my students to connect it to Farrell's purpose in writing an exploratory argument. Farrell's exploratory argument "probe[s] connections" and explores "links between personal life, cultural patterns, and the natural world" while leaving "space for readers to reflect on their own experience." In addition, Farrell's exploratory purpose "invites" readers "into a conversation about the meanings of college, and the personal and institutional possibilities of a culture of permanence" (10). I realized how I as a teacher and fellow student needed to provide space for students to plant and raise their own questions alongside the personal inquiry into the watershed I was interested in. My own inquiry could be a model for them, but only by inviting students to claim their own inquiry could I help them lay the groundwork for future writing for social change in our class, in other classes, and in suburban public life.[2]

2. Mary Birky Collier's concept of "preadvocacy" work, described in her contribution to this volume, has itself inspired and invited me into this realization.

As we continued, I asked students a series of questions: Is what Farrell suggests about the learned environmental ignorance of college students true of your experience at this university? How does his understanding of the purpose of a college education compare with your expectations, assumptions, and values? What do you believe a college education should do, and why? For my students, in one of our most lively in-class discussions to date, this exercise was a chance to articulate how a college degree is taken for granted, to posit the potential conflicts between a career-driven approach to education versus a life-of-the-mind approach, and to take into account the realities of cost, debt, and privilege. Students from in state and out of state, as well as from rural, urban, and suburban areas, shared and compared their reasons for choosing to attend UNL as well as their rationalizations, assumptions, and inherited knowledge about what college was for and how to navigate it. The result was not any answers; instead, it was some real questions about what *we* were doing *here*, on this campus and in this classroom—whether the matter of the classroom consisted of chairs and desks or screens and servers.

The way some of my students bristled at Farrell's tone in *The Nature of College*, as well as the way in which they instinctively gravitated toward social currents in the physical watershed of the university campus, suggested to me a pattern in students' relationships to their educational place: they were interested in and aware of group dynamics and structures of power in education and tended to see the university as a social rather than physical place. Solving for this pattern helped me understand why Farrell's questions about where their food came from or their trash went on campus were going against the grain in terms of student expectations. It also helped me see the value of these questions, which challenged them to consider the watershed when discussing social topics.

Finally, solving for this pattern of student response helped me see how Farrell's text did successfully provoke students into realizing their own rhetorical agency. Even though some of them were just becoming familiar with the university as a place, they felt informed and qualified to speak about their educational choices, learning goals, and social desires based on their position as students. Their firsthand experiences in dorms, classrooms, the student union, and the administrative building were relevant and valuable to their reading and writing. Their personal and locally situated knowledge granted them the authority to ask questions and construct claims, for instance, about whether they thought college students really should read *The Nature of College* as soon as they arrived on campus. In doing so, they began to craft a rhetorical engagement with the world around them.

This was one of the goals of WP1. For this assignment I asked students to identify an issue question about our local educational place that Farrell's text motivated them to ask and write an exploratory argument considering ways different stakeholders might answer that question before coming to their own conclusions.

Students conducted research on multiple community points of view by drawing on Farrell's points, completing an observation of a local place or an informal interview, recalling points made in class discussions, and imagining counterarguments. For example, during individual conferences I would ask questions such as "Does your question have only one possible answer, or is it open-ended? Could reasonable people disagree about the answer? What do you believe is the answer, and why?" to help them revise their issue questions and conclusions; questions like "Who else might know or care about this topic? Who else should be part of the conversation?" to help them come up with ideas about alternative viewpoints to explore in the bodies of their essays; and questions such as "What would X say in response to Y's argument? Why would A's position differ from B's on this point? Can you explain what Q would say after reading your conclusion?" to help them articulate the depth of the multiple points of view they found and to bring them into an appropriately complex conversation.

Students explored a range of issue questions: Do students party to escape responsibility, fit a cultural norm, deal with repressed emotions, or build social community? Do average college students know what they are putting into their bodies when they eat, and should they? What level of materialist consumption is necessary, and where do you draw the line of enough? Who should care about what college students do on campuses anyhow?

This last question is invoked in the title of student Olivia Reinert-Gehman's essay "Caring about Carelessness: Who Is Responsible for the

Mindset of Today's College Generation?" Reinert-Gehman opened her WP1 with the lunchtime insight that she had no idea what was in her hamburger or where it came from. She then listed more of her daily habits—flushing the toilet, logging on to social media—that she had never thought about before reading *The Nature of College*, pointing out Farrell's suggestion that "about 45% of daily behavior is habitual" (8). Her reflections culminate in a series of questions:

> Farrell does a great job of highlighting what most college students don't know, or don't think about. The question that arises in my mind as I read Farrell's thoughts on our carelessness is: what should be done to fix it? How can students learn to think of the big picture, and not just things that have a direct effect on them? To identify a solution to such an open-ended question, the source of the problem needs to be identified. Who is responsible for the widespread mindset among college students that convenience and disposability are more important than sustainability and a healthy future? When and what should we be learning about the environment and what it means for us?

In the essay Reinert-Gehman considers parental influences, the effects of convenient technology, demands upon college students' time, and the responsibilities of universities. She then perceives a pattern in terms of how education is linked to the environment and draws upon her own experiences to theorize the concept of a "disposable education":

> A lot of the classes that I have taken have consisted of lecture style class periods and a few exams during the semester. It teaches kids that all that matters is the grade. This makes it too easy for students to just gloss over the material and memorize a few phrases to receive a passing grade. Students aren't taking their education into their own hands, and aren't really taking an active role in their education. I have observed that the most common way of thinking among students is to study and memorize information for tests, and then most people forget the material by the time the course is finished. I feel like people have the same mindset about the resources they consume. People use products and then just throw them away and they only think about it from the cash register to

> the trashcan. They don't dig deeper to find out where it comes from, or find out about any more sensible alternatives.

Reinert-Gehman concludes that all people, college students included, have a stake in the issue she is exploring, but that the problem will not be solved by blaming anyone. She argues that students' "terrible mindset" and carelessness about the environment are learned: "Despite our independence, our school system or careers and the people around us shape us." Everyone is implicated and involved in this larger pattern of (non)environmental education, she suggests, so "it's up to everyone to make a change."

Reinert-Gehman's WP1 referenced the physical watershed on campus, but—more surprisingly to me—it deftly navigated the emotional waters of care, blame, acceptance, and responsibility. From her work, I was reminded of how solving for this social pattern, especially with regard to equity and justice, remains a central task of place-conscious education. Disposable information and places are also linked with disposable *people* into a larger pattern, and perceiving this pattern might help us see suburban developments as unsustainable watersheds both materially and socially.

Yet this work of solving for pattern was not taken up by all students in the same way. Reinert-Gehman's essay, for instance, was more reflective than the typical student project. More generally, one of my goals for WP1 was for students to write the opposite of a five-paragraph thesis-driven essay. I wanted them to ask questions and explore multiple answers in the process of coming to their own conclusions. In other words, rather than drawing on the habit of using the five-paragraph essay as the natural or normal solution for any writing problem, I wanted them to draw on what we had discussed about a new pattern—the rhetorical triangle (of audience-context-purpose)—to construct a different kind of essay in response to a college-level assignment. I see this latter model as more adaptable and thus a potentially perennial pattern for student writers as they move into future classes. I as the instructor sought to invite and reward solving for this new rhetorical pattern in the classroom community, as well as to recognize it through my own individual reflections and comments on student work, but students varied in their responses to the invitation. Some, including Reinert-Gehman, crafted essays in which they effectively tried out new ways of composing knowledge. Others, however, defaulted to the models they had used in high school or previous classes. During revision some of these students stuck to the rhetorical patterns they had brought to this course, but others were willing and able to tinker with these patterns based on my suggestions. At least all students had the opportunity to perceive their previous habits about writing and the form they had been taught that an argument must take. Doing so is the first step in recognizing their own rhetorical agency and in perceiving and solving for other patterns in their lives and the world around them.

Analyzing an Argument about a Global Issue

The second writing project (WP2) asked students to analyze an argument about a global issue. My goal here, building on the first assignment, was to extend students' ideas of who might be a stakeholder or have an interest in an issue as wide ranging and long lasting as global warming. If the first project invited them to look more closely at the immediate physical and social watershed of the world around them, this second project was designed to unsettle that level of comfort and familiarity by asking them to engage with an issue that reaches across watersheds and cultures, a phenomenon that can be difficult to imagine or depict.

Global warming is often communicated through numbers, graphs, scientific facts, expert discourse, and images of polar bears on melting ice. It operates on a planetary scale, and its existence is demonstrated through appeals to logic and authority. In addition, when put into stories and brought down to a national or individual scale, narratives of global warming's impacts upon the earth and human cultures often evoke strong emotions: fear, pity, anger, and grief come to mind, as do humility, resolve, and courage (a desire to act), even faith (a desire to transcend place or to find community here).

I chose Bill McKibben's book *Eaarth: Making a Life on a Tough New Planet* for us to discuss because I thought the topic was timely and educational. I found the text itself rhetorically rich as well as accessible. McKibben uses statistics as well as personal stories to appeal to logos, ethos, and pathos; he often predicts his intended American audience's responses and replies directly to them; he self-consciously reflects on his choice of tone and language; his rhetorical choices are based on his critical analysis of previous environmental texts that have not succeeded in bringing about the change he wants; and the imagery of the book is vivid. McKibben's main argument is that climate change owing to global warming is *already* happening (not something that will happen only to future generations), and we must recognize and learn to live on this "tough new planet."

Students diagnosed the book's cover as attention getting and off-putting, provocative and apocalyptic. It alternately made them want to pick up the book and put it back down. On the paperback version, a thick, black *X* stretches across the cover, the edge of a small planet earth peeking out from the white space behind. The globe seems to be crossed out. The title, *Eaarth*, is in white lowercase font against the black *X*, but the second *a* is in green, emphasizing both its weirdness and perhaps its potential. Other aspects of the cover assert McKibben's authority (for example, a line noting that this book was a *New York Times* best seller) and the urgency of his message (a blurb from Barbara Kingsolver implores readers, "Read it, please. Straight through to the end. Whatever else you were planning to do next, nothing could be more important.").

Because WP2 is a rhetorical analysis assignment, I tried to focus discussions on close-reading particular passages as well as tracing the overarching structure and summarizing the main claims of McKibben's book. For example, McKibben critiques the economic logic that demands continual growth: "On our new planet growth may be the one big habit we finally must break" (2010, 48). His reasoning is based on the fact that the economy relies on cheap fossil-fuel energy, which exists in limited quantities (30). This economic logic can be seen in systems of higher education and suburban development, and I tried to draw out this pattern in the classroom and make it visible for students.

As they drafted their essays, I challenged students to rely solely on evidence from the text to assess the effectiveness of McKibben's argument. I did so because in the past, students writing rhetorical analysis essays for the first time have tended to want to prove or disprove the claims of the author and so write a thesis statement saying that the text is right or wrong. They have tended to look to outside research to support their thesis. I instead have wanted them to focus on *how* the writer made those claims in the text, and specifically to write and support a thesis statement about *how the text works*—how it achieves (or does not achieve) its purpose in light of its audience, the context in which it functions, and its chosen rhetorical strategies. In other words, I want them to solve for the rhetorical patterns of the text rather than solve the problem of whether they agree with the text's argument. Often, these differing purposes (between student writers and me) mean that classroom instruction, group conferences, and meetings during office hours turn into a series of negotiations in which students share writing that I attempt to push in a different direction.

This semester at first seemed no different, but then one student's revision of the assignment pushed *me* to see rhetorical analysis differently. My comments at the beginning of Jarek Olivetti's essay were typical. He wrote: "Targeting Americans by saying they need to become smaller and more localized is contrary to [the] American mentality, as well as our capitalistic (over)drive, but this is what McKibben claims needs to happen in order to survive. Unfortunately, McKibben's ideal of small, local and dispersed is an unrealistic one. His is a world which cannot exist nor come to fruition in contemporary American times, not until laws are put in place. This is because of the American obsession with entitlement, money, and individual freedom." I commented in the margin: "Is this your thesis statement? If so, I'd like to see a clearer connection to rhetorical analysis. It seems like you're suggesting that the book's argument fails in its logical appeals because of the context in which it operates, and because of its audience's expectations and values . . . at least that's how I might translate this into rhetorical terms, so it's clear that you're evaluating the effectiveness of his argument. How might you translate it?" Later, when Olivetti wrote again that McKibben's "solutions are not realistic," I commented that it seemed to me that Olivetti was suggesting there was no good way to make the argument McKibben wanted to make. Therefore, Olivetti was not really analyzing McKibben's argument so much as making his own about the topic. A few pages later, Olivetti wrote, "McKibben is the alarm clock to wake up us sleepy Americans. But we don't care. Not enough yet anyways." At this point, rather than repeat my comment about the purpose of rhetorical analysis, it occurred to me that maybe *I* was not grasping the whole point of the assignment. Even though it was not the usual approach and he was not employing a rhetorical vocabulary, Olivetti was doing exactly what I had requested: he was analyzing McKibben's argument based on what he knew and believed about Americans as an audience and American economic and cultural systems as a context.

For the first time, I realized the contradiction in my approach to teaching rhetorical analysis: I was requiring students to use only the text in their essays at the same time I was asking them to write essays that evaluated that text in its broader global context and in light of its audience. In other words, I was saying that they should make claims about how the text worked in the world, but was not allowing them to bring *the world*, in all its messiness, into their analysis. The watershed and the commonwealth were being left out rather than engaged.

This approach is precisely what Olivetti did in his essay, titled "What is *Eaarth* Woorth?" Olivetti's title and approach drew from McKibben's reflection on the economic language of analysis McKibben deliberately chose for an American audience. For instance, as McKibben writes in *Eaarth*: "If it seems that I am callously reducing the danger we face to dollars and cents, that's correct. Money, in our system, equals information. It's how we understand risk; it's how we measure possibility; it's the only gauge we have for understanding our collective future. If you have a lot of money, you have a lot of options, and if you don't have much, your options narrow. On this new planet we'll have less money than we thought we would, and hence fewer choices" (2010, 69). In this way, Olivetti's process of composition and angle of analysis solved for a more holistic pattern, not limiting itself to what was on the page but thinking about how this argument fits into the material, political, economic, and cultural context of America and the way it is connected to global forces and the earth overall.

Based on what I learned from Olivetti's essay, I began to envision a pedagogy that utilizes a broader environmental or ecological understanding of context, one in which context goes beyond the immediate circumstances of a rhetorical event and stretches to include social, cultural, historical, linguistic, and material forces. Place-conscious pedagogy can seek the environmental context behind and around the human technology of writing. This realization of context encourages students and their teachers to think about basic concepts of purpose, form, and audience in new ways. As Thomas Hothem explains, "In calling our attention to our surroundings and the discourses by which we know them," place-conscious composition or eco-composition "helps to contextualize our written expression" (2009, 35). This context matters, Hothem argues, because it helps students "gauge their relationship to their surroundings, their backgrounds, their education, and hence their future" (38).

My rhetorical analysis assignment should be revised so that this possibility of a broader cultural and material understanding of context is opened for students rather than closed. When analyzing texts that discuss global warming, I can ask questions that compel students to think beyond the typical boundaries of the page, such as: What are the different connotations of the terms *climate change* and *global warming*? Who would be best persuaded by an economic argument about global warming? Who will be most affected by it? Who might be marginalized or speak another language than your own, but have something to say about global warming? How could we identify and listen to the perspectives of the more-than-human world when it comes to this global climate change? From a place-conscious perspective, these questions could expand the concept of community to include marginalized humans as well as nonhuman creatures and relations. When we broaden a local, suburban place-based perspective to consider a global environmental issue, there is an opportunity to also broaden our conception of which kinds of community members might be included.

Making a Public Argument That Connects the Local and Global

The third and final writing project of the semester (WP3) linked the first and second writing projects by asking students to make a public argument that traced a cultural, economic, or ecological connection between a local argument and a global issue in order to make an argument that mattered in Lincoln, Nebraska. In other words, at this point in the course, I invited students to draw on what they had learned so far about writing and arguments to solve for pattern in the suburban context of the university and surrounding community. My goal was for us to use writing to practice the political skills of argument—what Canadian political scientist Roger Epp names as "articulating a position, listening, strategizing, researching, finding a consensus, depersonalizing conflict, and building external alliances" (2001, 320)—that, along with claiming rhetorical agency, are necessary for composing and enacting place-conscious citizenship. WP3 is a community literacy project, in the rich sense described by Linda Flower (2008) and articulated in the introduction to this book.

We began the final unit by reading current public arguments in the context of each other, first analyzing the claims and rhetorical qualities of each individual text, then discussing the underlying patterns (of narrative, logic, value, and so forth) that may have linked the texts together, and finally considering the broader context the linked texts existed within (for instance, how are they responding in different ways to the same situation?). One grouping of texts I used to focus on education were the 2012 UNL chancellor's State of the University address, which outlined strategic plans for the university to expand its student body; a chapter on "The Nature of Politics" from Farrell's *The Nature of College*, which considers apathy, activism, and responsibility on campus and in classrooms; and headlines from the Lincoln newspaper and UNL newspaper that, for instance, brought up for discussion a student-generated blog that drew attention to racist and sexist social media posts by UNL students.

In an online discussion group, I asked students, "After reading all three of this week's texts, what have you learned or started to notice regarding the context in which we are learning, writing, and living at UNL or in Lincoln?" One student, Rex Burkhead, shared this response, which demonstrates his ability to solve for pattern across multiple texts:

> I would say just having a bigger picture or knowledge base on how education, politics, and the environment all kind of tie together. It seems in many instances that money pops up to be a primary motivator for many issues or changes in all three of these categories, whether it be tuition fees, university income, taxes, or cost of "going green." These examples have helped me to see a pattern of cause and effect relationships guided

> by our society locally and globally. Reading the Chancellor's University address has given me a new perspective on our campus and the activities associated with it. I often feel that I don't know too much of what is going on with university decisions. . . . So this was a nice read to come across and has given me a new perspective on many motivations of universities across the country and ours as well.

In addition, after exploring these different perspectives (as they did in WP1) and analyzing them in a wider context (as they did in WP2), students like Burkhead were able to use their insights about patterns to generate ideas about where and how they might intervene in or contribute to the patterns they had found. For example, in his WP3 Burkhead articulated and contested a pattern of negative perception of student-athletes' intellects by considering his own local learning experience as a student-athlete at UNL, interviewing an academic adviser about the university system's expectations and support for student-athletes' educations, and weaving in more global research from the National Collegiate Athletic Association and social science scholars. In WP3 students were able to generate ideas for the topics they felt were important to argue about and that they felt capable of writing about, the audience they wanted to write for, and the genre they wanted to write in. The first step, then, was for students to propose a specific topic and create a short annotated bibliography based on textual research and sources.

I extended this research stage by asking students to consider who was impacted in their topic, to interview a stakeholder, and to write a two- to three-page exploration essay in which they described his or her perspective. I wanted students to have a conversation outside of our classroom with an expert source, a member of the community they were writing for, or someone whom they expected to have a different stance than their own. In the prompt for their essay, I asked them to address these questions: What did the stakeholder share in terms of knowledge and experience? What were the stakeholder's beliefs, values, and underlying assumptions? What did you learn about your topic that you did not know before? Finally, how might the stakeholder's perspective influence your own writing project and argument?

In my comments on their proposals, bibliographies, and stakeholder exploration essays, I asked questions to guide students into developing their longer public arguments. At this stage I have also used Brooke and McIntosh's (2007) practice of deep mapping as a tool for students to draw the context of their arguments as they take shape in draft form, saying, "Draw a map of what surrounds your argument, who's involved in it, and what you're responding to." The WP3 prompt suggested that students might compose an exploratory argument, a thesis-driven argument, or an argument in a different genre than an essay, such as a narrative, series of opinion pieces, letter, or testimony. I expected them to choose a form effective for their intended audience; to incorporate their research, analysis, and reflections; and to cite all outside sources.

Asking students to seek a community readership for their work is a long-standing move in place-conscious pedagogy—for example, see Robbins and Dyer (2005)—and I asked students to "publish" their arguments by sharing them in some way with community members or stakeholders outside the classroom. Many students returned to the person they interviewed, which allowed them to renew the relationship that they were forming, but some found new readers to help them get a fresh perspective on the strength of their argument, and others chose to post their work through social media networks or in public blogs and solicit comments. Students described their publication choices and receptions in a reflective writing exercise. Through reading these narratives I have come to see the moment of "going public" as one that opens possibilities for accountability, vulnerability, and connections beyond campus in the local suburban community. The act of "going public" with their work influenced how my students placed themselves in relationship to the community and how they realized their own relational power and privilege as literate agents.

Student Hayley Johnson, for example, chose to write about bullying by college students on social media networks. Her multigenre argument—which included a collage of Twitter posts, an exploratory piece that culminated in a call to action for student readers, and a personal narrative in which she frankly reflected on the ways she was complicit in negative uses of social media—actually composed a digital place in which she rhetorically located herself as someone able to both teach and learn an ethical engagement with different community members. She concluded her piece with a desire to act *with* her audience, writing, "My plan to make this movement on bullying stop is to be an active listener to my readers," and finally inviting her readers to tweet or e-mail her and engage in conversation.

Another student, Aileen Lee, modeled this type of reader-writer dialogue by composing a series of frequently asked questions about her topic: bicycling rather than driving in Lincoln. She used information gathered in an interview with the city worker who manages Lincoln's trail system to anticipate common concerns and counterarguments about bike commuting and to reach out to community members across the city, ranging from students on campus to families in suburban developments. Lee was surprised to learn from the trail-system manager that many communities "would like to have a bicycle network like Lincoln's" and took pride in emphasizing the ways in which this system of transportation could safely and sustainably connect people and places. Her project, which sought to educate readers, composed a sense of place based on movement from knowing to doing. It thus supported her growth as a writer who—in her own words—could "[bridge] the gap between knowing the concept of an argument and actually being able to apply it into my own writing" and could make purposeful choices that "will make people more likely to consider what [I] have to say."

Student Junyi Wang also reflected on an issue of public concern: wind power. Wang, who came to the United States to study business, chose to prepare a report for administrators of the public power industry. "The Truth about Wind: An Analysis of Wind Power in a Local and Global Context" drew from an interview Wang conducted with a Nebraska wind developer, as well as news articles and government studies about economics, politics, and climate change. During the interview process, she was taken aback to find that the wind developer disputed some of her research findings. Reflecting on this surprising result, Wang realized she needed to revise her analytical approach in order to understand the investments of different stakeholders: "What I have been doing has been largely about looking at what [the stakeholders] think instead of why they think so." In her reflective narrative, she explained that solving for this pattern led to a new perspective on how to effectively construct her own public argument. "Before I start to make my own claims, it is important that I know why I came to this conclusion, just like how other stakeholders came to theirs," she wrote. "This may, to some extent, help me to make claims that can be better understood or accepted by my readers."

Finally, student Sam Helberg composed an informative article about the value of higher education in an era of rising tuition costs. Writing for an audience of suburban high school students (she shared her final project with the guidance counselor of the high school she graduated from in suburban Chicago), Helberg acknowledged her own privilege but argued that the majority of students, regardless of background, stood to benefit from making the investment in a college degree. Drawing on an interview she conducted in person with UNL's dean of students, Helberg traced a connection between educational knowledge and economic power that supported the university's plans for growth in terms of research funds and undergraduate student enrollment. In my comments on her work, I noted that McKibben traced a similar causative pattern but came to a very different conclusion about the logic of continual economic growth: namely, because of the environmental context that he also took into account, he argued that a plan of perpetual growth was flawed and bound to fail. Yet I also noted that Helberg, like McKibben, self-consciously and practically chose economic language to speak to an audience she believed would best understand her in those terms. Her essay concluded, "In a world ruled by money and success, the definition of value is measured in dollars and cents. And while it may seem dramatic or overworked, the value of education is truly priceless, something to never leave solely up to a manipulation of numbers." In reading these lines, I noticed how Helberg shifted from accepting an economic value system as natural to subtly denaturalizing it, suggesting with her final phrase that suburban high school students as citizens must take responsibility so that they do not make choices based on "a manipulation of numbers." She acknowledges the very real economic context that people must consider while making decisions yet also hints at the need for people to consider a broader context beyond that.

I emphasize this point because when I first read Helberg's essay, I felt frustrated that she did not follow McKibben's lead in considering environmental context. Yet as I reflected on her writing, I realized that the fact that she made her *own* claims about a topic—not the argument that someone else had made or that I might make—was more important. Like many of the students who enrolled in English 151, Helberg was gifted in writing a formal five-paragraph essay and in seeking to precisely meet her instructor's expectations. But over the semester, I witnessed her starting to define her own goals and expectations. She saw her drafts less as problems to be corrected and more as opportunities for experimentation, conversation, and negotiation between her and her readers. By the time she finished WP3, Helberg had grown in confidence and composed her own relationship to her place as a writer, student, and citizen in both the campus and Lincoln communities:

> After publishing my final work, I came to the conclusion that what I have to say is valid. It is something that I have struggled with all semester having been taught that I cannot use myself as a credible source. After sharing my argument with someone who is a clear stakeholder in my issue, I realized that what I have to say is indeed important and valid, and it was not until publishing it in some form that I realized that. I received an e-mail back from [her high school guidance counselor] who thought that my perspective was unique and took all that I had to say in consideration. He thought that my argument was extremely mature for my age, taking into account what is best for the academic institution and the student's educational experience. He shared with me that he would, "be more than happy to share my research with students deciding whether or not to continue their education."
>
> I learned that my strength as a writer has the power to change the course of a life. It may seem dramatic, but now that my work and voice may be shared with another person whose opinion may be undecided, I have the power to impact history. I know that as a citizen of Lincoln, I am a supporter of a controversial issue and am willing to support my university in this issue because I know the facts behind the matter. I now act as an active member, [an] adult in Lincoln [who] is willing to fight for what I believe in.

A New Crop

I continue to teach a "new crop of students" each semester, as part of an annual system of education in a suburban place. But I also continue to work with my students to enact a perennial pedagogy that plants the seeds of suburban place-conscious citizenship.

My students in the fall of 2012 challenged me, themselves, and their audiences to perceive rhetorical, cultural, educational, and economic patterns, and they offered new ways to solve for patterns through their own processes of composition. They engaged in resistance, response, and revision with regard to the texts that we read and the texts that they produced. By coming to their own conclusions about their roles as readers, writers, and citizens—based on their investments in communities and ideas that were sometimes different from my own—this particular group of students joined with me in cultivating the knowledge that solving for patterns is a perennial process, not an annual accomplishment. I now see this knowledge (rather than my students) as the real "new crop," which continues to grow beyond the end of the semester.

Administrators, teachers, and students of first-year writing courses at public land-grant universities could similarly take a longer view of the past and future and a wider view of the university and its surrounding communities. By doing so, we might consider how language and writing are tools for building communities of citizenship to *re*-place current suburban places in the here and now—and how we might begin this work by rhetorically engaging with the local imagination of watershed, an underdeveloped ability in suburban America. Like Linda Flower's long-term engagement with the Pittsburgh community literacy center, my inquiry into using argument to connect the local and the global attempts to seed a perennial relationship between students and the place they find themselves, a land-grant university in a suburbanizing city. By writing for a public audience that they interact with, students have the opportunity to grow their rhetorical skills beyond the increasingly privatized, transactional, and annual classroom community into the potentially public, conversational, and perennial community of citizens.

The possibilities of meta-awareness and of seeing rhetorical patterns suggest the need for a more in-depth exploration of the ways in which a perennial pedagogy relates to transfer theory, including models of transfer that consider genre theory in order to theorize transfer as recontextualization, such as Wardle (2007, 82) and Nowacek (2011). It must also be noted that a perennial pedagogy invites a longer-term relationship with students, extending the composition and learning process beyond one semester. But deep institutional and cultural change can be a slow process, and individual teachers (especially ones in precarious positions, not on the tenure track) may not be able to imagine being able to alter their departmental curriculum in such a way.

So in the meantime, a perennial pedagogy could also be used to invite students—especially students whom we interact with on an annual basis—to recognize the annual system that they are in and to begin to construct nonannual relationships to their places, particularly the suburban settings of land-grant public universities like the one where I teach. A perennial pedagogy places the first-year writing classroom in context, helping students and teachers make connections between the classroom, the places that envelop it, and the forces that work on and through it. Therefore, even on a short-term semester model, argumentative and reflective writing projects may be able to plant perennial seeds of place consciousness and place citizenship by encouraging students to make transfers across systems and between their education, professional goals, personal lives, public responsibilities, local places, and global position.

It is neither necessarily natural nor normal for writing to be a problem, for education to be unaffordable, for suburbia to be unsustainable, for watersheds to be invisible, for damage to social and ecological communities to be inevitable, or for citizens to be disempowered. Students and teachers can claim and use their rhetorical agency to call attention to and contest these trends. With each new semester, composition students and teachers can try to solve for perennial patterns. The knowledge, inquiry, arguments, and practices of citizenship they compose—the "new crop" they produce—could be for the benefit of all.

PART TWO

Writing from the Commonwealth

Claiming Local Place as a Cultural and Economic System

Introduction

ROBERT E. BROOKE

The second part of our book explores our place-conscious approach to the commonwealth in which suburban schools are located. *Commonwealth* is Wendell Berry's term for the cultural and economic "wealth shared in common" by a community, including the cultural traditions and histories, civic practices, employment patterns, and ethnic histories that arise from the region's resources and peoples. If the goal of suburban place-conscious education is to guide young citizens into a sense of belonging to the local community, then a crucial part of education is to help them notice and understand the rich "commonwealth" that surrounds them.

The key issue, of course, is how to guide suburban students to notice and understand what surrounds them. As with the physical realities of the watershed, the cultural practices and cultural wealth of a region are all too often obscured by the new construction and migratory life histories of suburbia. For us, the best place-conscious responses to the relative invisibility of the local commonwealth are the practices of regional inquiry and rhetorical agency.

Regional inquiry. To see the commonwealth that can give vitality to a community, a suburban student must see past the insular "newness" of new construction into the region's diversity, economics, and history. If, as Teaford (2008) takes pains to point out, a metropolitan area's *array* of suburbs is likely to be ethnically and culturally diverse while *any given* suburb is equally likely to be insularly restricted to similar peoples, then schools and individuals need to explore the location of the suburb in the region as a whole. In his article "Race and Suburban Sprawl: Regionalism and

Structural Racism," Ronald Hayduk goes even further: "[Suburban] isolation may be more of an illusion than a reality. The economic fortunes of suburban dwellers are in large part dependent on the health of the region they are within, whether they are aware of it or not. Regions are the economic engines in the global world, and the fates of cities and suburbs are increasingly intertwined" (2003, 158). We would add the exurban "working rural landscape" of Savage and Lapping (2003) to Hayduk's plea for regional connectivity. Understanding your own particular suburb as contributing to an interconnected, diverse "commonwealth" of a region made up of urban centers, other suburbs, and outlying rural communities may well be the most effective way of seeing the issues, possibilities, and challenges for local citizenship.

Rhetorical agency. Alongside a robust understanding of the region's collective commonwealth (and your own suburb's contribution to that collective), young citizens also need to develop an understanding of rhetorical agency. Secondary and college students need to develop a range of rhetorical practices that actually do the work of citizenship. We are guided in understanding this aspect of place-conscious education by Linda Flower's concept of rhetorical agency in community literacy work and by Nancy Welch's concept of claiming rhetorical space in activist rhetoric.

For Linda Flower, the recent pedagogy of public rhetoric has emphasized four attitudes toward rhetorical action: *speaking up*, or making your position heard; *speaking against*, or effectively critiquing polices you see as negative; *speaking with*, or negotiating shared understandings of the public good; and *speaking for*, or advocating for values and actions you see as positive for the community (2008, 78–79). While she sees all four as important, she sees the work of "speaking with" and "speaking for" as particularly crucial for community members and community vitality. She argues that helping ordinary people develop these rhetorical practices is a core goal: "Rhetorical agency can be the work of *everyday people*. Such people may indeed stand outside the discourse of privilege and power. But they are nevertheless carrying out the work of discovery and change that is at the heart of rhetoric. The teens, tenants, mothers, low-wage workers, and college students of community literacy take *rhetorical* agency not just by speaking up but by *acts of engaged interpretation and public dialogue carried out in the service of personal and social transformations*" (206; emphasis in the original).

Nancy Welch similarly sees engaged community rhetoric as an activity open to ordinary people. She argues that the local creation of *rhetorical space* for the discussion and shaping of public policy is a key skill and necessary outcome of education aimed at civic engagement. She writes, "*Rhetorical space*—that is, public space with the potential to operate as a persuasive public sphere—is created not through well-intentioned civic planning or through the application of a few sound and reasonable rhetorical rules of conduct. Ordinary people *make* rhetorical space through concerted, often protracted struggle for visibility, voice and impact against powerful interests that seek to deny visibility, voice, and impact" (2008, 477). Both Flower and Welch advocate for educational practices that guide students to the development of rhetorical agency and the claiming of rhetorical space. These practices and abilities are, we believe, core components of place-conscious education.

The four writers in the commonwealth part of our book all present educational units that sponsor regional understanding and rhetorical agency. Secondary teacher Mary Birky Collier divides her Advanced Placement Literature and Composition course around this distinction, immersing her students first in inquiry into the representation of our Great Plains region in literature and then in rhetorical action in her suburbs of Papillion and La Vista. Ralston High School teacher Daniel Boster describes his junior class's claiming of rhetorical space in the actual curriculum of the school, following their encounter with the history and diversity of the Columbus narrative. Dual-credit college and secondary teacher Cathie English presents her unit on three-generation work ethnographies in the exurban community of Aurora, Nebraska, through which her students trace and engage the shift from agriculture to service economies in their community. Last, university instructor Bernice Olivas describes her Native American literature class's engagement with regional understanding and rhetorical action as the students consider the local representation of and policies surrounding Native peoples in our region. All of these projects illuminate options for the place-conscious engagement with the commonwealth of suburban communities within our wider region.

Suburban Identity and Change

Place-Conscious Literature in the Suburbs of Nebraska

MARY BIRKY COLLIER

Papillion is a town of compromise, of halfway-ness. It has neither smog nor brushfires. There are no big holiday parades, but there are no cattle herds. People in Papillion may look you in the eye, but they may not know who you are, even if you live here. The air does not smell of either industry or animal waste. Papillion seems to straddle itself between the big city and the small town. Neither apply to it, and it lives out its existence somewhere in the middle of big and small. (Hannah)

Growing City

As the city grows
the cornfields and grassy plains
begin to be eaten up by big corporations and
shopping malls. The heavy machinery rumbles and billows out heavy
black smoke choking out the sun's rays.

Looking left and right,
there are signs of big money.
The metal girders and cement spread like a disease
plaguing one field after another caring not what it covers.

The wind that once
cooled our faces now throws
dust into our eyes in disgust. The sun never sets

as the parking lot lights shine through the night standing straight,
mocking the trees that once stood there.

Now instead of grassy plains and creeks full of wildlife,
we are stuck with the seas of concrete and drainage tunnels with
cold metal shopping carts as its only inhabitants.
(Tyler)

> The ever changing nature of creation itself can be frustrating. It is not unusual to hear a person lament social, economic, or physical changes in their environment. It may be unusual to hear such a lament from a teenager. Tyler is a life-long resident of Papillion. He and we have seen the city change rapidly with recent additions of Shadow Lake Towne Center, Market Pointe, and a number of housing projects. The population is expected to increase from its present 25,000 to around 60,000 in the next twenty years. In a poem ("Growing City") which Tyler was recognized for by the Nebraska Writer's Project, he laments this change. (Excerpt from sermon delivered May 25, 2008, Rev. Dr. Dan Flanagan, senior pastor, Saint Paul's United Methodist Church)

Hannah, Tyler, and Rev. Dr. Dan Flanagan are all residents of Papillion, Nebraska. Papillion, in many ways, is a typical growing midwestern suburb, with uniform housing suburbs, large shopping malls, good schools, low crime, and people generally happy with their suburban life. During the spring of 2008, my Advanced Placement Literature and Composition students and I read, dialogued, and wrote about what it means to live in suburban Nebraska. Hannah and Tyler were just two of several students who identified some of the underlying complexities of suburban living. Many students' journals focused on positive traits of suburbia: nostalgic family life and safe neighborhoods, for example. At the same time, in their poetry students began identifying complex suburban experiences: search for identity, land encroachment, metropolitan change, and isolation.

This chapter describes a two-year journey in my teaching experience when I began incorporating local place into my curriculum. First, my students and I mostly explored and described our local place. However, we eventually moved to engaging in social action. Our work together grappled with several ideas prominent in suburban thinking—how suburbs promote, support, and enact the American Dream; how our suburb is involved in suburban sprawl; as well as critiquing the "bubble mentality" that allows us, to some degree, to avoid or obscure (or both) problematic issues of our suburban living. As a result, my students began moving toward advocacy through their engagement with suburban place. This work added to their preparation for critical thinking on the AP tests they would take, as well as to their work at the local universities where many students find themselves the year following my senior AP Literature and Composition class.

My chapter also directly reflects the theme articulated in the introduction to this volume about freedom and self-determination versus responsibility being one of the biggest issues in the suburban consciousness. Many of my students endlessly struggled with how to be responsible citizens in the midst of their sense of personal freedom in choosing the main features of their environment. My project provided the opportunity for students to think about and articulate some of those tensions, questions, and potential new ways of being as active suburban citizens.

Papillion–La Vista Demographics

Papillion (population 23,800) and La Vista (population 17,000) are two relatively small contiguous suburbs on the southern edge of the Omaha metropolis. The two communities serve as bedroom communities for Omaha's large corporations and businesses, as well as for the Offutt Air Force Base, on the very southern edge of the Omaha area. The suburbs of Papillion and La Vista clearly draw on, depend on, and are in many ways affected by the commerce of the city of Omaha. Yet the southern edge of Papillion borders clearly rural landscape—vast acres of cornfields, working farms with large barns and tall silos, and even a herd of buffalo.

The City of Papillion's website (n.d.) advertises itself as offering a "healthy economic climate, lowest crime rate in the state, productive work force." The City of La Vista (n.d.) claims to be "one of the fastest growing cities in the State of Nebraska." Both suburbs are indeed experiencing a rapid growth of their commercial, industrial, and residential areas.

When I started exploring place in AP Literature, I focused only on poetry, especially the Nebraska poets I knew. I did so to help my suburban Nebraska students see how Nebraska was "named" by others and give them space to name their Nebraska experience through writing their own poetry. But over several years, I have moved toward not only a wider range of literary genre as textual location for this place-conscious engagement but also a wider critical engagement with suburban place itself. The second part of this journey in particular helped make visible for students that the suburbs they subconsciously wanted to protect as good and as perfect as the manicured lawns of their neighborhood were, in fact, temporarily isolating them from issues of poverty, race, socioeconomic class, and more. These issues were just underlying the surface of their own neighborhoods or just across the suburb lines into less affluent living spaces.

This lesson is just one of the many tensions of suburban living that became a crucial step in my suburban students beginning to take steps toward active citizenry in our suburbs in Papillion and La Vista, Nebraska.

Nebraska Poetry

In 2004 Ted Kooser, longtime Nebraska resident and poet, was appointed US poet laureate. At that point, many teachers across the state began reading Kooser's work with students in their classrooms. I also began assigning Kooser's poems in my AP class—initially as an example of a Nebraskan who became US poet laureate. I wanted my students to include Nebraska writers among great American writers and poets. Nebraska has indeed produced many talented poets, many of whom are still living and writing—among them Kooser, Twyla Hansen, and Don Welch.

At the same time, the Nebraska Writing Project's work with place-conscious education and writing had intrigued me for several years. From my colleagues on the Nebraska Writing Project Advisory Board, I knew about the place-conscious Rural Voices, Country Schools program across the state and had read about the place-conscious projects of several teachers in *Rural Voices* (Brooke 2003). Rural Institutes helped teachers connect their curriculum to their local communities. The Poetry of Place Celebration, launched in 2006 with Ted Kooser's sponsorship, is a program that focuses explicitly on poetry about rural Nebraska places.

This knowledge raised several questions for me. What does the majority of existing and most celebrated Nebraska poetry of place communicate about those individuals living in the state? Are rural writers more tied to and affected by their place in Nebraska than are suburban Nebraska writers? Are more densely populated areas of Nebraska dissociated from their place? Do suburban Nebraskans see their place, their people, their culture, and their experiences represented in Nebraska poetry?

Thinking about such questions, in 2008 my students and I began reading and dialoguing about Nebraska poetry. In the process, we defined key terms (*rural*, *urban*, *suburban*), freewrote about experiences living in Nebraska and comparing it to other places we knew, and dialogued about regional stereotypes. We read, annotated, and had long discussions about poetry written by well-known Nebraska writers, including Ted Kooser, Twyla Hansen, and William Kloefkorn, as well as Nebraska student writers whose poetry of place had been chosen for publication on the Poetry of Place website (n.d.).

Student discussion in class was nonstop. The discussion prompts I thought would last ten minutes filled the entire hour, with students responding and dialoguing aloud. Students who did not usually have much to say during previous literature discussions readily contributed their place observations to the dialogue. Several students had personal experience visiting (and some previously living in) rural, urban, or suburban areas. Some observations derived from stereotypical characters portrayed on television or in movies (*Desperate Housewives*, *Larry the Cable Guy*, *The Stepford Wives*). In both discussion of Nebraska poetry and Nebraska rural, urban, and suburban places, students exhibited real difficulty getting past images of rural Nebraska, especially images often used by those *outside* Nebraska to typify our state. They immediately resisted the rural images as stereotyping *them* as uneducated, backward, and without cultural sense. Part of students' resistance to the perceived stereotype of Nebraska as rural stemmed from their experiences with the media portrayal of Nebraska. Several students brought up the recent *American Idol* tryouts held in downtown Omaha just a month before. Andrew P. and Leslie sort of tag-teamed in their vehement response, "*American Idol*—that made me so mad! Yeah, there's a huge city right there, and all they show is the corn. They were in downtown Omaha! I was hoping they'd turn away from the stereotypes." This national portrayal of Nebraska was not *my students'* Nebraska.

Yet once students moved past their resistance to Nebraska stereotypes, students recognized in the speakers of the poetry a love for their Nebraska, even their rural Nebraska place. As we discussed and analyzed US poet laureate Ted Kooser's poem "So This Is Nebraska," Chelsea F. commented, "[The speaker] seems content, fond of, appreciates the relaxed rural atmosphere." Christine added, "Seems like people in these poems enjoy the simple, laid-back life. We're so used to rushing around, driving fast, [hearing] sirens." Matt M. observed, "This guy [Kooser] really likes [Nebraska]. He's enjoying the simple pleasures—his hand out the window. Haven't you ever done it? You put your hand out the window, and it goes up and down like this [Matt and Ryan demonstrated with their hands]. Yeah, he's just enjoying the simple pleasures." Megan C. wrote, "'So This is Nebraska' brings me back to my childhood. Whenever my family and I go to Colorado, we always drive through rural Nebraska. I can honestly say it is one of the most comforting feelings seeing those fields and just watching them fly by out the window. I love thinking about the warm air and sticking my hand out the window in the sun." Clearly, students were recognizing, and at some level identifying with, the pleasurable experiences of rural Nebraska life.

Furthermore, in her critical reading journal, Amy wrote, "'Scars' [Hansen 1992] was one of my favorites. I loved the way it cleverly hinted at signs of tension and then waited until the last stanza to reveal the source of it all; 'We were losing the farm that summer.'"

Jessica also observed in her journaling about "Scars," "The tone began the poem in a sad manner, 'It was the summer our well / was going dry and my brothers / both had jobs in town.' You notice right away that to them this must be abnormal and strange. It is finally revealed at the end that they are losing their farm. The tone is blunt when they say it, but she mentions that 'everything is going deeper/into the ditch, even/the last of the water.' This shows all of the sadness they are experiencing especially since a connotation of water or rain is sadness." Here students not only were closely analyzing the trajectory of the poems but were also recognizing the impact of rural Nebraska places on these poets—in this case, the impact of Nebraska drought on one farm family's economic plight.

Our Suburban Place Experience

Yet, again, this rural Nebraska represented in the poetry we read is not the Nebraska my students knew. So after our extensive dialogue about Nebraska place experience and Nebraska poetry, my students and I then moved to thinking, writing, and dialoguing about living in Papillion and La Vista—our suburban environment. To begin working toward understanding our place and how it affects us, we started with basic questions: What is "typical Papillion" or "typical La Vista"? What do we like about living in our town or suburb? What is good about where we live? What is not good about living here?

We also drew on students' experiences living in places other than suburban Nebraska. But ultimately, we were moving toward thinking about how living in suburbia, particularly Nebraska suburbia, shapes us.

The students' descriptions of their place emphasized both sides of the freedom and self-determination versus responsibility tension identified in the introduction to this book: the positive features of the suburban landscape focused on the personal freedoms students experienced; these elements were balanced by an emerging sense of the impact of those freedoms on people and places surrounding their suburban homes.

Students talked and journaled about suburban living in largely positive ways. Brian P. wrote, "The place of Papillion-La Vista is defined by friendly people, tradition of excellence in high school sports, golden cornfields, simple economy, freezing temps in winter and unbearable heat in summer, little traffic, slow life, and a history that dates back to over 150 years." Tyler observed, "Papillion is a great place. It is close to major stores and areas of interest. There are still cornfields nearby making it feel like

Nebraska. It has all four seasons of weather so that you can't ever get bored [with] one season. Big yards with three car garages, clean well-trimmed. Safe neighborhoods and good schools. I like how most people know each other but yet we're not a small town." Students also like the calm, the quiet, and the safety of our suburbs. Shannon wrote, "I like the security in being able to walk among strangers unafraid. I never have to hold my purse tight like I did in Paris."

However, the poetry students wrote, which was the culminating writing piece after all the other thinking, dialoguing, and journaling of the unit, was much more complicated. Like Hannah and Tyler, the student poets quoted at the beginning of this chapter, several students represented experiences of discomfort with suburban change and the land encroachment going on around them, of shallow neighbor relationships, and even of isolation.

Matt W., like Tyler, watches the edge of suburban Papillion taking over what little rural landscape exists around him in these stanzas from his poem "Papillion."

> The quiet rows of corn no longer exist,
> Now houses grow in the same formal rows,
> Trading gravel for asphalt and fields for neighborhoods,
> The ever expanding city grows like crops in spring
>
> Orange warning signs and scaffolding are everywhere,
> Especially in the south, drifting further outward
> Where did this mall come from, and this strange school?
> New neighborhoods explode from empty space.

Rebecca sees the lack of diversity in suburban landscape as producing shallow inhabitants in her poem "So This Is La Vista?"

> A town made up of generic knickknacks
> Carbon-copy colonies pop up like dreary daisies
> Another rectangular prism spring up, oh wait
> Just one more grocery store
> Make sure to tear down all proof of what used to be

And replace with cute trees and clever street names
Sunrise to sunset, year after year the horizon is a straight line
Who walks along the empty sidewalks?
Shovel them you must!
S.U.V. paradise
Offspring are safe to swim in a town this shallow
Plan on never becoming much more than average.

Katherine moves past the "acres of lawns and hundreds of two-story houses" to wonder, in her own loneliness and isolation, about the people "behind closed doors." Her poem "It's All So Peaceful" begins,

It's all so peaceful
in this little suburban sanctuary.
My homeland is sunny and familiar,
but why is it so lonely?

A few lines down, Katherine continues:

I watch for signs of life.
There is nothing but the sounds of automobiles
whistling down the street with stoic expressions through
weather-stained glass.
The emptiness of my neighborhood

In her last stanza, Katherine sees her coinhabitants of suburbia as emotionally dead as they disappear behind closed doors day after day.

acres of lawns and hundreds of two-story houses,
there are children and adults alike walking like
the undead to and from their cars to remain behind
closed doors until the sun
rises the next morning.

Through ongoing talk, questions, and writing, my students deepened their thinking and understanding of this suburban place. No longer were they simply describing the cleanliness, the calm, the apparent safety of their suburbia. Students were uncovering feelings of discomfort that addressed the hidden responsibilities of suburbanites: replacing our fields with suburban expansion neighborhoods, acknowledging isolation and loneliness behind the doors of these quiet suburban houses, and resisting the generic molds offered them by suburban idealism.

As my students and I were thinking about living in our suburban Nebraska place, I was also dialoguing with several colleagues who were also doing place-conscious work in their classrooms and reading theory about suburban living. Several things became clear. My students—in demographics, in behavior, in attitudes—matched many of the classic suburban images. They were mostly homogeneous in class and race. What little diversity the area has derives largely from the families connected to the nearby Air Force base. Families, primarily households consisting of married adults with children, live in cookie-cutter houses with meticulously manicured lawns. Students live in the midst of the strong consumerist pull—working part-time (some even full-time) at local fast food restaurants or discount stores to support their purchase of name-brand clothing and the cars they drive to school. Papillion and La Vista are very isolated from the societal ills of our nearby urban area. Therefore, these suburban students are preconditioned to not only avoid the problems of their urban neighbors but disregard them altogether. At the same time, Papillion and La Vista are also isolated from the rural landscape. Farms and cornfields are just outside our suburban border to the south. However, shopping malls, business parks, and numerous sprouting housing developments mostly block them from view.

Unlike teens from small towns and rural areas, many of my students are without the deep-rooted ties to the place where they live—for a variety of reasons. Fewer than half of these students have lived in suburban Omaha for more than ten years. Many of these students and their families have migrated to these suburbs seeking better jobs. As a community closely tied to a nearby US Air Force base, a notable share of students have lived the highly mobile life of military dependents. These suburban students lack the history of time, the connections to people, and the stories tied to this place where they currently live.

Furthermore, much of the typical literature AP students read in many ways fits the dominant American education model where instruction is designed to be portable and contextless to serve the "migratory intellectual" thinking framework (Brooke 2003, 7). This model asks students to imagine themselves migrating from place to place (as many of my students already know from childhood experience) for the best experiences in postsecondary education, jobs, and job advancement. The AP Literature Test, which many of my students take and for which many receive three hours of college English credit, asks students to write three literary analysis essays on contextless pieces of literature in a two-hour period. Therefore, students read much of the course literature in a "portable, contextless" way, preparing to write literary analysis essays for the AP exam in similar portable, contextless ways. Furthermore, most of these students do "migrate" to universities around the nation the next year. So again, AP Literature teachers and students find little immediate reason for reading literature in ways that root them in the specific community in which they live. They read literature in much the same way they live suburban life—using it to serve the purpose of their next job or move to another similar suburb.

At the same time, I was also struck by the lack of community and political awareness, care, or involvement of my students. The year 2008 was the time of a particularly highly charged presidential election, but students were very apathetic, rarely talking about or giving other evidence of political awareness about presidential candidates, issues, or other local and state political races. Furthermore, this apathy was despite the fact that for several of these high school seniors, it was the first year they were legally able to vote. In addition, whatever community service or action students were involved in happened to meet requirements for National Honor Society membership or for résumé building.

These complexities about suburban living experience and suburban education manifested themselves more clearly for me as I discussed my students' thinking and writing with my place-conscious teaching colleagues. I wanted to draw out more explicitly the suburban consciousness of students, to help them name more clearly the tensions of suburban living and, therefore, to better understand the complexities of our suburban experience. I ultimately wanted my students to engage more actively with this suburban place as a vehicle for personal understanding and, even further, for possible civic participation.

In the process, I began to see some of the major responsibilities of advanced writing classes in high school as doing the work of cultivating what I call *preadvocacy* thinking. Whereas many college composition classes focus on public writing and positioning students toward the work of inquiry and finding ways to enact personal and public agency, high school (and often early college) students have little experience with this type of thinking and writing. Writing classes in high school can be a crucial place for this kind of work to begin.

Place Location and Place Critique for Action

In order to help my students more actively engage with our suburban place, the next year I developed a larger inquiry project. As part of the AP Literature program, students primarily practice writing as argument—in the form of formal literary analysis. However, writing as inquiry, a major mode of thinking and writing in which students also need preparation for college, had not been part of my current high school curriculum. Yet critical thinking was often an overarching curricular goal at my school. Therefore, I decided to experiment: could inquiring deeply into the shaping effects of our suburban place, critiquing those effects, and finding ways to address resulting civic issues emerge as a clear and rich way to help students hone their critical thinking abilities? For the purpose of the place-inquiry project, I divided our place-conscious thinking into parts: place location and place critique for action.

For any of us as writers to locate ourselves in a place, we often begin by identifying the ways we live in our place, as well as how the place defines and shapes us. Furthermore, in preparation for the types of public writing classrooms many of my students will find themselves in as they enter college, I wanted to begin gently pushing them toward dipping their toes in the waters of inquiry and *preadvocacy* thinking through our place-conscious work. So my students and I first talked through a series of questions, including the following: What do you like about living in Papillion/

La Vista? Dislike? Compare Papillion/La Vista to other places you know—places you have lived, where family and friends live, other "Nebraska places" you know (Nebraska small towns, Nebraska rural areas). How is it different? How is it the same? Think about what defines a place. What about Papillion/La Vista defines it? How do you think living in Papillion/La Vista shapes us? Shapes people around us?

As in previous years, many students, especially the half or so who have spent a good portion of their lives in Papillion and La Vista, framed their location in terms of nostalgic childhood memories. They saw our suburbs as good and safe places to grow up, to bond with other neighborhood children, go to good schools, and live among good people. Several students commented on the kindness and politeness of our citizens. Amber commented, "I work at a Hallmark store . . . and I see kindness of the heart from all sorts. There are people holding the door for older ladies and gentlemen or helping her or him out to their car by carrying her or his bags. Every so often some people will have extra coupons and will give one to another person at the checkout counter to just be merry. One does NOT see this in Omaha!"

After expressing their great liking and almost affection for their communities, however, some students took an additional step toward inquiry and critique. Erin describes what she sees as our suburb's landscape, as well as the kinds of citizens one finds:

> The crisp, cut grass, the clean and tidy roads, and the well-kept housing and buildings are all possible signs that you live in Papillion, Nebraska. If the cornfields weren't enough indication, maybe you can tell by the politeness of its inhabitants. We are a kind people. We say our "pleases" and "thank yous" and like things to be kept in order. Our streets are free from crime and mischief. It is said that Papillion is the perfect place to raise a family. There are many young tikes who have lived here their whole lives and have grown up to be well-bred citizens.

The ways Erin, in the beginning stages of place inquiry, renders our landscape and kinds of citizens clearly match the stereotypical ways most suburbs are depicted—on the surface.

In small ways, students began to critique some of the problematic sides of living in this place. Many students lamented the lack of "anything to do," and some went so far as to suggest this factor as a reason for a growing number of area teens getting in trouble with the law in our suburb.

Nebraska Literature

In addition to poetry, I wanted my students to read some prose literature to expand their sense of ways our region is represented. However, finding literature of place for suburban students in relatively new suburbs can be problematic. Our state is nationally thought of as rural, so much of what is known as classic Nebraska literature is rural as well. My Nebraska Writing Project colleague Sharon Bishop, who has been teaching place-conscious Nebraska literature courses for more than two decades, writes, "[Classic] Nebraska authors . . . Willa Cather, John G. Neihardt, Mari Sandoz . . . reflect the early settlement history of Nebraska, and the authors often describe the prairie that the first settlers found—huge open spaces open to an endless sky" (2004, 66). The place suburban students now inhabit looks nothing like what the first residents of Omaha or Papillion or La Vista found. Yet within the last decade or two, more pieces reflecting my students' experience of Nebraska have emerged. Robert Vivian's (2007) essay "Hereafter in Fields" describes his hour-long commute on Interstate 80 between Nebraska's two largest cities, Omaha and Lincoln. It is a familiar route for many of my students—one they travel frequently to state sporting tournaments and Husker football games every fall or to visit friends and siblings at the University of Nebraska–Lincoln, the state's largest university.

As my students and I discussed Vivian's essay, students recognized not only the description but also the ways the landscape in Nebraska shapes people. Amber commented, "It's like an escape for him—free of all worries. I get that [feeling] too—you're concentrating on the road, but you start thinking about stuff." Irwin connected his driving experiences to Vivian's. "I love driving places. You get to see different things. [But] sometimes I turn off the music and just listen to the road." Furthermore, Matt M. observed, "When I'm driving through something, I'm a part of it."

Alex commented on the power of Nebraska's landscape—both in Vivian's essay as well as in his own observations. "He [Vivian] sees Nebraska as majestic—it has its own majesty. In its own way, Nebraska is beautiful, too. There is power in its plainness." Matt M. added, "It's like a love letter to Nebraska. He sees deeper meaning [in Nebraska]. He sees Nebraska as mysterious." Clearly, these students were beginning to see the beauty and power of living in this place.

Deep Mapping

At this point, my students were ready to try representing their own relationships to place. Deep mapping was something I had seen work powerfully among teachers participating in the Nebraska Writing Project Institute: to explore—and write about—ways place shapes us.

Deep mapping is a kinesthetic thinking strategy that helps individuals dig deeper into the many ways—geographically, emotionally, psychologically, spiritually—we are affected by a place. This exercise is especially crucial for suburban students, who often do not see themselves as tied to the place in which they live. Jason McIntosh describes deep maps as "drawings of psychological locations (both literal and abstract) created by writers to represent their relationship to place" (Brooke and McIntosh 2007, 131). In his University of Nebraska–Lincoln sophomore writing course, Robert Brooke describes deep maps in the following:

> A Deep Map is a drawing of psychological locations (both literal and abstract) created by writers to represent their relationship to place. A deep map is a map of the place where you are now, showing what makes up that place, indicating the forces that have led you to be the kind of person you are in that place, representing the tensions which create the energy of that place (positive and negative). A deep map represents understanding of location, not just description. A deep map represents celebration and critique of where you locate yourself. (Brooke and McIntosh 2007, 141–42)

After discussing deep-map definitions and instructions, I handed out large sheets of white paper and pointed out the boxes of markers and crayons, and students thought, sketched, colored—descriptively and symbolically. At the end of the hour, we conducted a walking tour of our maps, noting that many maps included houses of friends and family, school and job places, as well as some places important to people in the larger Omaha area—the historic Old Market, the Qwest Center, and even Lincoln's Memorial Stadium, home of the Nebraska Cornhuskers and an hour's drive to the south.

The next day we used our deep maps to further our thinking about our location in this suburban place. Adapted from McIntosh's idea of map-legend narratives, I asked my students to use some of the following questions to analyze their deep maps:

- What images and/or locations are most prominent on your map? What is the centermost "thing" on your map?
- What is at the edges of your map? Why?
- Is the place you currently inhabit concentrated in one part of your city? Does it extend beyond the city limits?
- What people or groups of people do you associate with different locations on your map?
- What places do you walk, ride, or drive by regularly but never enter (outdoor and indoor places)?
- Who does not inhabit your map? What is not on your map?
- List three places you would like to know more about so that you include them on your map.
- What would you title your map?
- What do you most like about your map? Dislike?
- What new things have you noticed about your map after finishing it?
- What questions arise about your map?

Students observed a variety of noteworthy features as they analyzed their deep maps more closely. Perhaps most significant was Brad's observation about the isolation his suburb was producing. Brad, like many of his classmates, astutely observed that the literal borders of our suburb bound his life and interactions. "I could go within this small square all my life and never have to leave. It's . . . Giles to Centennial [Streets] and 72nd to 84th [Streets]. All three of my schools [have been] in that area—Hickory Hill Elementary School, La Vista Junior High School, Papillion-La Vista High School. That's where I do everything in my life." As is common in many suburbs, students like Brad were beginning to observe that our suburban space promotes isolation from our neighboring urban areas.

Even more significant were the maps of students who have *not* lived long in this place. These students constituted a good half of our suburban population. For instance, Raveena, whose father's job transferred her family from their lifetime in India to La Vista two years before, drew her map in the shape of two thought bubbles. She noted that her thought bubble containing India was much larger and more concentrated with people, places, and events than her La Vista thought bubble, clearly representing the level and kind of difference in impact of these places.

These students, very representative of the large population of the mobile suburban student, were recognizing their strong lack of connection to this suburb, one of many places making up their mobile life experience.

Robert Vivian's (2007) fascination with the landscape of Nebraska in his essay "Hereafter in Fields" clearly inspired several students to look at Nebraska differently, as they describe in their essays. Matt P. reflected Vivian's wonder about Nebraska as he writes about a newfound appreciate for cornfields, "When one looks past the plainness to see something else, they begin to see the beauty they missed in the dull and the common. I've come to appreciate the cornfields. They have a mesmerizing, trance-like beauty in their simplicity. It just takes time to come to love."

Students also explored the ways *other* places shaped the way they viewed living in *this* place. Eric wrote about what he learned about Papillion after spending summers in Iowa. "There is an old expression that goes, 'You don't know what you have until it's gone.' By leaving your hometown you can learn a lot about yourself. I started to see Papillion as that place which showed me how to be a responsible and good member of society."

Furthermore, several students also used the location writing to begin exploring tensions and real problems of living in our midwestern suburban place. Jessie, who identifies herself as ABC (American-born Chinese), described one of her first experiences in Papillion that highlighted how the lack of diversity had impacted her as minority:

> About ten years ago, a second grade classmate approached me with a question that would forever render me self-conscious: "What are you? Chink? Jap?" he demanded while slanting his eyes and incessantly spitting obscenities at me. I had just moved to Papillion, a city drowning with white and had never been confronted by such a humiliating question while being physically mocked. I had never felt so embarrassed and so repulsive.
>
> Nebraska has shaped me in, ultimately, a negative way. Nebraska has caused an identity crisis for me. Raised in Nebraska, I've been confined to the suburban lifestyle; yet I've also grown up in a Chinese-culture household. When I seriously reflect upon that question, "What are you?" I find myself unanswered. Who am I?

For students like Jessie, the isolationist and segregated life of suburbia emerged in their writing as discomforting and disturbing, and our place-conscious work was crucial in providing space to uncover and explore those problematic experiences.

Place Critique for Action

Although several students were beginning to uncover personal and community tensions in our suburban place, I wanted to make visible for them what critiquing our suburban place and working to change it could look like in a collective way. Robert Brooke writes, "Place conscious students need experience identifying local issues they want to affect and the knowledge they need in order to contribute" (2003, 13). This idea of affecting our local place is also an excellent place to begin giving high school students opportunities to exercise what Linda Flower calls *rhetoric of engagement*, which she defines as "the art of making a difference through inquiry, deliberation, and literate action" (2008, 75). This idea, again, is crucial in the work of preadvocacy thinking that begins in my classroom. The beginning steps of this kind of rhetoric often involve *speaking up*, or discovering and expressing oneself through personal and cultural identity, and then moving to *speaking against* something—against dominant ideologies, institutions, and oppression (78).

However, again, the problematic nature of place-conscious work in suburbia arises. Suburbs are generally where people *choose* to move—to avoid issues of crime and safety or for better economic opportunities. For Papillion, Nebraska, the larger of the two suburbs Papillion–La Vista High School serves, this point is exceptionally highlighted by its status as number three in the magazine *Money*'s (Bluestein 2009) "100 best places to live in America." Papillion is especially cited as a *good* place to live for its strong economy, affordable homes, open space, almost no traffic problems, and safety for children. Suburbs generally are *not* places with problems, at least readily apparent problems. The issues with suburbia often are responsibility issues for groups of people impacted by the freedoms that suburban dwellers take for granted.

Critical Lens

For this reason, it is even more difficult for high school students, whose civic awareness and sense of responsibility are often just developing, to identify problems. So a critical lens to help highlight some of suburbia's issues seemed necessary. Therefore, my students read an early draft of the article that became Robert Brooke's introduction to this collection of place-conscious essays to help them in their critical thinking.

Students' reactions to Brooke's article were very strong: they were strongly resistant to several portions and fiercely protective of their suburbs. Several students defended why their families live in the suburbs—defending, in short, their own "freedom and self-determination" as people who choose suburban living. David wrote, "Sure, we aren't like New York or Chicago but the suburbs aren't supposed to be. The suburbs are nice friendly communities. The suburbs are places where parents come to raise their children."

Kasey expanded from personal experience: "I do agree that suburbia is . . . sheltered from the 'real world' issues, but that doesn't mean we don't know about them. My parents know what's out there and just choose to be away from it."

Beth wrote about the suburbs as part of the American Dream. She said, "We are taught to pursue the 'American Dream,' which actually takes place in the suburbs. So really, we would have to reverse decades of idealism to overcome this. Note this hasn't stopped children from aspiring to greatness and questioning their world."

Beth also analyzed what she saw as the negative impact of stereotypes, both affirming and resisting the stereotype of suburban inhabitants.

> Just because suburbia looks like a cookie-cutter society, it does not breed such individuals. I find this [article] greatly objectifies suburbanites. I simply do not think we are all the same: look in the hallways of the school and you'll see that. Sure, the majority of kids are white, from middle-class families. But looking past that, we have the gothic kids, the atypical jocks, the nerds of academia, the crazy speech kids that talk to walls [a satiric reference to Beth's speech team], the future political activists, the druggies/alcoholics, the list continues on and on. All of this from suburbia. Additionally, I think stereotypes are counter-productive because one of two instances will happen: people will either rise above it or they will accept that they "obviously" cannot be any better and thus will not try just because someone told them they couldn't.

Craig, though, made some of the most significant observations between perceived lack of problems in suburbia and civic participation. "People tend to be more politically active when they have problems. Only when they have something to complain about are they active. Perhaps the less active suburban folks are content with their policies. The crime is low, the education systems here are decent. We don't have an abundance of problems (and that's a good thing), and thus, we don't need to be running around with signs yelling that things are horrible."

Alex made the transition in his thinking even clearer. He wrote, "[Brooke] made it sound like we are overly sheltered and even rather ignorant. This got me thinking about how much I loved my community. I was angered by what he wrote and argued for it, but people in the discussion brought up other flaws. The one that stood out most to me was how big business was taking over the community. I found myself not finding much to say to argue this point because the sad truth is that we are being taken over as a community."

In reflecting on student responses to Brooke's writing that began naming the issues, problems, and complexities of suburban life, my students exhibited some of the classic first stages in the journey toward advocacy. Students were strongly resistant to ideas of problems in their "bubble of suburbia" and intensely protective of their view of "normal." In "writing through" these feelings, their writing showed their lack of exposure to diversity of race and culture, much less recognition of the dominance of whiteness in their suburb. However, as students came to class and discussed Robert's intro along with their written responses, they began the transition from defensiveness to recognition and agreement. As their fellow students and suburban residents, whom they trusted over "outsiders," began admitting and naming the issues and problems of suburban living, they, too, began to speculate about problems and, ultimately, solutions. Through our place inquiry, students like Alex clearly were moving from the previous fierce protectiveness of their suburban place to critiquing the neat-and-tidy facade of suburbia and the true problems lying just beneath the surface. Most of those problems involved naming the responsibilities they held, as advantaged suburban dwellers, to those individuals indirectly impacted.

Nebraska Literature as a Critical Lens

In addition, students also read some of the poetry written by students from previous years highlighting some of our suburban problematic issues. Interestingly, the few students who had not always lived in our suburb, who knew what it was to be *other* in suburbia, responded most thoughtfully to these poems. Matt P., who moved to Papillion from Iowa the summer before his senior year, responded to Katherine's poem "It's All So Peaceful," excerpted earlier in this chapter. "Everyone in my neighborhood keeps to themselves. Many times I've seen neighbors 'walk like [the] undead' from their cars to the house. Not once has any of them greeted me in the seven months I've lived here."

Erin, who moved five years ago to Papillion from Albuquerque and whose writing describing our suburb's landscape and citizens is excerpted earlier, began to understand Tyler's critique of suburban expansion in his poem "Growing City." She wrote, "The tone in this poem is full of shame and disgust towards the human race for letting companies tear down and cover up the natural beauty of the town. This poem does a great job of showing how our environment is affected because many of the inhabitants don't really notice all the new changes because we have been in cities and/or suburbia our whole lives."

We also read part of Mary Pipher's *Writing to Change the World* (2007). Pipher is a best-selling author who resides in Lincoln, an hour's drive from our suburbs. Her book suggests that writers can be change agents and offers several examples from writers she knows. Jessie, whose story about being taunted in elementary school I quoted earlier, wrote about the strong connection she felt to how Mary Pipher dealt with negative experiences in her childhood. Jessie wrote, "I also feel that I have been strongly influenced by the negative experiences I have faced. The race issue has always been a sensitive topic for me because of the negative experiences I've dealt with. When [Pipher] described her personal experience during elementary [school], I really empathized with her inward personality and lack of social prowess. I feel that way as well. The fact that [Pipher] later accomplished her goals and the fact that everything turned out 'okay' for her gives me hope for my future because I feel so unhappy now."

During class discussion more students identified issues as problematic in our place. Many students talked about the inequity of the new outdoor mall and other strip malls going up on the edge of town, while a large strip of malls on Eighty-Fourth Street, formerly known as the "Golden Mile" and former home of Walmart (presuperstore), a large chain grocery store, and numerous small businesses, now stands vacant.

Place-Action Writing

As the culmination of our inquiry into place, students dabbled in the roles of change agents by writing place-action pieces. I asked students to use writing to in some way *affect, define, shape, or influence* (or some combination thereof) some segment of our Papillion–La Vista population. I wanted my students to move beyond simply recognizing and responding to their place and work toward affecting our place in some way through their writing.

Before we wrote, however, I asked students to use several questions to think about in preparing to write:

- What ways can we use writing to *affect, define, shape, and/or influence* Papillion and La Vista?
- What issues or tensions could we offer solutions for?
- What would make our community better?
- What aspects are in danger of disappearing that should be sustained?
- What of our best features need to be maintained or improved?
- For the percentage of our suburban population who move here every year, what can we do to help them care about Papillion and La Vista and understand what is so valuable about living here?
- What audiences might we write to who could support our solutions and/or help enact change?

Students targeted primarily four audiences in their writing: their fellow students, school or school district administration, community leaders, or potential residents of our suburbs. Many students wrote about the recently escalating community tension since the addition of a second high school in our school district. Students saw the two high schools as polarizing our suburb into two communities—the "haves" (the new high school) and the "have-nots" (our high school). Brad wrote a well-articulated letter to a specific elementary school, whose students' parents that year were publicly "outraged" by the boundary switch that would require their students to attend our "old" high school rather than the newer high school. Brad advocated for the value of education at our high school: "I have . . . spent my last four years with some of the best teachers in the state in arguably the best district in the state. Not once have I thought I was getting an inferior education or something less than students at [the other school]. As I speak, a multi-million dollar renovation is taking place at [our school] to better equip it and give it better facilities." Clearly, Brad felt this tension and advocated it vehemently in his writing against the perceived discrimination he felt against our suburban high school.

Many students recognized growing problems among their fellow teens—growing vandalism and teen pregnancy rates, as well as one of the highest rates of sexually transmitted diseases in the country. For this reason, many students advocated for a community center for teens for supervised productive activity. Interestingly, many advocated that the vacated "Golden Mile" strip mall be used for such a purpose, thereby relieving some of the suburban blight while keeping their peers from destructive behavior.

Students seemed conflicted about the housing and commercial expansion in our growing suburb. Some students wrote letters to the editor of the local paper, defending the expansion and the jobs and shopping opportunities it was bringing, while other students wrote to decry the destruction of their parks and the green space formerly adjoining their backyards. Although most students could identify issues of tension and struggle in our suburb and articulated them fairly well, few offered clearly articulated solutions. However, a few were beginning to understand the importance of real action for citizens of a community. Jenny wrote about our "throwaway society" and the impact of trash at her favorite park: "I propose that the two high schools should take the lead in keeping the park clean. It can start with the clubs in the schools and they can organize a day of clean up. Citizens can be invited to help. This would bring generations together and add to our sense of place and community. If this happened on a seasonal basis, we could keep Walnut Creek Park clean and continue our investment in the future."

One of the most creative and powerful pieces was Kay's poetic children's book, complete with illustrations. In her author's note, Kay wrote, "I chose to write a poetic children's book because the children are the future. I have childhood memories of volunteering with my school, family, and church. Today, I am still an active volunteer in our community. My hope is that all children will be able to say that they did their part to better their community." Below are some lines from her poetic children's book:

Excuse me dear
But would you volunteer
There is so much to be done
Some of it is even fun

There are people here in need
Will you do a good deed?

The park needs some cleaning
Will you get it gleaming?
You can start by picking up trash
It can be fun if you do it as a dash

Collect new or used toys
They can be for girls or boys
There are animals at the shelter
Will you lend a hand?
Even in this helter-skelter
Play pals are in demand

There are people at the nursing home
Will you make it so they're not alone?
Perhaps you can read them a book
Or give their old pictures a look
Or maybe you can just bring a smile
As you sit and visit for awhile

One of the most satisfying results of this type of writing was the public feedback several students received. Both Michael's and Jeremy's letters to the editor were chosen for publication in the *Papillion Times*, our suburb's local newspaper. Michael wrote advocating community involvement, while Jeremy defended expansion in Papillion. Taylor received a note from the mayor's executive assistant, inviting Taylor to speak with the mayor about her proposal to fill the vacated strip mall on Eighty-Fourth Street with a teen center for after-school programs. Kamrie received a letter from Rick Black, Papillion–La Vista superintendent of schools, with a long personal and detailed response to Kamrie's request that students receive physical education credit for participating in varsity sports. Dr. Black ended his letter to Kamrie with the following words: "I . . . wanted to let you know how much I appreciate you identifying a concern and also offering a suggested remedy. Most folks simply stop at identifying the concern. . . . What Papillion-La Vista [School District] will attempt to do is continue working to find ways to be sure we are offering interesting and useful experiences to promote a healthy lifestyle."

Black, both a school and a community leader, affirmed Kamrie's thinking and writing, as well as Kamrie's use of her writing to influence her school and community leaders. Clearly, Kamrie saw in this letter that her writing was shaping thinking in her school community about a problem she saw within the school system.

By this point, students were seeing their relationship to this place as much more complex than they had started out believing. They were seeing more deeply into issues needing wrestling with and were practicing, perhaps for the first time, ways of being *active citizens*, helping to find solutions for these problems in their place. And in a variety of ways, they were acting to shape their suburban place.

Place-Conscious Impact on My Teaching

Place-conscious inquiry in my classroom enhanced the work of my classroom in multiple ways and on many levels. Students were engaged at new and deeper levels because they were directly connected to the place represented in the literature we read. Strong resistance slowly turned to identification of problems. For those individuals worried about the time issues and the mandates of the Advanced Placement curriculum, my students' place-conscious thinking clearly continued the work of careful reading and critical analysis of literature. The only difference was some of this literature was rooted in our Nebraska place. Students read even more carefully and deliberately the literature of our place because they *knew* the place and were invested in how their place and they were being represented. In addition, my students' AP test scores rose again that spring. Several of these AP Literature seniors, in the throes of applying to colleges and honors programs, used their place-inquiry writing for the application essays as thoughtful representations of who they are and what they contribute to the places they inhabit.

Furthermore, the next fall Myriah saw me in Walmart and stopped me to say that she and another of my students, Kyle, were in the same composition course at a local university. Their class was at that moment doing inquiry writing, very similar to the thinking and writing they experienced in our AP Literature classroom the previous year. She expressed gratefulness that she and Kyle "knew what they were doing" as they continued their inquiry work at the college level.

My own journey as a teacher has been greatly affected by this place-inquiry work. I understand my students in new ways—as fiercely protective of this suburban place and as valuing the values of their fellow citizens and the good education our schools provide. Yet I have worried over their isolation, even civic and political apathy, with some students going so far as to identify their place as a "protective bubble," a few saying they "like it that way." When several students strongly resisted the idea of the existence of significant problematic issues in our place, I worried again—until our thinking, reading, discussing, and writing slowly turned to identification of problems and what we as participatory citizens could do to create awareness of those problems and propose solutions to make our suburban place a better place to live and act. As a result of inquiring deeply into our suburban place, my students took many significant steps toward becoming participatory citizens, even advocates for their community. They thought deeply about how they were affected by suburbia, identified many of the problematic issues in our suburb, and used writing to take action to stand against and remediate some of these issues. Most important, students *actively* connected the work of our classroom to local concerns and issues mattering to them, engaging in learning at new levels.

"Why Didn't We Know?"

High School Students Learn, Act, Teach, and Write

DANIEL BOSTER

It was an activist teacher's dream come true, really. In the fall of 2011, in the first week of an eleventh grade American literature course, my students and I were discussing explorer narratives, including primary sources written by the explorers themselves, entitled "First Encounters: Accounts of Exploration and Exploitation" in our textbook. Although this "unit" of this course's curriculum is typically an overview to provide context for literature of the Puritan era, these students, troubled by their lack of knowledge about these stories and after reading some alternate versions of this history, decided they wanted to teach. In a project that spanned a month or so, my students and I developed curricular activities for a sixth grade class in our district that explored the complex realities of the myths of these "first encounters." In doing so, my students claimed a rhetorical space for entering local public discourse (see N. Welch 2008) and perhaps learned about community literacy as Flower (2008) defines it. In a suburban school district, these students felt the responsibility of helping educate younger students in their community. These students saw their suburban community as a place, as a town, as their home. Whereas most people in the Omaha area see Ralston as a typical insulated suburb populated by people who have the luxury of being unconcerned about diversity and justice issues, the students know a different reality. They know that attitudes about race are complex and dynamic in their town. They wanted to have a voice in shaping those attitudes among their younger peers.

Throughout my teaching career, I have taught an American literature course, which is usually a chronological survey built around a standardized curriculum focused on an anthology that includes short selections and excerpts. The American literature course I now teach is no different. However, at my current school, teachers have the freedom to swerve from the textbook to some degree. We have about one week of flexible planning time built into each quarter of the school year in our standardized literature courses for ninth, tenth, and eleventh graders.

The selections at the center of our work concerning these "first encounters" are excerpts from "La Relacion" by Cabeza de Vaca and "The Log of Christopher Columbus," both first-person primary sources. De Vaca recounts the explorers' misadventures as they get lost, almost die trying to come ashore, and are finally saved by the Karankawas. De Vaca's story is one of bad navigation, incompetent sailing, and mistaken identity. The Karankawas eventually rescue de Vaca and his men and nurse them back to health. At the end of the excerpt, de Vaca tells the story of how the Karankawas become very ill and demand that the Spaniards become "medicine men." And, as my students almost always note, despite the fairly obvious fact that de Vaca and his men would have died without the Karankawas, de Vaca's tone throughout is superior and condescending.

After de Vaca, we move on to Columbus. Of course, they already know all about the mythology of Christopher Columbus. I begin by asking them about their earliest experiences studying Columbus. They can all sing the *Niña*, *Pinta*, and *Santa Maria* song; a few mention the old episode of *Schoolhouse Rock*. They wonder why they used to get Columbus Day off of school but do not anymore. Every once in a while, there is a student who says something along the lines of, "Yeah, but didn't he, like, kill a bunch of Indians and stuff?" I bring in several children's picture books that fictionalize the Columbus story. In almost all of the books for really young readers, "Chris" is just a boy like all kids, hungry for adventure and fun times. The books for more mature readers explain, to some degree at least, the political and financial motivations of the Spanish monarchy and the purposes of Columbus's eventual trip. These books include information that matches most of what my students know about Columbus.

We then read a short excerpt from Columbus's log. In this excerpt, he describes the physical traits of the Arawaks. He writes, "I want the Natives to develop a friendly attitude toward us because I know that they are a people who can be made free and converted to our Holy Faith more by love than by force." Columbus goes on to describe idyllic scenes of the "Natives" swimming and trading trinkets with the Europeans. At one point, Columbus mentions that the Arawaks seem unwilling or unable to engage in physical resistance and are often taken slaves by neighboring peoples. He continues writing about his desire to convert the Natives to Christianity. At this point, my students do begin wondering about and discussing Columbus's motivation. They are bothered by his attitude toward the Arawaks when they are seemingly without guile in their interactions with Columbus and the Europeans who continue to land on their shores.

About ten years ago, at the recommendation of a friend, I read Howard Zinn's *A People's History of the United States, 1492–Present*. This recommendation arose from a conversation in which I was bemoaning my lack of a quality history education, something that bothers me. I have always been a conscientious student, but I have never liked a history class, including the six courses I took as an undergraduate. These thoughts were often on my mind actually, since my wife, during a large part of her teaching career, was a high school social studies teacher. I heard about all the cool things she did with her students, and I was jealous. For her students, she seemed to be shedding light on some "hidden" history that I knew nothing about. What she discussed with her students was actually interesting. So, after my friend explained a bit about Zinn's book, I picked up a copy. I read the first few pages; I was hooked by words like the following, in the opening chapter about Columbus and other early explorers, when Zinn is explaining the frame for his book:

> The history of any country, presented as the history of a family, conceals fierce conflicts of interest (sometimes exploding, most often repressed) between conquerors and conquered, masters and slaves, capitalists

> and workers, dominators and dominated in race and sex. And in such a world, a world of victims and executioners, it is the job of thinking people, as Albert Camus suggested, not to be on the side of the executioner. . . . My point is not to grieve for the victims and denounce the executioners. Those tears, that anger, cast into the past deplete our moral energy for the present. . . . I don't want to invent victories for people's movements. But to think that history writing must aim to simply recapitulate the failures that dominate the past is to make historians collaborators in an endless cycle of defeat. If history is to be creative, to anticipate a possible future without denying the past, it should, I believe, emphasize new possibilities by disclosing those hidden episodes of the past when, even if in brief flashes, people showed their ability to resist, to join together, occasionally to win. (1980, 11–12)

I decided then that the next time I taught Cabeza de Vaca and Columbus in an American literature course that I would also be teaching the first chapter of Zinn's book.

So, after hearing from de Vaca and Columbus and exploring the students' previous learning about Columbus and the "discovery" of the "New World," I hand out photocopies of a few excerpts of the first chapter of *People's History.* I spend some time helping my students through the somewhat difficult (for them) syntax of Zinn's prose, but afterward, I simply give them time to read Zinn's version of the Columbus story. This version, based on primary documents, including that same log by Columbus excerpted in our textbook, explores Columbus's motivations once the initial moments of contact with the Arawaks were over. My students read of the European lust for gold and their mistaken and violent plans to turn the Arawaks into gold gatherers. Zinn goes on to tell, again using Columbus's own words, of the European desire to convert all Natives to Christianity and the barbarous treatment of the Arawaks. This violence included the chopping off of Arawaks' hands for failing to gather the right amount of gold and random killing of children to sharpen swords. My students eventually read of the spread of disease and the dramatic decrease in the Arawak population. I watch them as I read along with them. It is always one of those beautiful moments in a classroom when everyone is into it, when there is no need for a teacher to "manage" the classroom.

Finding ways to provide students with these types of moments seems to me like something that all teachers can do. As a teacher I was allowing my interest in reading Zinn's book to shape the materials that I would ask students to work with. While we were still exploring the materials stipulated by the curriculum (that is, primary sources, early explorer literature), I, as the individual teacher, was tapping into my understanding of what it feels like to learn something new about something I thought I already knew about. This embrace of ideas outside the textbook seemed to propel the project forward.

After they read, we discuss. Their reactions are what one would expect: "Wow, that sure changes my ideas about Columbus" and "That's sick" and "Man, those dudes were bad." We discuss the Zinn excerpt for a while and also talk about how primary and secondary sources function. We have a great conversation about who gets to tell history and how they tell it. But then there come words that I often wanted to hear but did not: "We should have known this sooner." Later, "What can we do about this?"

In previous years, I enjoyed teaching this material and found it rewarding that students engaged in this conversation. That point is usually where the lesson ended. It is public school after all. We have to move on to the next thing in the curriculum guide. As most teachers would tell you, all of us, perhaps especially English teachers, in traditional public school settings often have difficult decisions to make about how much time to spend on each part of the curriculum. In some schools teachers have no control over this aspect, as curricular maps are developed at, and mandated from, the district level. But even when teachers do have some freedom to choose, there is always a nagging thought: "If I spend time on this subject, I'll have to skip something else later." There is a certain art to knowing when to allow student interests to dictate the day's lesson as opposed to just moving on.

But this time it was different. In this moment these students were not content to have this knowledge and then just move on. They were not happy.

In fact, they were angry, in the abstract, at their teachers, at the system. They could not imagine how they had made it to eleventh grade without any sense of what Columbus was really up to. They were upset about Columbus Day. A few were even sad that what began in 1492 continues today in various forms of oppression, ethnic strife, and general social injustice.

In my seventeen years of teaching, I have found, despite the pervasive public (mis)perception otherwise, a lot of adolescents do care about their schools and their communities. Even in a suburb like Ralston, a place that many may view as temporary or transient, many students see it as their home. Although they may have a vague sense that suburbs are ahistorical (not a word they would likely use), they do seem willing to make efforts to see their town as a unique space. Most will say they are "from Ralston" rather than "from Omaha," as many adults do.

They do think about why they have to learn certain things and do not learn about others. During these particular class sessions, my students began asking questions about curricular decisions. They wanted to know how these decisions were made and by whom. They wondered why some teachers will tell them the "truth," while others will not. They started to question the versions of history that the curriculum offered them. They realized that this history might have local implications and were willing to engage in trying to change things for students younger than them.

Inevitably, the conversation took a turn toward the idea that "the stuff [they] learn in school" is often only partly true, that they are lied to. As Linda Flower (2008) suggests, my students "offer[ed] an inside perspective," in this case on the nature of their own education, but did not quite know how to respond to their own developing understanding of their education.

So, back in the classroom, I started to ask them what we could do. I talked a bit about Zinn's words about the "hidden episodes of the past when, even if in brief flashes, people showed their ability to resist, to join together." Some talked of making T-shirts and posters. Cool-enough ideas but likely to be lost in the "noise" of high school life. Perhaps inspired by images they were seeing in the news of the Occupy Wall Street movement, a few students proposed a protest to take place on Columbus Day. I liked the spirit of the idea, but anticipated that we needed something a bit more organized.

I have to admit that I also saw this project as something that probably would not pass the "What is the curricular purpose?" test of my administration and could even endanger my job. This latter concern is another aspect of teaching in this way that teachers must consider. Teachers are often conflicted about and torn by the competing pressures of encouraging our students to take action, to pursue "civil disobedience," to speak up for themselves, and to be activists and, on the other hand, the necessity of keeping their jobs. Additionally, a teacher should be conscious of the community's expectations and find ways to connect students' impulse toward activism to mandated and approved curricular ideas. To do otherwise is clearly problematic and, in my opinion, violates the agreement a teacher makes with the community when he or she signs the contract.

I started asking them about what seemed to be their main concern: the fact that they did not learn this earlier. Again, they started to slip into discussion about poor teachers, boring classes and textbooks, and so on. I wanted them to move beyond this point and to work toward "develop[ing] strategies for entering a public discussion as partners, not just to vent or state personal opinions" (Flower 2008, 49). While tapping into adolescent energy to attempt to change things can be powerful indeed, students often need direction and channels for this energy. Although I was interested in working with them to "do something about it," I was not willing to spend precious class time simply engaging in complaint. I explained this fact to my students and started to ask more questions. By this point, we were doing the important work of dialoguing and "work[ing] collaboratively to build a better, more inclusive, more complex understanding" (49). My students were realizing that the content of their classes and the decisions about the curriculum teachers worked within were not simply matters of an individual teacher's whim. Instead, they seemed to be moving toward understanding that there were always things left out, always things that they did not learn. After a brief discussion about how textbooks are developed and adopted, my students seemed almost stunned by how little choice students and their teachers are given. Ultimately, we returned to Columbus, and, finally, they started contemplating action that matched their desire to make sure others in their community knew about this history sooner. They realized that the stories they had been taught were the stories of the dominant culture. They were aware that their textbooks excluded voices. They wanted to do their part to encourage listening to other voices and other stories.

Again, in the classroom, I asked, "What can you do with this realization you've had?" I also talked to them about the idea of "thinking globally, acting locally" and what type of things they were capable of doing. There were a few students in this class whose parents are teachers, so it did not take too long for them to come to the idea of teaching. They could teach!

"But who?" they asked.

"Well, who do you think could handle this information? Who is old enough to get it?"

Someone offered something along the lines of, "Probably fifth or sixth graders. We do a lot of stuff with this history in those grades."

"Okay," I went on, "I'll help you get it set up. But this is the deal. If I do, you will do this work. Teaching is hard work. It takes a lot of planning. I can tell that you are excited about this, and that is great. However, I can tell you from experience that the excitement you feel now can give way to frustration when you are doing the work that this will require. So, you have to think it's really important. You'll have to stick with it if we get teachers and students from another school involved. The stakes are more important than simply not completing an assignment or failing a test. It's not just about you and your grade. You are doing this for others. You have to follow through."

There were a couple of murmurs of discontent, and some students voiced sentiments along the lines of "Never mind." But eventually, one student, Breann, spoke up. "This seems important. I think it would be fun to teach. We will do the work, Mr. B. Can you help us get it set up?" Bre is one of those students whom other students will follow. This time that was a good thing.

To get started I asked students whom they would like to work with and what their role in the group would be. With their input about who they could and could not work with, I set up the groups and designated some different roles: leader, artist, writer, and organizer. Everyone had a clear set of responsibilities, and, during designated times over the next few class periods, they got together in groups and began working.

My first priority after they were working was to find some elementary students for us to work with and get approval from all the appropriate administrators. I did not have too much concern about my ability to get approval because I do have good relationships with my administrators as well as several elementary school principals and the assistant superintendent of curriculum. Soon enough, I arranged for us to work with two sixth grade classes at one of our district's elementary schools. I also asked Kristi Gibbs, Ralston assistant superintendent of curriculum, to come talk to my students about how curricular decisions are made and answer some of their questions.

On the day of Gibbs's visit, she was clear and open with the students. She answered their questions about how teachers decide what to teach, especially when the topic is potentially controversial or troubling for students. She mentioned that high school teachers in our district do have a great deal of freedom to decide, but that the curriculum is often more standardized at the elementary level. Gibbs asked students about their motivation for doing this project and what their plans were. My students were able to answer these questions intelligently and thoroughly, and Gibbs seemed impressed by their preparation and work and gave a final seal of approval to the project.

After she left I asked students to write about their impressions of the meeting by asking them, "What did you think about Dr. Gibbs's visit? What did you learn?" Audrey wrote, "I think she was really smart." Amber continued along these lines and added, "I think it was cool how she was supportive of what we wanted to do," and Taylor added, "I feel like my opinions were heard." Other students, like Saul, appreciated that she "taught [them] about how teaching is evaluated in schools and about the pros and cons of [their] project as well." Shawn wrote that her visit confirmed that they should do this project "because it is the right thing to do and we wouldn't have to be living a lie that this is our land." So, now, the students, with perhaps a more finely tuned sense of purpose, got to work planning activities for the sixth graders. They had become more historically aware and conscious of the multiple influences on how and what they were taught. These new realizations seemed to energize and focus their work.

Throughout the days leading up to our visit to the sixth grade classrooms, my students expressed genuine concern with the idea that they do something for the sixth graders they would "teach." They wanted the younger students to remember what they learned. They were very much concerned with what I will call an "authentic learning experience" for the sixth graders. They felt empowered to reflect on their experiences as younger students (which they found lacking when it concerned social studies) and responsible for "telling the truth" about this history. As they talked casually while working, I wondered about their desire to work to "fix" this "mistake," as one student expressed it, to take this stand.

Our society provides many opportunities, even some public ones, for us to express our opinions. Most current high school students, raised on a steady diet of social media, are quick to "speak up—to discover and express themselves, their personal and cultural identities" (Flower 2008, 78). As one who spends a lot of time with adolescents, I can say confidently that most of them are comfortable expressing themselves; some do so loudly and publicly, while others do so quietly. However, rarely do I work with a teenager who does not have anything to say. But in this case, my students also seemed to be moving toward Flower's more complicated versions of "speaking."

In our conversations they were also "speaking against something"—a history curriculum that hides harsh realities, textbooks that do not include the "truth," and the fact that their teachers do not push students toward a "real" understanding. Although this conversation involves issues that are more complicated than my students seemed to desire pursuing, they were starting to ask some crucial questions about how school works. At the time I remember thinking, *I hope they remember this when they are parents, when they are voting.*

However, for me, the most important transformation in their thinking was their moving toward what Flower calls "speaking for something"

(83). As public school students, they were subjected to the versions of history presented by editors at textbook companies far away from their town, from their school. The interpretations of history in the few books they were "forced" to read did not match their interpretations after reading from multiple sources, from multiple voices. With just a few days of study, they began to wonder about the complicated narratives of history, about whose voices are left out. Whereas a few students were simply doing their work because it was an assignment, I had several quiet conversations about the implications of decisions about textbooks and curriculum being made by "people in offices far away," as one student put it. Ultimately, what became most important for them was developing ways that they could help a few students in their town understand more than they understood when they were children.

Again, they saw the importance of helping the other individuals in their local community. They wanted to help the younger students of Ralston. For them, the fact that they had not "learned the truth" early enough was deeply troubling. They wanted to fix what they saw as an injustice, a failure—perhaps a relatively minor one—in their community's education system. Their schoolwork during this time became local activism and, even without their knowing, spoke against the idea that young people in a suburb were not concerned about social issues.

On October 7, 2011, the Friday before Columbus Day that year, these students entered a classroom as teachers. My students ended up in four different groups and designed four distinct activities for the sixth graders to experience. The two classes of sixth graders were divided into four groups, and each group rotated through the four activities designed by my students. I will summarize the activities briefly to provide a sense of their work.

One group used colored pencils and maps to show students all the different routes that Columbus and other European explorers were using to get to the "New World." They also had students make little boats out of apple slices, toothpicks, and candy corn, which ended up providing some fun for the younger students. Then the high school students asked the younger students to reflect and write on the effects that this sudden influx of people must have had on the Native groups. This resulting conversation was a fascinating display of empathy and seeing history from the point of view of the oppressed.

The next group led a conversation based on some actual excerpts from the Zinn piece. They wanted to understand the sixth graders' emotional response to this material. This activity lacked a clear structure that I hoped for, but the discussion went relatively well. The last two activities I will describe in a bit more detail because they seemed to get at the heart of what my students gained from reading and discussing Zinn's work.

The third group created a version of the game Life. Sixth graders could choose for a game piece either a compass for European explorers or a feather for Natives. (Perhaps, not surprisingly, my students were not able to be free of all of their own stereotypical thinking about Native Americans.) People with compasses chose from a purple set of cards that always had positive messages such as "Found gold. Move ahead 4 spaces." They moved around the board quickly. Those students with feathers chose from an orange set of cards that always had negative messages along the lines of "Didn't meet gold quota. Hand chopped off. Move back to start" or "Got smallpox. Move back two spaces." Students with feather game pieces moved nowhere. After a while, the sixth graders got the point. A great discussion about fairness and cruelty followed.

The last group did an activity that built upon the themes of the board-game group. Sixth graders were divided into two groups. Both groups were given instructions to build a pyramid out of playing cards. One group was given about forty cards, tape, and Popsicle sticks. They could also have candy while they worked. The other group was given only seven cards and nothing else. They were told they could not talk. Of course, the choruses of "That's not fair" started right away, but the disadvantaged groups always tried to get started on the building. After a while, a student in the advantaged group would be instructed to go to the disadvantaged group and steal something. This theft could be the cards or even a person from the group. Naturally, after a while, one group had constructed an elaborate structure with the help of their "slaves" from the other group. They, with the exception of the students taken as "slaves," were laughing, talking, and eating candy. On the other hand, the two or three people left in the other group sat there with a few scattered playing cards. After the groups finished or quit working on the structures, the high school students facilitated a productive discussion about how it felt to be treated so unfairly.

After each sixth grade group went through all four stations, we wrapped up the morning with a brief group discussion. The sixth graders were able to list several new things they had learned. The high school students seemed proud of what they had accomplished. We said our goodbyes, briefly outlined our plan to return in mid-November to talk about the myth of the first Thanksgiving, and the sixth graders returned to their classrooms. After they did so, I asked my students to sit down and reflect on a few questions and do some writing. I asked, among other things, "What frustration and successes did you have today while being a teacher?" After the expected musings about some sixth graders being "smart alecks" and "refusing to listen," many students wrote in ways that spoke to the rewards of the work they had done. Some simply enjoyed the experience of being a teacher. Brittany "love[d] being a teacher," and Audrey added, "I felt like I actually taught them something." Michael, a student who said very little in class, wrote, "I felt shy at first but knowing I was expected to teach, I got involved and just did it." Others seemed most interested in the content and were happy that the information they shared seemed to actually shape the sixth graders' thinking. Makayla wrote, "Students now understand the *real* story" (emphasis in the original). Amanda agreed, writing, "They learned the truth." Kennedy pointed out that the sixth graders "wanted to share what they were learning [and] seemed enthusiastic." Nate added, "I loved seeing the kids learn something new." Some other students mentioned that being in the role of teacher allowed them to learn some things, too. Nicole wrote, "It was cool to actually talk to them and hear what they have to say and know," and Amy shared, "I was able to think of questions of my own on the spot. I was into it, Mr. Boster!"

As we walked back to the high school, we were abuzz with energy from the experience.

After a weekend I wanted the students to reflect more deeply on their work once they had a little distance from it. I knew that the writing from the day of the event was likely tinged with the excitement from the completion of a task long in the works. I asked them to take their time and put some careful thought into this writing. I asked them to write about a few questions, so they could have an opportunity to articulate their thoughts and emotions now that the initial glow of the event had dimmed.

How did you feel when you were working with and teaching the sixth graders? What did you learn during this experience? As I have already mentioned, many students were enthusiastic about the experience. As I expected, many students mentioned feeling "nervous" about being the teacher and that they did not realize how hard it would be to be the "authority" figure and to get younger students to listen. These responses were common themes in the answers to this question. However, there were many more positive responses. Almost every student reported feeling "good" or "great" when they were teaching. Ashlee wrote, "When I was teaching I felt happy because I felt proud that I was actually teaching something to someone." Shawn concurred but spoke to the importance of community when he wrote, "I felt good because I was telling the future of Ralston about the real Columbus." And Tonio seemed to be summing up the frustration of teachers and activists everywhere when he wrote, "I learned that some people actually care and will listen to what you have to say and some won't."

There were also some more nuanced responses. Andrea wrote, "I have realized that some people react differently than others when it comes to hearing about Christopher Columbus' actions." Pat seemed to be exploring a similar idea when he wrote, "It's hard because sometimes they don't believe you because they want to believe the fairy tale story that everyone else knows."

What do you think the long-term effects of this will be for the sixth graders? This question seems to be the one that both challenged and interested my students the most and led to many intriguing responses. Quite a few believed that their work with the sixth graders would make them "where they won't believe as many lies" (Shawn) and that "they will remember this for longer than if it was taught in their regular classroom" (Shane). Shay hoped that they would be the type of high school students who would "want to do something like we did with younger students, or tell friends and family about what they learned from what we all did." Pat wrote, "I think we set an impression on the kids, but I also think it needs to be reiterated so that they won't forget." I also asked the sixth grade teachers to have their students write about this experience. I will not provide a detailed account of their responses here, but, as I shared with my students, many of the sixth graders were able to explain several new things they learned during the activities. As their teachers reported after, the sixth graders clearly had a more complex understanding of Columbus and the "discovery of the New World." They remembered the details, and many of these students repeated the themes of unfairness, violence, and mistreatment that characterized those "first encounters." And like my students, many wondered why we have Columbus Day.

Many of my students' responses speak to the beginning of a sense of activism. Although some might (and did) question spending this much time on a project that would impact only about seventy students during a lesson that is supposed to last only a couple of days, I like to think that my students and I shared an experience of moving from new knowledge to action. Their desire to teach was invigorating to me after having taught this material for many years without having students deciding they wanted to do something like this project. I know that this desire is not something that I could have created and would have been short-lived had I been the one to come up with the idea. Naturally, I encouraged it and helped shape their enthusiasm, but, ultimately, the entire project was their idea. In addition, they had to contemplate their pedagogy (even though they would not have used that term) and develop the activities they would do at the elementary school. Furthermore, at this point, my role shifted. Instead of being the interpreter and deliverer of curriculum, I became a facilitator. I was able to use my connections to other district teachers and relationships with administrators to create a forum for their teaching. They could develop active learning sessions with my guidance but based on their own understandings of this material.

I now see this project as an example of a high school English class participating in a public act of composing and developing rhetorical strategies that create a space for students to have a voice in a school system that increasingly demands that they silently develop skills for learning facts that they will later be asked to repeat on standardized tests. A project like this one can provide students an authentic opportunity to learn while teaching, to feel empowered in and in control of their education. Furthermore, I believe that some high school English and composition teachers are uniquely positioned to do this type of project in their classrooms. My students clearly felt this moment and deserved to be encouraged in their pursuit of finding a way to share what they had learned. They knew something should be done and found a "fun" and interesting way to do it. And, of course, they seemed to feel like they learned and taught a great deal while doing this.

As is likely clear from my narrative, I did not begin teaching these lessons with the goal of turning students into activists. However, as a teacher, I am always open to students getting excited and proposing ideas for how I can best help them learn, especially when that learning involves critical thinking about a social justice issue. In the case of this project, I was even more enthusiastic because they wanted to use what they learned to engage with their community. I think my students' work here was a pragmatic example of what Flower calls "community literacy [as] a rhetorical practice for inquiry and social change," and I believe my students were learning by "hands-on experimental and strenuously intellectual engagement with the world" (2008, 16).

Nancy Welch's phrase "ordinary people" (2008, 471) seems readily applicable to students at a typical public school like Ralston High. The students in my class are indeed a microcosm of the changing face of Omaha, Nebraska, and, perhaps, even the shifting demographic nature of the country as a whole. In this class, there were several Hispanic students, a student who grew up in Togo, a few African American students, and several "working-class" kids.

Ralston, the community most of them live in and that all of them go to school in, was once a "small town" on the edge of southwestern Omaha, Nebraska. The city of Ralston, landlocked by Omaha and another suburb (La Vista), had a population of 5,943 people in the 2010 US Census. Ralston has avoided the fate of most area suburbs and has not been annexed by the city of Omaha, despite the fact that Omaha could legally do so. The town has its own mayor, city council, and police and fire departments in addition to its own independent school district.

Ralston is a town that prides itself on having a small-town feel. It has a relatively vibrant downtown area, a well-funded public library, and an array of community events. It is what people who live there consider a "middle- or working-class" community. Home prices are stable, and people who buy homes there tend to stay. Although new home building has stopped owing to our being landlocked within the city limits, there are also several large apartment complexes. Naturally, residents of these complexes tend to be more transient than those individuals who own homes.

While 5,330 (89.6 percent) of the respondents indicated "white" as their race, Ralston is an increasingly diverse community, and this fact is reflected most clearly in the schools. Ralston Public Schools is part of the two-county state-mandated Learning Community that was established in 2008 to address the increasing achievement gap in Omaha-area schools (Learning Community n.d.). Ralston High School is substantially more diverse than the city of Ralston. During the 2010–11 academic year, the school population was 989. In total, 29 percent of RHS students are "nonwhite," and 4.4 percent of students are English-language learners. In addition, although many in Ralston and in the larger metropolitan area consider Ralston to be a middle- to upper-middle-class community, the number of students on free or reduced lunch (a commonly accepted measure of student poverty rates) was 37.31 percent in 2010–11. This figure was up from 26.64 percent in 2006–7 ("Annual Estimates").

In the Omaha metropolitan area, Ralston is often misperceived as still being in the "upper-middle-class white" community that it was forty to fifty years ago. When I mention to people that I teach at the high school, people who have lived here often say misguided things such as, "Oh, it must be nice to not have to deal with any of the problems of urban schools" or "So your students probably don't have too many issues, do they?" But, of course, the reality is much more complicated. My students come from a variety of ethnic and socioeconomic backgrounds. It is a dynamic and shifting space. My students are aware of this fact on a daily basis as they see people different from them and hear multiple languages in the hallway.

As we worked on this project, I often wondered why the "facts" and "lies" of the Columbus story seemed so important to my students. After all, they lived in a metropolitan area that is troubled by all kinds of social issues from gun violence to segregation to child poverty. In fact, many of these same issues often creep into life in Ralston, where there have been a few murders and drug busts in the past couple of years. Over the years, I have mentioned some of this to students when we study texts that allow a discussion and exploration of racism or poverty and the other issues of contemporary life. Students sometimes engage with these ideas, but, more often than not, they seem to see the purpose of reading and discussing as the way to make a good grade on a test or a paper. I often wonder if these contemporary issues seem too overwhelming for them. Even when they do come to the realization that something should be done, they (understandably so, I think) do not believe there is anything a kid can do about these problems.

Perhaps thinking about Columbus allowed them to think about injustice in a more tangible way. They saw the fact that students spend most of their school years without knowing the "real" story of Columbus as an injustice. They saw it—the fact that young students in their town were not taught this information—as something they could do something about. They were able to envision ways to make change.

The way most students are educated in our era of assessment works against students and teachers pursuing projects like this one. I think this fact is especially true in suburban schools where there is a great deal of pressure to compete with neighboring districts. Increasingly, students in the United States are in school systems that, while encouraging critical thinking, reading, and writing in official mission statements, are actually reducing the school experience to a place to prepare for standardized tests. Authentic learning experiences that actually allow for critical engagement are becoming rare in many school systems and actively discouraged in some others. This emphasis on standardized testing and curriculum is at the core of a "neoliberal education reform" (Hursh 2007) that seems oriented toward reducing opportunities for authentic engagement. While giving lip service to encouraging teachers to challenge students to become better critical thinkers and innovative creators, these "reformers" insist that the only way to evaluate whether teachers are successful and students have learned is to judge the entire educational process by scores on tests. Of course, many teachers have been concerned about this notion since 2000 and the implementation of federal No Child Left Behind educational policies during the second Bush administration. Researchers such as David Hursh are expressing concern about how this neoliberal influence on education may eventually affect the country's schools and students. In a "democratic" and "civil" society, "teachers would not merely employ the curriculum, pedagogy, and assessments as determined by others but would become educative leaders engaged in deliberation with the community. . . . Instead of subjugating education to the goal of producing workers who will increase our productivity within a globalized economy, we would engage students in continually working to answer the questions how we best develop a world that supports human welfare and planetary health" (2007, 515).

David Hursh's words speak to many of the issues that can come to the forefront for teachers when they encourage students to do work in the "real world" rather than only in their classrooms. First, he speaks to the importance of engagement with the community. My students, even if in a small way, did something to improve the education of their fellow citizens in their town. Those sixth graders will be the people they live with, the people they vote with, the people they raise their own children with. For my students, it became important for them to understand the potential for coming together as a community to engage critically with the texts and ideas that they confront in and out of classrooms.

The thinking about the teaching of writing is important here as well. Although Ralston has a composition class, I was working with this group of students in a literature class. But, as became clear, they became interested in this literature when we began exploring how it was composed. Their explorations of how history is composed, how it is created, and who gets to do the composing and creating are what eventually led to their passion for reaching out to younger students in their community.

In addition, they then turned their attention to composing themselves. Their development of lesson plans connected to state standards for both sixth and eleventh graders, activities, and discussion prompts were also acts of composition. They were writing the lesson that they felt cheated out of. To use Nancy Welch's terms, they were "refusing to play their assigned role" (2008, 481). They were seizing the power to develop and implement a learning activity normally reserved for their teachers.

Welch argues that there is a great "reward [from] student projects leading to substantive action beyond the classroom" (2005, 476). I think what Welch is referring to here is key for students living in a twenty-first-century world that seems to be confronting constant reminders of desperation from many different places. Our politics are dysfunctional on national and local levels, many students face uncertain futures, and schools often fall short in finding ways to help students connect what they do with the reality that meets them when the dismissal bell rings. They feel disconnected from their places, their institutions, their classmates (despite the simulacrum of connectedness created by reliance on text messages, Facebook, and Twitter), and many of the adults in their lives. Although a class project like what I have described here is unlikely to create change that is immediately evident, it is clear from my students' writing that it did make a difference to them. They believed that their work had an effect, and students believing that what they do during their time in school makes a difference seems crucial in their engagement as students.

The conversation about and the reflection on this event were crucial, too. Welch points out, "Class discussion needs also to focus . . . on the policed boundary between permitted and prohibited acts of speech and protest" (2005, 481). Although few of my students would consider what they did an act of "protest," I believe it is. Although they might be drawn, especially as adolescents, to flashier and perhaps louder forms of protest, they do come to understand that the seeking and discussion of the "truth" of Columbus are, in some ways, a speaking back to the curriculum they have experienced. These students were also invested in the idea that they should do something to make sure younger people in their community have an opportunity that they did not have. This motivation is very much in the spirit of serving a community of people who do not have the advantages that they have. It was inspiring to read their reflections and hear what they had to say after they had spent time with the sixth graders.

Education in the neoliberal model becomes about preparing students for an agenda that is delivered from afar. Anything that allows students to engage on a local level has a much greater potential to lead to other acts of engagement. As students have opportunities to take action—something like teaching younger students—in their local communities, I believe they will begin to see the potential value of their contributions. Even though many may see the suburbs as "isolated" or places without social issues, students in suburbs, perhaps because of these towns' size, actually have opportunities to engage in a way they would not in a larger arena. As they develop a sense of responsibility for their local "small" community, they might come to see that their activism has a place in a wider context.

If, as educators, we say that we want more engagement, more critical thinkers, even when those thinkers may be critical of the institutions around them—including their schools—we must allow these students opportunities to show that they can act, write, and think in their society.

Of course, educators can also be energized and inspired by projects like this one. Such projects allow teachers to feel a sense of social engagement and to encourage their students to see themselves as activists or at least as active participants in their communities. They can find fulfillment in their teaching lives that simply cannot be found when spending day after day delivering a mandated and standardized curriculum that serves the interests of those individuals who want students to perform well only on standardized assessments. There is the possibility of seeing teaching as genuine learning with students. In such projects, many voices are heard. Instead of a teacher serving the interests of external institutions by being simply a dispenser of information to be memorized by students, education can become a conversation where all are expected to talk but also to listen, to teach, and to learn.

In high school language arts and literature teachers seem particularly well positioned to do this work. We will always have the responsibility of "preparing" students for the writing and reading they will do in college or the workplace. These teachers seldom have reservations about doing this work. In addition, most of us accept the reality that standardized assessment preparation is part of what we are expected to do by the public. Although there are some parents who are beginning to voice concerns about the continual emphasis on standardized assessment in our schools, many in the public do want their students to do well on these assessments.

Teachers understand this fact, and we do what we can to support students in these efforts.

Nonetheless, teachers can find space for seeking out projects that help students develop authentic critical skills. The project described here is one example, and teachers are doing great work all over the country to provide students with experiences that transcend this neoliberal model. When these types of projects take place, communities are likely to be supportive. Our project was highlighted in the local paper, and, despite its being a potentially politically sensitive topic, I heard only compliments from people in our community.

With projects like this one, learning and teaching become acts of suggesting possibilities. Students see that there are real reasons for engaging with the texts they are assigned in their literature classes. Students have an outlet for the feeling that something should be done to change the world around them. My students were angry that they did not know about this history. They thought it was unfair that this information was "kept from" them. The act of wanting to know something is where authentic learning can begin. They then worked toward creating a more just and fair education, albeit about one text, for their younger fellow citizens.

For teachers, projects like this one might serve to reinvigorate us as we may see our students' work as evidence of one of the reasons we became teachers in the first place: to help students get excited about the possibilities of a literary text, to see that text as relevant to them. There are many possibilities in literature and the teaching of literature. We can begin to see the literary texts we teach as something more than ways to "check for comprehension" or as a tool to train "productive citizens."

Ultimately, teaching literature and composition can become about suggesting possibilities instead of searching for a "correct" answer. English teachers and students can be engaged in dialogue with one another, with the texts, and with their communities. In this model, teaching and learning become acts of activism rather than competitive tasks to be completed and then forgotten. And, hopefully, teachers will find themselves, in the words of Camus and Zinn, on the side of justice and truth.

Work Ethnographies

Teaching Economic Sustainability

CATHIE ENGLISH

> To live, we must go to work. To work, we must work in a place. Work affects everything in the place where it is done: the nature of the place itself and what is naturally there, the local ecosystem, and watershed, the local landscape and its productivity, the local human neighborhood, the local memory.
>
> —Wendell Berry (2003b, 3)[1]

David Sobel, in his definitional volume *Place-Based Education*, writes, "While we all started out thinking that our focus was on school improvement and academic achievement, we have come to realize that our focus is equally on creating vital communities and preserving the quality of the environment" (2004, 36). Sobel claims that economic vitality—the social capital and economic well-being of a community—is one leg of the "three-legged stool" that supports community sustainability.

In my place-conscious teaching in the high school at Aurora, Nebraska, I emphasized the connection between the economics of our region and the health of the community surrounding our school. In this chapter, I report on a "work ethnographies" unit I taught in various forms between 2005 and 2012. During this unit, my students and I investigated

1. Copyright © 2014 by Wendell Berry, from *Citizenship Papers*. Reprinted by permission of Counterpoint.

the world of work that supports Aurora. In every year I taught this unit, a centerpiece was an oral history interview with an adult community member about their work, which the students developed into a digital story to share with the class and the community. In the class I profile below, my students surrounded this community interview with a three-generation history of their own family's work in Aurora. We used both the interview and the three-generation history to explore the changing nature of work, as Aurora experiences the changes from rural agriculture to suburban service economies as a consequence of the growing micropolitan explosion of our region.

Aurora, Nebraska: A Community in the Midst of Micropolitan Development

I lived and worked for twenty-one years in Aurora, the county seat of Hamilton County, seventy-five miles west of the nearest metropolitan center of Lincoln and abutting the micropolitan area of Grand Island (Cantrell 2006, 2). Aurora's "downtown" is built around a historic county courthouse completed in 1895, constructed of redbrick with Colorado sandstone with a tall spire. A strobe light rests atop the spire in recognition of Harold "Doc" Edgerton, its inventor, one of Aurora's most famous native sons. There are several businesses on each side of the square. Some buildings are empty; some thrive. Within four or five blocks of Aurora's downtown, there are many majestic two-story houses that look like something out of the American South: palatial plantations surrounded by grand yards full of deciduous and evergreen trees.

Bailey and Preston define a micropolis as an area of counties "based around a core city or town with a population of 10,000–49,000. A micropolitan area may consist of more than one county depending upon economic, social and cultural connections" (2011, 1). Aurora has become a bedroom community to its nearby micropolis, Grand Island.

Grand Island is one of the micropolitan communities currently gaining population in Nebraska. The 2010 US Census confirmed that most rural Nebraska counties lost population, but the metropolitan Omaha area and two micropolises gained. Two Omaha metropolitan counties increased:

Douglas County increased its population 11.5 percent, and Sarpy County grew a whopping 29.6 percent. In central Nebraska two "micros" grew more than 9 percent: Kearney (including Buffalo and Kearney Counties) and Grand Island (including Hall, Howard, and Merrick Counties). Grand Island is a manufacturing center, with a Hispanic population of nearly 27 percent in the 2010 Census, up 11 percent since 2000. Bailey and Preston (2011) note that the Hispanic population increase for all Nebraska micropolitan counties was nearly 62 percent.

Hamilton County, and Aurora, is clearly a part of Grand Island's micropolitan growth. St. Paul, the county seat of Howard County, is twenty-two miles north of Grand Island, and Central City, the county seat of Merrick County, is twenty-two miles northeast of the city. Aurora is twenty-one miles due east of Grand Island. Aurora's 2010 population was 4,479, and the entire county was 9,124. Aurora experienced a 6 percent increase in a decade.

Aurora (and Hamilton County, Nebraska) is going through a population transformation of the sort Savage and Lapping describe: "Many people are attracted to a community on the rural-urban [and micropolitan] fringe because of the open-space amenities such places provide. . . . Those who are attracted by the suburbanizing landscape often have a desire to enjoy such open-space amenities, country lifestyles, and the provision of certain amenities and services, such as the perception of better schools or personal safety or cheaper and larger building sites" (2003, 8).

The old rural community is giving way to something new, something best captured by thinking about the effects of suburban sprawl on the exurban rural community. Joseph Goddard notes that Auguste Spectorsky first coined the term *exurbia* in reference to New York, "claiming that playground suburbs—'exurbs'—had developed 60 miles from Manhattan where the well-heeled Madison Avenue set enjoyed weekend farming" (2012, 22). In his work Goddard focused on Howard County in Maryland, Loudoun County in Virginia, and Niagara County in New York, counties close to the cities of Baltimore; Washington, DC; and Buffalo. What he observed in these eastern cities is reflected in the trends for Hamilton County and other rural counties on the metropolitan and micropolitan edges: "Farming landscape changed greatly between 1945 and 2000. Incomers claimed the countryside: they began envisioning and choreographing land for its intrinsic aesthetic worth rather than for its utility or production. New country people imagined the land as a setting that supported the countryside's role as a place to live in rather than work on" (54). Hamilton County has similarly changed. It was a landscape of the rural, a pastoral setting centered in farming. It is now being reimagined by "new country people" of the sort Goddard describes.

When I first arrived in Aurora in the summer of 1992, I was discouraged by the lack of housing available. The superintendent of schools sympathized, noting that daily he received phone calls from Grand Island residents seeking housing and residency in the community because they wanted their children to attend its school. The trend only increased over the past twenty years. In 1992 Aurora could not provide enough new housing to meet the demand. Currently, housing developments spring up on the western and northern edges of town as fertile ground and row crops disappear. Because of its pastoral attraction and sense of safety and its country heritage based on the traditions of farming, Aurora is ideally suited for the "newcomer" reimagining Goddard describes.

Rural residents have sustained a way of life for many generations, but growing sprawl changes rural communities. In the years I have taught in Aurora, I have noted that students increasingly live and work much like their suburban counterparts. Students work at the local swimming pool and grocery stores, but also in the fast food industry, holding jobs at Subway, Arby's, Pizza Hut, and McDonald's. Many students also commute the twenty-one miles to work in retail stores in nearby Grand Island. I began to wonder: What does it mean that students in rural Nebraska now live and work much like their suburban peers? How have political and economic decisions influenced job acquisition and economic necessity? How have these policies changed our students and the needs they have for the future?

Documenting the Dominant Work of a Community

As a place-conscious educator interested in the economic and cultural forces impacting my community, I wanted my students to have the opportunity to explore the changes we were experiencing. Borrowing from the twin strands of oral history (a staple in my classroom for many years) and work ethnographies (which I knew through my research), in 2009 and 2010 my classes conducted a study of the dominant work of Hamilton County through personal work histories over three generations and interviews with local farmers and business owners.

To engage my students in the study of work, I borrowed Linda Flower's (2008) strategy of researching the "story behind the story" in a community issue. Her strategy of finding and documenting the story behind the story is a means of bringing the narratives of everyday people to bear on issues affecting the community, finding out what stories lie behind the public narratives used to encode public policy. My students and I sought to uncover the story behind the story in the shifting nature of work lives in our community of Aurora. We collected the narratives of everyday people—that is, farmers, nurses, business owners, teachers, and the like—to contextualize how these changes would affect their educational and career choices on the cusp of their senior year and its inherent anxieties.

Wendell Berry writes in "Going to Work" that most modern work is done in "enclosures" that keep us from knowing how our work affects our place. But the work we do has a "precise and practical influence, first on the place where it is being done, and then on every place where its products are used, on every place where its attitude toward its products is felt, on every place to which its by-products are carried" (2003b, 33). Most of my students were oblivious to the effect their work had on our place or the influence that the work of their grandparents and parents had upon the community of Aurora. The influence was much more evident in the past, as small farms were self-sustaining and people traded goods and services. As farms became corporations with a credo of "feeding the world," the effect of mass production had a detrimental effect on our landscape and the type of work available for our citizens. In other words, the context of work shifted in our "neighborhood . . . and commonwealth." To understand effect and influence and contextualize their own work and with a "responsibility . . . to confront the problems and deal justly with them," students compiled a list of the jobs from their own, their parents', and their grandparents' work histories (33–34).

Examining a span of more than fifty years, students noticed a shift in where the work took place. Most of the grandparents described their jobs as ones that probably took place in our community, either self-employed or employed by a business in Aurora. Often they were vocations such as farmer or home builder (not a construction worker), homemaker, teacher, or beekeeper. Many of the students' grandparents also owned a business or a farm. The locale had to provide a market for less mobile people. Citizens could get just about anything they needed within a small community fifty years ago. (See table 1.)

In their parents' generation, the baby boomers, there was a marked increase in mobility. Many jobs could still be viewed as vocations, and many jobs may have been in our community, but it is in these work histories that we see the mention of many businesses or manufacturing plants in Grand Island. There were twenty-four jobs recognized by the name of the company, including Bosselman's, Swift, Excel, and Chief Automotive. We also noted that many of the manufacturing jobs were related to agriculture, including a John Deere dealership, New Holland (manufacturers of agriculture equipment), and Excel and Swift (meat processing plants). (See table 2.)

Much of the work in all three generations was related to the service or retail industries, but none more so than students' work histories. Of course, at their age, those jobs are the only ones available. (See table 3.)

Their work histories showed very little professional career opportunities in Aurora or the neighboring micropolitan of Grand Island, where many students commuted to their part-time jobs. The lack of professional careers may also be influenced by the demographics of my classes. The work ethnographies were not conducted in my advanced composition classes, where parents may have had these types of jobs. My students discovered that if they did go to one of our larger communities to pursue a postsecondary education (necessary for a professional career), they would have few opportunities to return to work in central Nebraska. For many students who may stay or insist on returning, there will be a commute. A recent Nebraska Public Power District (NPPD) study revealed that "54.4 percent of Aurora residents work outside the city. The most popular destination is Grand Island, which attracts 17.9 percent of the Aurora work

Table 1
Job Histories of Aurora Students' Grandparents

Agriculture	*Retail/service*	*Factory construction*	*Professional*
rancher, farmer, greenhouse owner, ranch land owner, John Deere dealership, beekeeper, center pivot repairman, dairy farming, well man, co-op worker, co-op manager, and irrigation	hardware store, restaurant owner, jewelry store clerk, bowling alley owner, gas station owner, wood maker (carver), appliance sales, ceramic shop owner, sales and services, florist, banker, bar owner, FFA Leadership Center, assisted living, city electrician, church secretary, church work, baker, homemaker, nursing home, bartender, apartment manager, logger, cook, truck driver, nurse, county road maintenance, fireman, bookkeeper, activities director of nursing home, occupational therapist, airport service, garage company owner, swimming pool manager, chief of police, housekeeper, and auto technician	home builder, grain builder, roofer, car restorer, repair, electric motor shop, and electrician	semipro race car driver, military (navy, army, marines, air force) teacher, librarian, and minister

force" (Johnson 2011b). The entire county's outflow migration percentage was a bit higher, at 66.6 percent. The flip side to this trend is that "Hamilton County has 43 percent of its work force driving into the county for work," which conveys that many citizens of even smaller villages in Hamilton County commute to Aurora for jobs to sustain their families.

My students were concerned about the change in the nature of work in Hamilton County and how it impacted their future. As students explored

Table 2
Job Histories of Aurora Students' Parents

Agriculture	*Retail/service*	*Factory construction*	*Professional*
co-op, seed salesman, dairy farming, pig farming, farming, thistle picker, well man, seed company, ethanol production, John Deere company, New Holland, MFS, Swift, Chief Industries, Excel, CF Industries, Case International Harvester, Hooker Brothers	Lincare, A1 Fiberglass, Iams pet foods, florist, car sales, auto body work, telemarketing, tire sales, Starbucks regional manager, coffee shop owner, grocery store management, gas station attendant/manager, butcher, day care, receptionist, medical receptionist, mother, anesthesia tech, police officer, fire chief, Bosselman's, Hamilton relay services, Chief Automotive, custodian, truck driver, FFA Leadership Center, welding, plasma cutter, gunsmith, Red Cross, insurance salesperson, restaurant work, dental hygienist, mechanic, paper route, fireman, office manager, para-educator, grocery store worker, waste management, truck driver, racetrack worker, restaurant manager, convenience store clerk, dental assistant, cemetery caretaker, director of emergency management, CNA, hospital housekeeping, waitress, bartender	Top Flite, electrician, CAD expert, Overhead Door, Larsen, Olsson Associates, grain bin builder, and bricklayer	nursing, military (air force, army, marines) pharmacist, teacher, endowment coordinator, lawyer, and financial adviser

Table 3
Job Histories of Aurora Students

Agriculture	*Retail and recreation*
irrigation, farming, greenhouse, detasseling, rogueing, well drilling	Subway, Arby's, Kohl's, bowling alley, tree service, FFA Leadership Center, McDonald's, construction, nursing home, pharmacy, airport, grocery store, restaurant, paper route, plumbing, swimming pool, lawn care service, babysitting, coffee shop, waitressing, housekeeping, flooring, floral, telemarketing, movie theater, corn maze, youth center, and tae kwon do

their own work histories, they asked themselves several questions: "What is the dominant work of our community? How has that work changed over a span of fifty years? How will work evolve as we explore the job market? What skills or training do I need to live well economically?" In asking these questions, we engaged in a community literacy inquiry that acknowledged my adolescent students' and community members' expertise about their locale (Flower 2008, 56). Students integrated their personal knowledge of work into their parents' and grandparents' histories, "showing how intelligent, effective, complex and appropriate these local literacies are to their context" (127). They identified the past and present work but also anticipated future work that may be available in Hamilton County.

In order to understand more about the dominant work of this rural community, I asked students to write in response to writing prompts from David Seitz's *Who Can Afford Critical Consciousness?* (2004). Seitz asked his college students to consider who had been good and bad role models for teaching about work, compile a list of jobs they had had and which ones they liked or disliked, and write about personal relationships with bosses, coworkers, and customers. Seitz also asked his students to list objects or tools they had to work with and to think about what careers they were contemplating. Finally, he asked his students to choose a positive or negative experience in which school experiences were or were not like work. In my class these questions elicited extended essays from all of my students on an academic continuum from the special-education student to honor-society member. Students wrote in depth about work role models and their jobs.

In answering Seitz's questions, Whitney wrote extensively about her role models and the vital influence they had upon her. Whitney wrote mostly about her dad, Jonathan:

> My role models for work have been my parents, my grandpa, and my uncle. My parents managed a 200 acre farm, and took care of it extremely well. They worked long hours mowing, weeding, and feeding animals. My dad has had many jobs. . . . [H]e always wanted change, and to try something new. He went to many years of college, and after college he was a pastor. Then he went to law school and became a lawyer. He worked as a lawyer in a prestigious law firm in Washington D.C. He then went on to work at several other law firms, while managing a farm. He then opened his own coffee shop while still doing all those other things. When we moved to Nebraska, he was a lawyer and the manager of several different Starbucks. Recently, he began working as a financial advisor.

Whitney selected role models that exemplify one of the discoveries we made over the course of our project: we come from hardworking stock. The work ethic of midwesterners is highly valued, as Kilborn noted in *Next Stop, Reloville* (2009). Large corporations hire from Great Plains universities for a reason: we work tirelessly and take pride in our ability to do so. Despite his mobility, Whitney's dad returned to his roots after the death of his wife in a farm accident. He raised his large family in Hamilton County, surrounded by his extended family.

It is clear that Whitney's father is what Carr and Kefalas term a "high-flyer achiever" who returned to his rural roots. Carr and Kefalas describe the types of students in rural areas as achievers, stayers, seekers, and returners (they subdivide the last group between high flyers and boomerangs). Achievers are the "homegrown aristocracy" of small towns whose parents often had college degrees. They are placed on a different academic "track" than other students and receive special attention from teachers and community members (2009, 19). Stayers, on the other hand, generally do not attend college and "quickly start looking like adults. They quickly transition to adulthood, families, jobs and grown up lives" (20). Seekers often leave the small town because they just are not cut out for it—they often go into the military. Seekers are often the solid average student who does not want to settle down but does not have the grade point average to get scholarships for a college education (22). Returners are divided between high flyers, who "return with college degrees and entrepreneurial ambitions" (they had been achievers), and boomerangs, who are more like the stayers (they temporarily left the small-town life to join the military or attend community college, but returned after their tour of duty ended) (23). Carr and Kefalas argue that a brain drain happens because small rural communities groom the achievers to leave because of the changing nature of work and wages available in communities like Aurora.

Whitney, like her father, was certainly an achiever. She had several jobs in her work history, including farm and yard work, fast food service, and nursing-home employee. Her favorite job was farming and her least favorite fast food. She alluded to the ability to become independent with "new responsibilities" or "exploring" connected with a place. Since finishing our class in 2009–10, Whitney has pursued a career in medicine in Omaha. Through the work ethnographies, Whitney observed that her father was mobile and restless, with several changes in occupations. She also explored the work history of her maternal grandfather, a physician, and although her mother was not alive to conduct the work history, Whitney was aware of her career as a nurse. This knowledge and the knowledge that our work landscape was quickly changing led Whitney to a degree in nursing in the closest metropolitan area and life in the suburbs.

Jessica shared one of the most poignant work histories in the 2009–10 class. She told the story of the difficulty her grandfather Larry faced at a very early age:

> My grandpa was one out of six kids. His mother left when his younger brother was two. So after that, my grandpa took on a lot of responsibility. He got his first job when he was eleven by local farmers asking for help. He received five cents per hour on a milk farm. At the age of fifteen he made one dollar per hour. He saved his money to get parts to build his own car. When he was eighteen, he wanted to get married and to

> farm his own farm. He ended up doing both. Money was short most of the time. He did not need schooling for the jobs he has done. He had twelve jobs from the age of fifteen to fifty-five. In 2001 at age of 48 he went to college for heating and air. But at the age of fifty-five he is still continuing his work history.

Jessica's grandpa represents several discoveries my students learned about the differences between their work and the work of their parents and grandparents. Most students agreed that both previous generations had fewer job opportunities than they now have. Many were surprised that their grandparents had a "need" to work (rather than a "want") because of economic hard times. Most grandparents began work at very young ages. Consequently, some of them did not have a high school education. Some students noted that college was not as important to their parents' generation as it was for theirs. All my students recognized the difference in wages with a sense of incredulity. Students noted that parents and grandparents had served in the armed forces through the draft. Some of their parents (but very few grandparents) had the hardship of single parenthood.

Most students recognized that there were some job opportunities in Aurora and Hamilton County. A few also realized that beyond working in fast food establishments, there were not a lot of jobs for teenagers. That realization made them understand that pursuing an education was a migratory necessity. For a four-year postsecondary education, some would have to leave and live in one of the cities of the three major universities, Omaha, Lincoln, and Kearney. Some students also recognized the need for what secondary schools label "tech prep" and opted to attend a nearby community college where they would learn a technological skill such as welding, dental assistance, cosmetology, or tool and die.

Through work ethnographies, students were able to see the economic realities of their changing rural-to-suburban landscape. High-paying occupations were few and far between. Most farms had become extensive "farm operations" or corporate farms with large profits, not the small farms their grandparents knew. Many local businesses were also started by families, and many passed down to family members. Most local businesses were struggling to survive, and employee pay was minimal and without benefits. Hence, much of the populace was commuting to the nearby micropolis for higher-income occupations, often manufacturing jobs with health insurance benefits. Because most of the commuters shopped on their commutes, they were less likely to support local businesses, and thus local workers (Savage and Lapping 2003, 11).

Overall, then, my students' stories of the dominant work of our community became a means to understand the issues of economic sustainability affecting our region. My students' projects, the histories and personal narratives of the work of local community members, brought about awareness of the economic realities and the influence of suburban sprawl on this exurban community. Students reexamined what skills they might need in the future, whether they live in a rural, suburban, or urban place. Culturally, they learned that the past had influenced their work ethic for the jobs they presently held. Students also explored why Berry's concepts of vision and efficacy are vital in light of the changing nature of work. It was important they understand who their community is and why it is the way it is. Without this kind of knowledge, they could never imagine what the future may hold for them in regards to making a living.

The Changing Nature of Work

Following the three-generation histories, my students conducted an oral interview with a local adult worker. These oral interviews with elders in the community helped solidify the changing nature of work in Aurora, as traditional agriculture gives way to a more suburban migratory and service economy. These same issues, of course, are ones the community's business leaders have been thinking about for decades.

The community leaders in Aurora recognized this trend over the past fifty years. In a series of 2011 *Aurora News Register* columns, Kurt Johnson documented the community's thinking:

- The shift in farm production patterns means Aurora must embrace a shift to town-centered jobs: "With the farm community as sophisticated as it is we know it is going to require fewer people to farm more land so if we want to keep the community growing we're going to have to find more jobs for people in town" (Johnson 2011c).

- The development of manufacturing jobs is crucial for Aurora's future. Citing a 2010 Nebraska Public Power District study for Hamilton County, Johnson writes: "16.8 percent of non-farm employment is in manufacturing . . . [and its] location along the interstate has been prime for the manufacturing and transportation industries" (Johnson 2011a). My students' parents' work histories documented a shift of commuting to manufacturing jobs in nearby Grand Island.
- One of the challenges for Aurora economics is what business leaders call "retail leakage." Often, people commuting elsewhere for work "shop in their location of employment before heading home" (Johnson 2011b). According to Jenny Overhue of NPPD, residents of Hamilton County report "greater income levels than the average non-metropolitan county." Overhue's study showed Aurora's median family income is the midpoint in the ranked distribution of the sum of income for all family members fifteen years of age and older. The median income for Hamilton County in 2009 was $58,900. "The trick is getting them to spend it within Hamilton County instead of other areas" (Johnson 2011b).
- Despite the fact that the economic landscape of Aurora and Hamilton County continues to change, it is difficult to attract Aurora graduates back to the community after completing their postsecondary educations. Jim Koepke notes, "We invest about $150,000 into each student. Our kids need to return to the community, but we need to create opportunities that allow them to come back—we need the engineers, lawyers and physicians but we also need plumbers and electricians. We need to remind them: Don't forget about Aurora."[2] Young people tend to go where the best-paying jobs are. The income levels praised by the Overhue study as reasonable for Hamilton County were still $3,100 below the state average and

2. Jim Koepke (retired banker) in discussion with the author, May 2011.

> $14,600 lower than metropolitan Nebraska (2010, 29). Most colleges in Nebraska and across the country prepare their graduates for careers most predominant in the current job market. Many of the jobs in metropolitan areas they might seek will be in leisure, hospitality, financial services, natural resources, and construction (Johnson 2011a).

My students conducted their oral interviews in the context of this community-wide discussion of the future of work in Aurora. Once individual students completed their three-generation work histories, they partnered with another student and began to formulate specific questions about the nature of work for the adult worker they chose, focusing on the adult's actual work. For example, if interviewing a farmer they might ask, "How many hours do you work? How many acres do you farm? What is the most expensive piece of equipment you own?" If it was a local business owner, they might ask, "When did you begin your business? How much did you first invest to get started? How have prices changed? How has technology changed your business?" Once students compiled their questions, they scheduled visits with their adult worker and took notes, tape-recorded the interviews, and took ample photos of their place of work. Once the interviews were completed, students wrote the workers' narratives and then integrated a spoken narrative with images to create a digital story to upload onto our school website. Once the stories became publicly accessible (after revision, fact-checking, and digital fine-tuning), I wrote a letter to the editor of the local newspaper, thanking the community members who took part in our study and included the URL for the website so community members could view the stories.

Investigating the three-generation work histories helped my students contextualize their writing before they ever began the process of interviewing local farmers and business owners. Like many of their parents' and grandparents' stories, these oral histories were filled with the difficulty of the work itself. When students developed the questions they would ask farmers and business owners, they thought in terms of what actual jobs were performed, the length of the workday, the type of equipment needed, or how much money was invested in starting a new business. Students also recognized through their investigation how the community's landscape was changing: the rural was succumbing to the suburban and exurban influences, the nature of work was shifting, and job opportunities were changing. Students also had to consider the implications of these changes, that is, how do the changes affect generations fifty or one hundred years from now?

One student, Jake, discovered that much had changed in Hamilton County in the past fifty years. Both Jake and his grandpa Walt grew up on the family farm; like his grandpa, Jake was completely immersed in the work that had dominated Aurora and Hamilton County's past. In his initial reflection about the project, he wrote, "I learned a few things about my grandpa that I didn't know. There were some really hard times in the 80's and it takes quite a few years to get ahead in farming. Being a farmer is no easy task. There are long days and lots of work to do." Jake's grandfather embodied the cultural phenomenon of the midwestern work ethic, and through writing the narrative about him, Jake learned that perseverance is needed as we progress through enormous changes in our work environments.

Jake has a stake in Hamilton County. He is one of the fortunate ones who may stay in a place because he may inherit the family farm. Through farming he will experience what Owens calls "forms of hard labor with obvious rejuvenating benefits, especially labor that brings one in contact with the earth" (2001, 78). Jake's narrative depicts this sense of hard labor in association with the earth.

> When he has work to do during the summer, he gets up at 5:30 or 6 in the morning to go out to the field. He works all day long doing many different things and doesn't quit until 8:30 or 9 at night (daylight to dark). Planting is the most stressful part of the year. You have to get the crops in the ground or you won't have anything to grow and that is the most important thing he said. Picking the corn is another stressful part of the farming year and the weather doesn't always agree with when corn needs to be picked.

Jake's grandpa had lived as the quintessential Hamilton County farmer: early mornings, late evenings, financial risk, and anxiety over unpredictable weather that could result in dire financial losses. Jake will forge ahead with his eyes wide open into a vocation he knows well but also knowing it has changed dramatically. "Today, [my grandpa] feels that it is necessary for a person to have a college education and know how to work with computers and keep up with the changing technology." Walt's narrative typifies the agricultural trend in Hamilton County of newer technologies, which means less farms and the need for other jobs. This trend has an immediate effect on his grandson. The farm Jake may someday inherit will look very different from the one Walt knew—that is, if their family farm survives the coming influx of exurbanites or suburbanites from the Grand Island micropolis who want a lot of country space for leisure activities but do not want to work the land.

Even though farming is predominant in Aurora, many students do not know much about the actual process of farming, the technology, or the amount of dedication, perseverance, and finances needed to succeed. Most students would not know the difference between a combine and a planter. Students often do not see the connection between their part-time jobs and the farmers whose livelihood supports their employers.

Through writing work ethnographies, students were given an opportunity to see that they are part of the larger community in more than just an economic way. Continued micropolitan expansion and suburban sprawl will have an effect on their futures and generations beyond theirs. The changing nature of work gave my students pause. Three students wrote about how the nature of work changed for their fathers. Cheyenne, whose father could not maintain a farm without an extra job at the local pet-food plant, noted: "He worked a twelve hour work shift at IAMS and would then come home to feed and water all the animals on his farm, along with all the upkeep it took to keep the farm running. At IAMS my dad would work days for two weeks and then he would switch to nights for two weeks, this took a toll on my dad but he never stopped working, and I can't say I can remember a time that he would call in sick."

Another student, Gabbii, explored the change in the nature of work through her father's experience. Gabbii's father shifted from manufacturing to independent home construction. In the past, he worked a variety of manufacturing jobs, including for a local company that built prefabricated homes. But Aurora's need for new single-family dwellings as a bedroom community enticed him to start his own home construction business:

> He has worked for Bonnavilla homes, now known as Chief Custom Homes, and he also started his own construction business two years ago, McLamb Construction. Bonnavilla isn't doing too well right now and lots of people are talking about how it might close down, but dad has faith that it won't. Every winter it gets like this, nobody wants to build a home in the winter. We're hoping for the best with Bonnavilla, if it doesn't last though, a few people have offered my dad a job and he also still has his own business, so he thinks we'll be okay.

Through their fathers' experiences, these girls could see how the nature of work changed within their own families. Cheyenne's and Gabbii's narratives express the anxiety that accompanies changes in work, that is, the uncertainty of job security especially for those workers without an education or intense training to become employable in the new market. Both girls understood the immediate implications of career changes informing their deliberations for future careers as they contemplated skills they may need or the necessity of acquiring new skills within a short of amount of time.

LeAnna's father also represents the change in the nature of work influenced by the exurban influence on our rural community as the kind of "newcomer" Goddard (2012) describes. He is a well-known artist who lives on acreage outside of town. His daughter describes his work: "Many of the tools he uses while he works are brushes, paint, pencils, paper, copy machine, printer, computer, books, magazines and his desk. With most of these things there are various associations that come with them. With the brushes and pencils I always have a comforting feeling of hearing the water slosh as my dad washes the brushes out, or the pencil sharpener sharpening. I have always loved hearing those sounds because it reassured me that he was working, and I could watch him while he worked." LeAnna's experience differs from the other two girls' experiences in that her father's career was atypical from most residents. As an artist, he represented the limited professional class, while most careers were related to agriculture or manufacturing. However, he grew up on a farm in Hamilton County. This one-generation shift from agriculture to art is indicative of the farming landscape change from 1945 to 2000 noted by Goddard. But what are the implications for LeAnna? She did not experience the anxiety of a parent's loss of a job, but she was exposed to a career that has its own set of anxiety and trepidation. From her narrative, there was a serene sense of security evoked and the assurance that as long as her father was working, all was right with the world. LeAnna is a talented artist in her own right, and she may well follow in her father's footsteps.

Even if my students do not return to Aurora, I wanted them to take with them wherever they go a connection to the men and women who work in their community. I wanted them to be aware that they are influenced by the places we inhabit (by human beings, fauna, flora, and geography). "Others" influence our livelihood and the way we live out our lives in a particular place. As my student narratives attest, "We are all influenced differently, but we are the products of our connections with an array of locations and the inhabitants thereof" (Weisser and Dobrin 2001, 86).

Through inquiry into the work in Hamilton County, my students came to understand how important it is to be concerned about the economic sustainability of their future places, whether they are rural, suburban, or urban. As educators, we "have a responsibility to invent a locally based, pedagogical ethic informed and inspired by an awareness of the need to think and act sustainably" (Weisser and Dobrin 2001, 86). As an educator, I considered Berry's concept of the public good. What was I doing to contribute to the general welfare of the people of Aurora, Nebraska? What did I see as the wealth in common? For me, there was a "wealth in common" in our most impressionable citizens, our young people. Through the work ethnographies, I learned that our community's identity was rooted in agriculture, and, using Seitz's model, I asked students to "get at" the historical implications of that agrarian past. I considered, "Is our identity lost or is it just evolving? What happens to a community during that evolution?"

Carr and Kefalas advocate for "economic gardening" where the focus is "on planting multiple seeds for local growth in the hope that some will bear fruit" (2009, 155). The "economic gardening" I gave to my students was a rhetorical space where they could "speak with" community members about the economic changes at a time when a standards-based curriculum is the norm. I offered students an authentic inquiry, authentic writing, and an authentic audience. I offered them a chance to join with other "real" voices to tell stories of our community.

Ardean Andersen, ninety, a retired farmer who lived and farmed near Marquette, ten miles north of Aurora, began a dialogue with me after students and I sent him a personal thank-you letter. In letters to me (clearly typewritten on an "ancient" typewriter), he noted how challenging it must have been for my students to come to their farm and interview total strangers. He commended our community literacy project, writing, "I do agree that you as Educators/Teachers have a great responsibility in presenting farmers' philosophy . . . but as time goes on, this unique position is being diminished as the rural population is shrinking and as large corporate entities begin to dilute the best interest of land usage for shareholder and personal profits, the whole picture becomes counter-productive for the benefit of society in general. . . . While there is a wealth of information easily available, it takes a 'hands-on' approach such as your projects to give the younger generation a personal knowledge of our environment."

Together, that is, my students, farmers like Ardean, and other community members, learned that "leadership, youth, entrepreneurship, and charitable assets" are a goal to "increase the capacity of residents to improve and sustain their community" (Carr and Kefalas 2009, 156).

Sustaining an Economic Future

Citizens of Aurora understood Smart Growth long before it came into our nomenclature. The community understood what city dwellers wanted: a lot of space, places to walk, places to play, a good school, and a short commute. But the biggest need in any community is a job market. A community simply cannot progress without gainfully employed residents. Brooke acknowledges, "To participate fully in a community, individuals need a livelihood. Students should know about the options for livelihood available to them in their region, about the skills, knowledge, and experience necessary to sustain those livelihoods" (2003, 11).

Aurora has many small business owners who have maintained a concern for the common good of this community. Aurora citizens associated with the Aurora Area Chamber and Development Corps have often supported entrepreneurial endeavors because they care about the economic sustainability of their community. In 2011 the *Aurora News Register* began a series of articles disseminating and evaluating data from the 2010 Nebraska Public Power District's Economic and Demographic Trends Report. Kurt Johnson, publisher of the *Aurora News Register*, emphasized in his first column that the report "offers some must-read information for non-farm wage and salary employment by major economic sectors, as well as per capita personal income comparisons of area counties" (2011d). One of the biggest eye-openers of the report was that "non-farm employment grew by 16.6 percent in Hamilton County in the last decade" (Johnson 2011b). This growth in nonfarm employment was consistent with my students' findings in their work ethnographies. Their research matched the research of experts. They discovered what Brooke noted in 2003 about them: "If they are to make a living, they will need training and experience that helps them understand other options, especially entrepreneurship. They will need to understand how businesses are formed and sustained, how to identify skills and resources they can offer personally, and how to locate markets they can tap" (11).

Current statistics show that many of my students will migrate to urban and suburban areas in the eastern part of our state, but some students will stay in Aurora, but because of our study, the ones who stay have to ask themselves some very hard questions: What will happen when prime farm ground is consumed for expanding housing needs? What kinds of jobs will be available when the community is less agriculturally based? What happens when food production or farm equipment production wanes? What happens when the ethanol plant closes?

Asking these questions enabled my students to project the future. I gave them a real everyday problem, asking them to consider how the community was changing. I asked them, "What's the big deal?" Many adolescents cannot see past their noses, but I wanted them to imagine themselves ten years into the future, so I asked, "What kind of work will you do?" My students achieved a goal of producing citizen narratives that were contextualized within the community. We preserved the past through collecting stories about our work, but in the process of interviewing, listening, writing, and examining our data, we learned a great deal about citizenship and what it means to "do unto those downstream as you would have those upstream do unto you" (Berry 2003a, 135).

Did our study of work ethnographies influence the community? Did it change my students? The impact and changes are difficult to measure. It has been my experience that authentic inquiry and subsequent writing are measurable in both formative and summative ways, but assessing the deep learning or changes in thinking is immeasurable. The impact of this study may not be evident within the next decade or even several decades. I concur with Stone that "students can understand a community better by seeing it through the eyes of people who live and work there" (2010, 38). I believe work ethnographies, or the study and observation of the types of livelihood in our community, enable all students, whether suburban, urban, or rural, to find ways to strengthen and sustain their own communities through the investigation of local work and the issues they may discover through that investigative lens. Through this ethnographic study, I have fulfilled a civic duty paramount in most educators' eyes, that is, preparing our students for the workplace. My goal was to "provide contexts where students might critique and reinvent the idea of work so that it is no longer a four-letter word but something spiritually fulfilling, supportive of more free time, environmentally defensible, and most importantly, sustainable" (Owens 2001, 78).

Teaching Native American Studies in Midwestern Suburbs

Place-Conscious Education for Land-Grant Universities

BERNICE OLIVAS

In my early childhood my daddy ran crews for the biggest farmers in the area, working potatoes, beets, corn, and soybean. The rest of my extended family—aunts, uncles, and cousins—often traveled migratory paths that followed the work. My Teja family "came up" from Gloria Anzaldúa's (1999) borderlands, working citrus, berries, and tomatoes until they showed up on our doorstep to work the potatoes. My family *norte* "came down" from Minnesota, working in slaughterhouses and factories—apples in October and Jenni-O in November. On the job the workers called my father Jefe, and the white community called him Matt. No one called him Mr. Olivas. This naming exemplifies the ways in which migrant workers, even migrant workers with relatively high status, exist in a constantly shifting middle ground. We lived somewhere between the dominant mainstream community and the mostly invisible class of unskilled, often undocumented labor in the United States. When I was twelve my father lost his job, and we began to bounce from one Idaho town to another—always following a job or an opportunity.

Because of my connection to migratory workers and my own migratory experience, my sense of place is very expansive. Members of "my community" are spread across the country. We live everywhere: rural places, urban places, and suburban places. And everywhere we live, we experience many of the same concerns, frustrations, and civic struggles.

Consequently, whenever I encounter a new teaching method, approach, or theory, particularly one intended to encourage students to embrace ways of thinking about civic duty and citizenship, I question how it accounts for the issues of colonization, oppression, and marginalization because these components are critical in the lives of so many of that invisible class of people to whom I once belonged.

What I discovered about place-conscious education is that it is a pedagogy of seeing. It demands that we see and take note of all of the beautiful complexities of the places we name home. These complexities include the historical and the present-day contact zones (Pratt 1991) where peoples grapple with the lasting impact of colonization, slavery, and marginalization. Truly *seeing* our places facilitates loving, sustaining, and enriching those places. This knowledge is a political truth as well as a physical one. Truly *seeing* the peoples who share our places facilitates coming together as a community. Too often the evidence and aftermath of colonization, marginalization, and oppression are whitewashed away, cleared from the surface, rendered invisible. Place-conscious education has the potential to strip that whitewashing away, to reveal the things our communities normally overlook or ignore. The work, then, of place-conscious educators is to find that evidence, to uncover the things we do not see, to lay bare the things we walk by every day and never notice.

Contextualizing the connections between the places where we live, the places we come from, and the significant places in both our individual and community histories has incredible potential to broaden the way we see the world. Place-conscious education can be the focal point in building solidarity among community members with little else in common. Becoming place conscious includes becoming conscious of the history of displacement, loss, and injustice lived by communities of color. By its very nature, learning about place, learning to love our places, demands we account for the legacy of racism and colonization in those places. Therefore, embedded in teaching place consciousness is the simple fact that if we are going to talk about place, we must, at some point, talk about race. (Robbins and Dyer 2005; Gruenewald 2003; Somerville, Power, and de Carteret 2009).

As Greenwood points out, "Place matters to education because it provides researchers, practitioners, and all learners with a local or nearby focus for cultural study, and because it expands a cultural landscape to include related ecosystems, bioregions, and all the place-specific interactions between the human and more-than human-world" (2011). Within this dialogue of place and race, suburban communities present a unique challenge because, at the surface level, they seem to lack diversity and support homogenization of the inhabitants. We worry that the nature of suburbs obscures difference by creating an oasis of sameness within fenced borders. The concern is that the mosaic nature of the suburban landscape (Teaford 2008), a terrain that is collectively deeply diverse yet at the neighborhood level made up of homogeneous enclaves, hides and obscures the "contact zones" (Pratt 1991) created by diversity. We worry that this obscurity will facilitate the same narrow worldviews in our students that segregation and later white flight once facilitated in earlier generations. If students are separated by a buffer of sameness from the places where, as Pratt says, "disparate cultures meet, clash, and grapple with each other, often in highly asymmetrical relations of domination and subordination—like colonialism, slavery, or their aftermaths" (1991, 34), how can place-conscious education widen that perspective?

If suburbia acts to narrow the perspective and to diminish the possibility that our students will participate in those awkward meetings with the "other" that facilitate a widening of their worldview, how can we use that space to teach social engagement or social justice? This issue resonates with the fear that Americans are becoming less, not more, ready to embrace the globalized nature of the world we live in, and less, not more, concerned with social justice. It also resonates with the concern that the suburban space facilitates a way of living that *is not* living well and *is not* living sustainably.

In reality this social myth presents a skewed and myopic view of the suburbs. Diversity is as real in the suburbs as it is in the city or in our rural places. Teaford argues, "Given the fact that an ever-increasing portion of Americans are destined to live, shop, and work in suburbia, this diversity is bound to survive, but the forces of exclusion and inclusion seem destined to meet in many future clashes. Suburbia is the America of the present and the future; it is also the battleground of coming decades as the friction mounts between those who must be accommodated and those who dig in their heels" (2008, 222–23). What Teaford is pointing out is that the suburbs *do* offer a rich and diverse but often unseen "commonwealth"—that cultural and economic "wealth shared in common" referred to by Wendell Berry. This commonwealth is deeply diverse, even if the surface seems to be utterly homogeneous. Considering our national history, the commonwealth is often complex and intricate and old. Layers of human systems are stacked one on top of the other. The suburban commonwealth demands to be both celebrated and critically examined. Place-conscious education suggests that, in order to encourage our students to practice a citizenship that radiates outward from the local, we must bridge the space between what we *see* and what we *know* and the social and civic issues that are *unseen* and *repressed* in the same space. By creating opportunities to delve into the rich "underground" realities of local ecology, place-conscious education becomes a vehicle for social justice and community literacy (Brooke 2003; Bruce 2008; Gruenewald and Smith 2008; Juneau and Broaddus 2006; Tolbert and Theobald 2005; Winter and Robbins 2005).

Place-conscious education is a pedagogy that encourages, motivates, and sustains a way of critical thinking about ourselves and our local spaces. It develops rich and fertile ground for both community literacy and social justice work in the suburbs. By showing students the diversity in their local places, and encouraging them to take an interest the commonwealth, we do not widen their worldviews as much as we deepen them. By becoming aware of the cultural traditions, histories, civic practices, employment patterns, and ethnic histories embedded in our local places, we also address issues of tolerance and acceptance, racism and intolerance, ableism, and homophobia along with other issues impacted by human migration, immigration, and displacement. Locating ourselves within the commonwealth encourages the kind of active citizenship that place-conscious education considers crucial to living well.

Seeing Smoke

One of my favorite pastimes is to walk around town and people-watch. So, as soon as I settled in Lincoln, Nebraska, a city of 250,000, well within the average population range for suburban cities in this country, I grabbed my notebook and began wandering around downtown. I enjoyed the familiarity of the grungy little blues bar with decades of memorabilia on the walls. I fell in instant eggheady love with the used bookstore and its big fat cats. (All good used bookstores should have a nonhuman inhabitant.) I enjoyed the Thai place that a friend referred to as "truck-stop Thai food." Then I walked smack into a picture of an Indian in war paint on the window of a smoke shop. The painting was an updated, cool-dude version of the old cigar-store Indian. His Pan-Indian features grinned through a layer of war paint and smoke. At the time I registered, momentarily, how sad it was that the old image was alive and that it seemed to be evolving. As an indigenous woman, I see such images all the time. They act as microaggressions, inflicting small wounds and reminding me in small ways of the complex, frustrating nature of race in America. However, I do not always get thoughtful about these small incidents of misrepresentation or appropriation because they are so common in everyday life. They are on book covers and commercials, in music lyrics and cartoons. In fact, most days I react to such images only when they were particularly startling. So, as much as I hate to admit it, I promptly forgot about that Indian in the window, and it became a part of downtown I chose to simply "not see" when I walked by.

Fast-forward a couple years and to a time when I am grappling with the complex task of teaching a Native American literature class. Ethnic literature always contains texts that do not allow us to "not see" the aggressions the writers have experienced. I am teaching in the Midwest on lands that were once tribal, in a university with a mostly white suburban population. So it is inevitable that I find myself standing in front of the class talking about the history of the physical place of our classroom, our university, our town. Teaching Native American literature means taking on the responsibility of accurately introducing students to the ongoing stories of modern Native American peoples, stories that illuminate and expose injustices that are often hidden from the view of members of the dominant culture. In Lincoln these stories ask us to think about a variety of Plains tribes as well as folks who were pushed from their own homelands and onto the plains. It means thinking about our homeless population and about the controversy surrounding the interaction between Whiteclay, Nebraska, and the Pine Ridge Reservation. It means water rights and land disputes. It means facing that Indian in the window.

Unit 1: The Writing

Considering my own habit of walking around town and people-watching, I use the first writing project in my Native American literature class to encourage reseeing the city through a digital camera. I ask them to find the Native American presence in their local places, to find modern Native America in their America.

Essay 1

STEP 1: RESEEING

> Take a day and go into Lincoln. Look for the "Native American Presence"; the good, the bad, the beautiful, and the ugly. Take a camera (your phone or a digital camera) and take lots of pictures. Speak to at least one community member of your choice about Native Americans. At the end of the day, you will write up your notes about the experience in your reading notebook.

- Go to the mall—what is being sold as "Native"? Who is buying it?
- Go to the Sheldon Museum.
- Go to the Great Plains Museum.
- Go to a bookstore—what kind of "Natives" do you see on book and movie covers?
- Look for Native American food in the city.
- Go to the Museum of Nebraska; check out the exhibit on the second floor called "The First Nebraskans."

STEP 2: WRITE AN IMAGE ANALYSIS

> The goal of this essay is to gain a better understanding of how Native American identity is represented in our own local places and spaces. Pick the most startling image you took when you explored Lincoln. Write a short formal critical essay (1,000 words + the image) about the image. Answer the following questions:

- How and why is this image startling?
- Consider the readings we have read. Pick one or two that you think interconnect, intersect, problematize, or complicate this image. Tell me how and why.
- According to this image, are Native Americans justly and accurately represented in Lincoln? Why and why not?

Most of them bring back pictures of the Indian in the window and outrage. One student writes, "This image on this store's window of the cigar smoking Indian, unjustly and completely inaccurately represents Native Americans. This image to me shows Native Americans as substance abusers, chain smoking and alcoholics. Not to mention what the character is wearing. A headdress and what appears to be an animal skin outfit. I don't even know the last time I saw anyone wearing an animal skin outfit, let alone a Native American (NEVER). This image that all Native Americans wear this type of clothing all the time, I think, is offensive" (Michael Menish).

Suddenly, we—me, my students, and that damn smoke-shop Indian—are knee-deep in a space we usually choose to not see, or if we see it, we choose to ignore it. Inhabiting the commonwealth makes the unseen not just seen but felt. We feel personally affronted by that smoke-shop Indian, by an image we overlooked, did not see, and ignored over and over again. Once we see it, we cannot help but feel represented by it. Because it exists in our downtown, lives on one of our shiny glass windows, we own it—or maybe it owns us.

In class the discussion quickly turns to frustration at how easily things like that smoke-shop Indian just become part of the landscape, become normalized. Over and over again hard questions are asked. Do images like the smoke-shop Indian mean Lincoln is racist? Does it mean we are racist? How did it happen? How did we miss it? Why didn't anyone tell us about it? In response I ask them to think about the process we have worked through and how it has impacted the way they think about themselves and their town. I ask them what it might take to help other folks change the way they think about the single story of Native Americans. I ask them to think about it—not to talk about it, not yet.

The Class: Reading, Writing, Speaking

It was my goal to use place-conscious assignments in order to develop "habits of the mind" that encouraged students to recontextualize issues that arose in class by localizing them in their local spaces. We did so in a number of different ways. First, I created reoccurring work that we did daily. At the beginning of each class I presented a text by a Native writer, activist, or artist, usually a poem or a short essay, often in video format or from our textbook (Trout 1999). I asked them to journal their responses. These texts exposed them to the work of local and Native voices speaking about local issues. Through this medium we discussed the Key Stone XL pipeline, the Violence against Women Act, and homeless Native youth. I also asked them to write a "Where I am from" poem that they would eventually revise as we worked through the semester so that they could see how their understanding of place expanded over time. Finally, I asked them to create a public document that spoke out about one of the issues we had talked about in class. The goal was to continuously encourage them to locate themselves in the commonwealth, to see the ways that improving relations with our neighbors bettered the lives of everyone in the community. Each writing project was intended to build on the everyday work we were doing to encourage empathy and a genuine connection to community members and the literature we were reading.

Unit 1

The Reading

On the first day there is a sense of wariness as I read my spiel about the way this class will work. I start with my disclaimer; it is written into the syllabus, but I read it out loud anyway. "As an instructor I believe the classroom represents a space dedicated to promoting a better understanding of the world around us and dedicated to promoting social justice. This means that while I respect your worldviews and belief systems, please expect to be challenged as thinkers, learners, and writers. This course includes difficult and frustrating subjects and text. Please expect to occasionally find yourself frustrated and conflicted." They tense up, and I continue on to the class description. I do not read it all; I paraphrase. Some key points I pause on are: "The purpose of this class is to help you build a better understanding of the historical, cultural, and individual lived experiences of Native Americans in modern North America. We'll investigate the ways Native American writers reflect their cultural histories through their writing and listen to the voices of Native intellectuals as we work to develop a Native-centered understanding of both Native history and Indian-white relations. Many of our readings will challenge the mainstream cultural understanding of Native American identity in modern America." I ask them if they are willing to agree to some ground rules, right here, right now, on the very first day. These rules, I say, will help us navigate this material. They agree, and I give them the following rules. We will always approach the literature from a place of believing. This place of believing requires, I explain, that we always begin with the assumption that the writer knows more about what it means to be Native than we do. We will approach the literature with acceptance. That is, we will begin by accepting that the writer has a valid claim to whatever emotions he or she is offering up in their writing. And finally, we will try to approach the literature without making it about us. Then I explain that these rules will make better sense as we work through the semester and that I am asking them only to try this approach. They agree, and we move on to the policy, attendance, and typical syllabus stuff. I let them go early, knowing not all of them will return. In the next class there are eighteen students: ten suburban white students from Lincoln or Omaha; five students of color, including three Native Americans; and three white out-of-state students.

Next I ask them to watch Chimamanda Ngozi Adichie's TED Talk "The Danger of a Single Story" (2009). In her talk Ngozi Adichie discusses the idea of a meta-narrative, or a grand narrative, a term many theorists and philosophers such as Jean-François Lyotard defined as "totalizing stories about history and the goals of the human race that ground and legitimize knowledges and cultural practices" (Woodward 2005), without ever using the term *meta-narrative*. Instead, she tells the story of her younger self, narrating the way she understood a single story about a young boy who worked for her family. She understood that he was poor, and it was the only way she could define him until she went to his house and saw him in a different light. She argues that if a person knows only a single story of a people, then that is the only way they can see those people. I use Ngozi Adichie's term *single story* to ask my students to think about the meta-narrative that Americans have formed around Native Americans. She argues that by starting stories in "the middle," we make it impossible to understand the larger picture. In an effort to start the story in the beginning, we start not with Native American literature, but with representations of Native Americans.

We read accounts of Native Americans written by white people; we watch movie clips, commercials, and music videos. We watch cartoons that they loved as children, and we talk about their own experiences. Over and over again we look at the ways Native Americans are portrayed in the mainstream. Eventually, they begin to understand that the meta-narrative that most affects Native Americans is not a kind, flattering, or fair story. Instead, it is a story designed to dehumanize and trivialize folks. It is at this stage, about two weeks into the class, that I give them the first "real" piece of literature. They read Vine Deloria Jr.'s "Indians Today, the Real and Unreal" (1999). This essay takes up the issues of Indian identity and representation. At the same time, I ask the students to begin looking for Native representation on campus, in town, and near their homes.

Once we had the single story, I approach each reading with the same question: How does this writer disrupt, challenge, or reinforce the single story? It is a term we come back to over and over again. I do so in hopes of negotiating the paradox of what Linda Flower calls "contested agency." Flower defines students with contested agency as "people who stand within circles of privilege . . . [who] may also be standing in need of empowerment." She continues on to argue that students who are used to standing in circles of privilege need to be shown a different way of expressing agency, must be shown how to stand in solidarity with members of the community without speaking over those community members (Flower 2008, 216–17). In this class, contested agency is made more complex by the combination of guilt and frustration my white students feel when confronting the difficult realities we must take up in order to honor the literature we are studying. In order to give them the "capacity to speak publicly for something of value in a committed but critical way" (216) as allies, which does not encourage them to speak over or in place of Native Americans, I remind them that they did not write the single story. Our goal is to learn to recognize it so that we can stop supporting it. Through the semester I ask them to point out things they see in their daily lives that reinforce the single story.

Unit 2

The Reading

For the second writing project, we read Richard Van Camp's novel *The Lesser Blessed* (2004), which is a sharp, wonderful look at a traumatized Dogrib teenager reclaiming himself through sex, drugs, and heavy metal. I have taught this book before and found that the difficulty with it often lies in resisting the urge to "other" the characters, to simply say that "those people" are too different from me and mine or to simply reject its reality as too harsh, too ugly. Because of the nature of our national history and our present-day race relations, it is critical to acknowledge the special difficulties embedded in teaching ethnic literature. I am naturally inclined to leave these things unspoken because we (teachers, students, and people in America) are trained to not speak, not hear, and not see race, but it is not possible to discuss or reflect on the way I used place-conscious education in this class without explicating talking race. Ethnic literature is race. It is the story of race; often it is the story of injustice. Folks approach the teaching of it in many different ways; some focus on using it only as a vehicle to teach the literary arts. Here is a metaphor; here is a trope; here is an analogy; this poem uses iambic meter; and this one does not. Others take a more historical perspective—here is what happened, and here is what was written about it. And still others teach it from a sociological perspective. I chose to take up a different rhetoric, a Native rhetoric, and teach the literature through the traditions of storytelling as a mode of teaching empathy and building unity in a community. I hoped to offer each piece of literature with an invitation to the reader to embody the story, to consider how they might exist in the world of the story, and then to ask them to critique the way they embodied the story and how they might have impacted the world of the story if they lived it. Finally, I hoped to offer them a chance to ask themselves if they wanted to continue embodying these stories in the same way as they would have in the beginning of the class or if they wanted to change it.

In order to teach it this way, it was critical to consider Linda Christensen's (2009b) argument, that in any story of injustice there are four roles for the characters to take: ally, target, perpetrator, and bystander. I had to acknowledge that the stories I was planning to tell are hard stories, and no one becomes an ally without first coming to terms with their historical roles as targets and perpetrators and bystanders. This truth is unavoidable in a space devoted to stories about race in America. This truth must be laid bare in order for us to become ready to truly invest in the commonwealth. At the same time, we also have to deal with issues of agency. Who may speak is a critical question in any conversation about race. Therefore, it is critical in the Native American literature classroom, as it is in any classroom dealing with issues of race and colonization, to create space and opportunity for everyone in the room to grapple with and complicate those roles. We cannot ignore that my classroom physically exists as part of a land-grant university where three days a week we sit in a room built on the homeland of the peoples whose literatures we are studying. We cannot ignore that the university employs an ability-only admission policy instead of an open admission policy, has a specific admissions process for home-schooled students, and offers a legacy scholarship to the children and grandchildren of its graduates—but bans any kind of race-based admissions. Our relationship to literature has the potential to be a bridge that connects us to such hard stories, but it can also become a stumbling block, the elephant in the room, and the guilt monster in the closet. That relationship can hold us back from genuinely having the deeply needed conversations with such stories. By connecting them to local places (our classroom, our university, and our small suburban city), we can create a common drive to do better than those individuals who came before us, a drive to become allies with each other in service of the places we love.

With *The Lesser Blessed*, students who have experienced deep poverty or complex family structures find it easier to identify with the characters, but most of us find it difficult to find an access point into this story. Linda Christensen's (2009b) four roles become more apparent in class. Students begin to side with characters as target, perpetrator, bystander, and ally. The large majority of the class acts as bystander—some of them as judgmental bystander. They get frustrated with the writer because as one student wails, "He's proving the stereotype." Frustration stems from the dual roles we are trying to play—we are acting as witness to the story, and we are also trying to place ourselves into a story no one wants to be part of. In many ways working in the commonwealth begins with witnessing stories of injustice. Grounding ourselves in the commonwealth means figuring the role we were born to play. Investing in the commonwealth means choosing to change the role we were born into.

At the same time, we begin to research the issue of Whiteclay, Nebraska. According to the Battle for Whiteclay website:

> Whiteclay is an unincorporated village of 14 people in northwest Nebraska bordering the Pine Ridge Indian Reservation, home to the Oglala Lakota (also known as the Oglala Sioux Tribe). The Pine Ridge lies almost entirely in South Dakota.
>
> Whiteclay lies on disputed land, merely 200 feet from the official reservation border, and less than 2 miles from the center of Pine Ridge, South Dakota, the largest town on the reservation.
>
> The number of people living on the Pine Ridge has long been controversial. The 2000 census reports 15,521 residents, but in 2005 the U.S. Department of Housing and Urban Development (HUD) revised the

> figure to 28,000. The Oglala Sioux tribal government maintains that the true population of the Pine Ridge is around 40,000.
>
> Sale and possession of alcoholic beverages on the Pine Ridge is prohibited under tribal law. Except for a brief experiment with on-reservation liquor sales in the early 1970s, this prohibition has been in effect since the reservation lands were created.
>
> Whiteclay has four off-sale beer stores licensed by the State of Nebraska which sell the equivalent of 4.5 million 12-ounce cans of beer annually (12,500 cans per day), mostly to the Ogalalas living on the Pine Ridge. (2013, n.p.)

Whiteclay is a particularly difficult moment because we are faced with a situation in our backyard that is creating the conditions much like the one we are discussing in our literature. It is in these weeks that we begin to see how dangerous a single story really is. My hope is to connect these components—the frustration about the novel to the anger and outrage about Whiteclay. I hope to connect the uncertainty of our own roles to empathy and then to transform it into a desire to speak for Nebraska as a place and as a people who are better than Whiteclay.

The Writing

STEP 1: PERSONIFICATION POEM

> For this project you will use poetry to help you better understand the characters of *The Lesser Blessed.* Personification poems are types of verse in which inanimate or nonhuman objects are given human attributes. For example, "The wheat danced to the beat of the distant thunder." Clearly, everyone knows wheat can't dance, but it has been given human qualities for the purposes of this unique and entertaining poetic form.
>
> For this poem you will pick the characteristic, such as pride, courage, love, that best describes your favorite character and personify that characteristic.

Because this assignment came after the photo essay, my students' writing reflects a willingness to read these characters with empathy and to read them outside of the single story of Native Americans. I do not believe my students would have written the same poems if they had not begun to find their own voices and explore their own responses to the injustices they were seeing in the literature and in our home spaces. These poems are about characters that my students could imagine being, could imagine living next door to, imagine loving, not about "others," not "those people," not stereotypes. The poems, in many ways, speak for themselves.

Ambition: Juliet

By Lexi Cudmore

(Juliet is the female lead. She is young white woman who has survived sexual abuse and who is part of a love triangle with the two male leads. In class, we spend a day discussing the Violence Against Women act and the ways it does and does not protect indigenous women. We talk about rape, abuse, and poverty. We talk about slut shaming. At one point a male student points out with disgust and anger "this is just easier for people to deal with if they can blame her." The room falls silent as we digest this truth.)

Ambition is Fort Simmer's high school skank
Ambition's reputation is corrupt
She encourages it by drinking her sorrows away, acting as if the lies
  don't exist
Ambition is hurt but no one sees, she drinks until the pain goes numb
Ambition carries an odor of sour sting in her breath, with a cigarette in
  one hand,
And a joint in the other
Ambition desires the lust and fantasizes the love
Ambition sacrifices her body as it is to barter
Ambition teases Romance, and gives the Goon what he craves
Ambition is the pure, white caribou, she has the face of an angel,
Porcelain skin and magical lips
Ambition is beautiful . . .

In these poems my students not only offer a solid character analysis, but are also clearly viewing the characters with a great deal of empathy, even though it would be easy to fall into the default response to this story. Over and over again my students show a willingness to write about these characters from a place of empathy.

Humor: Donny

By Michael Menish

(Donny is a young Native boy, six or seven, who is already deeply scared by abuse, neglect, and poverty; it is this character that draws the most frustration and anger from the class. Why is his mother allowed to keep him? Where are the authorities? Somebody should be held responsible. A heated debate breaks out about mothers' and their role and responsibility. "It's not just her fault. It is her fault, yeah, but not all of it, why does she have to do it all by herself?" We leave early that day.)

Humor protects his broken heart
Scars left by neglect, abuse
burns from the damn cigarettes
she let them extinguish on his hands
Diminish with laughter
Humor creates barriers to prevent more pain
Humor cracks a joke to try and look tough
Maybe then, things will be alright
Humor minimalizes others to make himself look strong
Humor is smart, unwilling to show it
Messing with the other kids to show who's top dog
Finally feels powerful, in control, putting others down
Maybe they'll know what Humor's been through
Humor shields
Can't look weak in front of his brother
Dad won't come if he thinks we're weak
He won't love us like she doesn't love us
If Humor doesn't keep a brave face
He'll be stuck in this hell forever

Part of the success of these poems is owing to the fact that poetry automatically shifts our perspective away from the impersonal, objective, academic voice we are used to using in the classroom. However, the success is also owing to the fact that in preparation for this work, we wrote about our own families. We wrote "Where I am from" poems and drew deep maps of the places we loved best. We wrote about our histories and wrote about discrimination, hate, pain, and misperception in our own lives.

STEP 2: STORYTELLING

> The goal of this assignment is to connect the current issue in Whiteclay, Nebraska, to *The Lesser Blessed*. Please consider the impact a town like Whiteclay, with the same business practices as Whiteclay, has on the lives of the people it touches. The goal is not to argue for or against Whiteclay or to take a political stance but to explore the human cost of business practices we see in Whiteclay. You will take on the voice of your favorite character from *Lesser Blessed* and rewrite their story. You will begin by placing your character next door to a fictional town based on Whiteclay, Nebraska.

Consider these questions:

- How has addiction affected the characters in our book?
- What effect might it have on teenagers?
- How might it affect children?
- What would your parents do if they lived next door to Whiteclay?
- Consider your initial response to the Whiteclay readings or *The Lesser Blessed* and "speak" back to it. Do you still feel the same way? Why or why not? What changed your mind? What do you think now?

Most of the students choose to begin their stories where *Lesser Blessed* left off but change the location of their character to Whiteclay. We become political, exploring through fiction the politics of Whiteclay, a place in our state, a place we choose to not see most of the time. We explore the way it impacts characters we care about. We get angry when we cannot imagine or write or pretend good outcomes for our characters in that place. Suicide, addiction, loss, pain, and failure haunt these stories, even though we are trying to write happy endings. We do not learn to write good poetry or good fiction in this unit, but we begin to think about the literature and about issues in our own state that reflect the same issues and themes we find in the literature in a language that is focused on character, on the human element of the story. We discover the human cost of the alcohol business in Whiteclay, Nebraska. We can move into an earnest conversation about human rights.

> [This short story by Olivia Johnson depicts the life and death of the character Juliet at the end of the book. In this version Juliet moves to Edmonton, which becomes like Whiteclay for the sake of the story, to be with family and to try to raise her daughter.]

Goodbye, Edmonton

I wasn't expecting the town to be perfect by any means. In fact, I had heard it was a rough place. And my aunt—well let's just say she was exactly like my mom, except she drank *more* (if that's even possible). I didn't mind her drinking though, because it meant she was always hanging around one of Edmonton's three liquor stores, and I had the house to myself. Being alone so much got lonely, though. I often thought about Johnny, which only made me angry. If he hadn't bailed on me everything might be different. I might not be here. . . . One afternoon I couldn't take the depression anymore. I had to find something to stop the pain. All I wanted was something to give me some relief, *just* for a moment. All I needed was a little bit of time to calm down and think things out. That's all I needed.

I went outside into the garage. My aunt kept a second fridge out there for her alcohol. The stash was usually in low supply, which is why she was generally at the bar. It was freezing outside, and I knew I shouldn't be going out there. Hell, the only reason I knew she kept booze out there was because I opened the fridge out of curiosity one day.

"Don't get any closer to the fridge, Juliet. You're *pregnant*. You can't have alcohol. Just wait a few more months and then you can drink again."

> My mind raced every direction. I had already made it to the garage. The cold pavement was freezing my feet. I had made it this far, so I might as well just check to see if there was anything in the fridge. If there wasn't, I could just go back inside. I opened the door and there was one Hurricane on the top shelf. Without another thought I grabbed it and went back inside. What I didn't know was that I was beginning my worst battle yet.
>
> I couldn't even last a few hours after I'd drank it. Once I had that taste again I couldn't stop. I felt like a different person, zoned out from reality. When the buzz dulled, I had to have more. Why couldn't there have been just one more in the fridge? I had heard rumors that the stores downtown sold to minors. I had no choice. I put on my coat and boots and went out the door. I didn't even stop to think about the baby.
>
> Well, the rumors were true. All I had to do was smile nice and bat my eyelashes real pretty and a brown paper sack with a 6-pack in it was mine. It wasn't even until later that I stopped to realize that the salesman had to have noticed my pregnant belly. Businesses will do anything for a sale I guess.

Speaking

The biggest difficulty in this unit is in finding ways to nuance or even disregard what we, the dominant culture, see as normal. This issue becomes particularly poignant as we discuss motherhood. In the student sample above, Juliet drinks her baby to stillbirth and then commits suicide. In the last paragraph she denounces the town and the businessmen for their part in killing her baby. This taps into some core issues for marginalized peoples. In a world where good parenting is marked by how much time we spend with our children, folks who lack the privilege that allows us to do so are vilified, particularly mothers. In the book we have three mothers, one who has given up and is allowing her sons to attempt to raise each other; another who is going to college, which takes her away from her son; and Juliet, who sees motherhood as a way out of her cycle of self-destruction. It takes a great deal of conversation in order for my students to see any of these mothers as good mothers. Over and over again I hear how good parenting is "paying attention" or "being there." Finally, I offer up the suggestion that, in a place where hope is almost nonexistent, perhaps the greatest gift a mother can give her children is the hope of a better future, even if it means she cannot "be there" or "pay attention." The student stories, at the end of the unit, revolve around hope—the lack of it and attempts to regain it, while living in the shadow of a place like Whiteclay.

The Final Project

In the final unit we imagine and design our own projects. The only requirement is that the project be something that we can present to the public as part of the discourse of Native American literature. Together we negotiate the ways the projects will meet research and page requirements, and every project is different. Many students are attracted to the immediate audience offered by the Internet and choose memes, blogs, or Tumblrs. One student creates a series of memes. His full project includes a photo essay that discusses the rhetorical choices he made as he designed the memes, the writers that influenced his work, and his hopes for the project. He writes: "For my final project I have created a series of five memes. . . . Memes on the internet are meant to poke fun at cultural aspects and behaviors. . . . Although some knowledge of history about what Native American people have endured would be helpful in fully understanding and interpreting these memes it is not critical. A major component of a meme is the simplicity of it. To me, the simpler the meme the funnier it is and more critical it is of the subject."

Others play to their strengths by thinking about how they can bring what they learned in this class into their other classes or majors. Those students who are interested in becoming educators are particularly interested in taking what they learn into their future work. Over and over the projects show a genuine desire to pass what they learn in class on to people in the larger community.

> My final project can be found at: http://nativeamericanstoday.tumblr.com/.
>
> (Olivia Johnson)
>
> My Tumblr account has worked really well for my final project. I debated over a theme, but decided on breaking the "one story,"

specifically the misconception that Native Americans aren't around today. I chose this theme because it's the one I'm most passionate about and one I think the world needs to know more about.

My first entry in my Tumblr blog is called "What is the One Story, Anyway?" It's filled with background information and it gives me my purpose for creating the blog. I relied mostly on information I recalled from class discussions, plus information from http://www.shadowwolf.org/misconceptions.html. The first resource I offer readers is the Ted Talk we watched in class since it gives such a great overview. The second resource I offer is Vine Deloria's *Custer Died for Your Sins*, particularly "Indians Today, the Real and Unreal." I really liked this reading because it discusses what the culture is actually about, while pointing out the false things.

My second entry is titled "The Rez in Lincoln, NE." It's all about redefining the popular tailgating site near campus. I think this entry is important because every one on campus knows "The Rez" but I doubt very many know what the "Indian Center" is. My purpose is to inform readers that this common drinking spot is about a lot more than partying. The first resource I offer in the entry is to the Indian Center's website, which gives a complete rundown of the purpose of the center, as well as a lot of great pictures to show Native culture in action. The second resource I offer is Diane Burns' "Sure You Can Ask Me a Personal Question." This is one of my favorite readings from the semester. I thought it was appropriate for this entry because it's about being a Native American living in a world where people act like the culture doesn't exist anymore.

My third entry is titled "Thanksgiving: The Holiday Exposed." The purpose of this entry is to give readers a more realistic view of the holiday, including the history and how to celebrate it respectfully. I thought the entry was pertinent because I wrote it the week of Thanksgiving. The first resource I give is a link to a really great article by Jacqueline Keller that gives a more accurate history of the holiday. The second resource I provide is a link to an article designed for school teachers. I think it applies to this entry because it provides good tips for everyone on how to educate others about the truth about the holiday.

My fourth entry is titled "Modern Issues & Modern Stories." I explore the issue of Whiteclay in this entry. I try to give a good overview of the issues surrounding the town, designed for someone who knows nothing about it to begin with. I provide a few resources for readers, including the "Battle for Whiteclay" documentary on YouTube. I think this video gives excellent background and present day information about the issue. It also delves into the attempted legislation to correct the issue. Another resource I give is a link to purchase "The Lesser Blessed," as well as a link to a quick synopsis about the book. I think this book explores a lot of the real modern issues surrounding Native American spaces, even though it's a fictional book. At the end of the entry I also cite one of the Whiteclay articles, which is an additional resource for readers.

My final entry is titled "The Pop Culture Problem." I look at some of the big controversies in pop culture like the No Doubt video and the Victoria's Secret Fashion Show. There have been so many issues with pop culture I could've compiled an endless list. The first resource I offer is an article by Walter C. Fleming that takes a really good approach to breaking stereotypes built by pop culture. Mr. Fleming is a professor in the Department of Native American studies at the University of Montana. I think his article does a much better job than I could do explaining the flaws in the way society thinks of Native Americans. The second resource I give in the entry is a link to buy Silko's *Ceremony.* I think *Ceremony* works with this issue because it looks at the roles of Native Americans and Whites, and their roles in the world. I also wanted to recommend this book at some point in my blog because I enjoyed reading it so much.

I also included some pictures along the way. I have really enjoyed compiling this blog and have been able to gain some Tumblr followers along the way. Some interesting people have followed my blog, which must mean they took the time to read my articles and liked what they saw! I think this proves that people are interested in hearing insightful things about Native Americans. It will be interesting to see if I continue to gain new followers.

The one common requirement for each of these projects is that the students have to create a resource list. They are asked to create lists of Native or local writers, artists, and activists to offer to their audiences. We attempt to focus on what Native members of our community are saying about the issues we are taking up instead of speaking for them. This assignment is one of the most useful exercises of the semester. In searching for Native folks who are speaking about these issues, we can clearly see how complex the community is, and occasionally, when no Native voices agree with a stance or claim, it offers an opportunity to illuminate the reasons the Native community is in disagreement with the stance or claim. We are engaged in dialogue.

The final project is the hardest for all of us. Many of the projects are more ambitious than we realized, and in many cases we struggle and even fail at getting the results we hoped for, particularly those students who envisioned invading public space in a way that would create a public reaction. Poster and art projects fail to draw audiences; Facebook pages fail to draw comments or reactions. Many of our projects are simply not seen by the public. Even though most projects do a great job considering what it means to take an issue to a public space, it is difficult for us to use that space effectively. We suddenly find ourselves in a new role. We are no longer on the outside looking at the Indian in the window. We are the Indian in the window, and our fellow community members are walking past us without meeting our eyes or stopping to ask questions. Online, we have trouble envisioning our audience or accounting for the amount of information our audience will need to engage with our projects. We struggle to meet the goals we set and find that the projects we envisioned are harder to produce than we anticipated. We run out of time. We run out of energy. In many ways, the projects that struggle impart the final lesson of any place conscious–based classroom: creating rhetorical space is hard; getting people to listen is hard; working for social justice is hard—but we do it because we are deeply invested in living well in the places we love, the places we call home. If, in fact, the American suburban landscape is spreading and growing, morphing and changing, then it is even more important than ever for all of us to invest in the commonwealth of our communities, to commit to living well, living sustainably, and to commit to speaking with those members of our communities who face social injustice. It's not because we are somehow outside of that injustice, but because we all exist within that commonwealth and we are all part of this ongoing story.

After Class

Place-conscious teaching appeals to me because mine was a migratory childhood and mine is a life still in transition. It appeals to me because I am still searching for a place of my own. I am indigenous Mexican American. My people are some of the first people to live on this continent. We have been displaced, pushed out, and marginalized. We have no family farms; we have no city streets named after grandfathers who achieved the American Dream. I am the newest manifestation of the migration story. I have amassed some cultural capital, I am building a life that will be more financially secure than my mother's, but my chosen profession will eventually put my feet back on the road to the next house, the next neighborhood, the next town, the next state. Many people like me build homes in suburban spaces. It is crucial for me and people like me to be seen by the dominant community because we live in those contact zones that are so carefully hidden by all that glass and landscaping. Place-conscious teaching can help build the kind of solidarity that facilitates a healthy, thriving commonwealth, and a healthy, thriving commonwealth is deeply beneficial to any community.

It is critical, I think, to view the suburban space from "the long now" perspective. The term *the long now* comes from the Long Now Foundation (1996), a collaboration of intellectuals who argue that we have become pathologically shortsighted in our ways of thinking about everything. They argue that we no longer think about the next fifty or a hundred years; we no longer work on long-term projects. Instead, everything is counted in seconds, minutes, and days. It began with a member, Stewart Brand (1996), who, after hearing computer scientist Daniel Hillis, proposed a long-term project that included building a clock that "ticks once a year, bongs once a century, and the cuckoo comes out every millennium." The foundation hopes to encourage people to think of the long now through projects including a clock that, like the pyramids, will stand on its own long after its makers have passed on. A long-now perspective demands that we look to the commonwealth as a starting point in the discussion of sustainability (Long Now Foundation 1996).

By becoming aware of the long-existing histories and cultures of our local spaces, place-conscious education acts to create exigency, a desire and need, to speak to the concerns and issues that were once hidden. Place-conscious education locates us in our physical space and asks us to resee that space as a citizen. By shifting our view to the microcosms of society that our neighborhoods often represent, we are encouraged to critically consider the public work of being a responsible and contributing member of that microcosm and, by extension, larger society.

By asking our students to explore the commonwealth and to take a long-now perspective of all of the experiences and stories we find there, we can encourage and sustain habits of the mind that can develop into rich and fertile ground for both community literacy and social justice work. Teaching Native American stories to suburban white students, many who do not even realize that they are part of a culture that continues to benefit from national policies that include cultural genocide, broken treaties, and historically traumatic relations with Native Americans, is no small thing. Place-conscious teaching offers me a small patch of common ground where we can begin and acts as a place to recenter when it is needed. Place-conscious teaching offers me a way to serve all of my students no matter which of Christensen's roles they embody upon entering the class. It gives me a way to navigate the issue of contested agency by redirecting our speech and writing so that no one in the room is speaking for the other; instead, we are all speaking for the places we love.

Afterword

Place-Conscious Education in an Age of Assessment

ROBERT E. BROOKE

Now that you have reached the end of this book, we hope our presentation of watershed and commonwealth projects in suburban schools has helped convince you of the following big ideas:

- It is possible to link school projects to community issues, at least across the English curriculum.
- A place-conscious approach to learning helps students become more active and engaged citizens of their local community, often acting as community members in their own right.
- Place-conscious learning has the potential to combat the migratory and isolationist tendencies of suburban living.

If you have followed our collective argument thus far, you have seen how a variety of classroom projects have the potential to develop student citizenship while still meeting the curricular goals of the specific class. From these examples, we hope you can imagine the possibility of widespread place-conscious education and the different kind of civic life that might result from it.

In this afterword, we want to help you with that imagined possibility by taking on the main obstacle to place-conscious education in our national culture: the push for national standards, a core curriculum, and routine assessment of student achievement on standardized tests. These three elements of the "assessment reform movement" make up the main challenge to place-conscious education in the current national consciousness. The assessment movement is the elephant in the room as far as place-conscious education goes. If we do not address it, we cannot move forward.

In this afterword, we want to make three points:

- The push for national standards and a core curriculum is antithetical to a place-conscious vision of education. As educators, we need to recognize the differing visions of the cultural goal of education clearly so we can make our choices. National standards and a core curriculum serve a migratory, placeless model of education serving a largely migratory business sector. By contrast, a place-conscious education system serves an educational model of an active citizenry.
- In our experience, local communities themselves value the opportunities of place-conscious connection. Place-conscious education is a way to bring the people of the community back to school and give new vitality to education.
- In an era of assessment excess (like the one we live in now), the place-conscious alternative to teaching to the test is "meeting and exceeding" the existing standards. This educational maneuver is the activist hope for place-conscious education.

Rethinking the Assessment Agenda

There is no way to sugarcoat this point: place-conscious educators and the national standards assessment agenda offer radically different views of the purpose of education. At some level, educators, policy members, and parents will have to choose between them.

In a nutshell, place-conscious education views the purpose of education as the creation of a sustainable, informed, contributing *local citizenry*. Place-conscious educators strive to develop young people who contribute to their local communities, understand the natural and cultural forces that shape and challenge those communities, and have the rhetorical skills to engage in the vibrant local debates that imagine and create a sustainable, thriving future. By contrast, the current national standards assessment agenda views the purpose of education as the creation of *a migratory workforce*. This workforce will be, in the words of the Common Core State Standards Initiative (2014), "college and career ready." One of the core planks in the standards and assessment agenda is that essential skills are contextless—in the new global workforce, what matters is that the individual has the ability and knowledge to do the job, wherever that job is located and whoever the hiring authority is.

Diane Ravitch, the Bush-era advocate for school reform turned preeminent critic of the standards and assessment movement, identifies the problems with the current reform movement in geographical terms. She sees the current reform agenda of standards, assessment, and school choice as promoting a different geographical form of public education:

> The "reform movement" . . . seeks to eliminate the geographically based system of public education as we have known it for the past 150 years and replace it with a competitive market-based system of school choice—one that includes traditional public schools, privately managed charter schools, religious schools, voucher schools, for-profit schools, virtual schools, and for-profit vendors of instruction. Lacking any geographic boundaries, these schools would compete for customers. The customers would choose to send their children and their public funding wherever they wish, based on personal preference or on information such as the schools' test scores and a letter grade conferred by the state (based largely on test scores). (2013, 19–20)

For Ravitch, there is a direct connection between "standardized test scores" and the reform movement's attack on "the geographically based system of public education." The purpose of standardized tests is to allow comparison between schools anywhere, because the same material is covered. The specifics of local place, and local citizenship in that place, drop away. As she points out, the move to standardized tests and curriculum means, finally, that the design of education does not even need to happen in our nation at all: "[The Gates Foundation] supported the creation, evaluation, and promotion of the Common Core State Standards. . . .

In addition, the Gates Foundation has joined in a partnership with the British publisher Pearson to develop online curriculum for teaching the Common Core standards" (23). When a multinational publishing firm, located in Great Britain, can design a curriculum to be delivered online to any state in the American Union, we have clearly reached an educational agenda where local place consciousness does not matter at all.

Ravitch's critiques of the assessment-based "reform movement" in our country are supported by a healthy range of other scholars. Paul Gorski and Kristien Zenkov's 2014 collection, *The Big Lies of School Reform*, for example, gathers the critiques of twelve nationally recognized scholars, all of whom address the curious mythologies of the current reform movement. The book takes on several of the "big lies" of current educational reform, including the achievement gap, the Common Core, the evils of teachers' unions, Teach for America, and federal School Improvement Grants for turnaround policies for school. Central to the book's argument are these claims:

1. that the testing movement sees the problem as "low standards" for schools, rather than systemic issues of poverty in the communities surrounding schools;
2. that the testing movement sees a market-driven "business model" solution for education rather than a humanitarian "whole citizen" solution; and
3. that the testing movement is not research based, has been proven *not* to work in other countries, and hence is a sham that cannot achieve the ends proposed for it.

Some of the exciting findings from the book:

- Early returns for Common Core tests in Kentucky showed a 30 percent *decrease* in proficiency levels in the first two years (Cody 2014, 37).
- The "skills gap" for college-educated workers in our country, so central to Common Core's "college and career readiness," is "a myth."

Bureau of Labor Statistics projections of job openings in 2018 suggest 23 percent of all jobs will require a college degree, while 67 percent will require a high school diploma or less (Cody 2014, 36).

- The Journey for Justice Alliance (2014) has filed Title VI complaints against policies and practices for school closing. They argue that these practices are "discriminatory" in much the same ways as the segregation policies of decades past (Renée and Trujillo, 2014, 161).
- Teach for America retention rates are only 10–15 percent after four years in New York and Houston and overall 27.8 percent after five years—compare this number to more than 50 percent teacher retention from traditional education programs after five years (Zenkov 2014, 88).
- Finland, the poster-child country for school reform (going from poor performance to very high performance in a very short time), has done so *with no high-stakes standardized tests at all.* Instead, teachers have to have master's degrees and are highly paid, unionized, and respected. Public schools are well funded, and there are no private schools (Au 2014, 148).

Summarizing this material, editor Paul Gorski cites "the mother of all lies" in school reform: "that we can equalize educational opportunity and outcomes without addressing fundamental economic inequalities in the United States and its schools" (2014, 130). He sees poverty, not low standards, as the fundamental problem facing American education. He points out that a core curriculum and a battery of high-stakes tests are unlikely to address communities of poverty. Instead, he offers a list of "things we can do right now" to address poverty in local communities. His list is interesting, for two reasons. First, he points out that schools in wealthier communities already provide these things (although he does not say so, we suspect he is thinking of many suburban schools in this comparison). Second, most of the items on his list imply a healthy interface between the local school and the surrounding community—suggesting that many of the "things we can do right now" are place-conscious things.

- Incorporate movement pedagogies and other opportunities for exercise across the curriculum;
- Adopt higher-order, learner-centered, inquiry-driven, rigorous pedagogies;
- Incorporate the arts, including visual and performing arts, into the curriculum;
- Make the curriculum relevant to the lives of students in poverty;
- Analyze and encourage students to analyze learning materials for bias;
- Make opportunities for on-site school involvement accessible to parents and guardians who are most likely to work evenings, to not have paid leave, and to struggle to pay for child care;
- Fight to protect dedicated nurse positions. (138)

Clearly, Gorski's ideas for direct work on poverty share much with the suggestions for place-conscious education in this book. A curriculum "relevant to the lives of students" is almost by definition a place-conscious curriculum. The opportunities for adult involvement, for movement and the arts, for inquiry-driven analysis of bias—all sound like the active, community-engaged, local inquiry–based projects offered by the teachers in this book.

It is useful to see, in such stark contrast, alternative agendas for education laid out for us. Clearly, the preponderance of evidence is that the "reform agenda" of high-stakes tests, common curricula, and school "choice" is an agenda that is not attentive to local citizenry in local place. In Gorski's words, it is an agenda that "deflects attention away" (130) from important features of local community life.

Given these stark contrasts, it is important that place-conscious educators become aware of the need to present place-conscious teaching as an alternative. It is important to be able to articulate our different goals for education. It is important to be able to critique the reform movement, using some of the arguments collected here. And, in some contexts, it may be important to direct parents and community members to the many "opt out of testing" options legally available to them in most states. (See, for example, the resources for opting out on FairTest: The National Center for Fair and Open Testing 2014.)

The Local Value of Place-Conscious Education

Curiously for an era of assessment, suburban schools and communities seem eager to support place-conscious projects. As we have worked on this book and the pedagogical projects offered in it, we have been struck over and over again by the interest shown in our work by school officials, community members, parents, and local community agencies. When presented with educational programs that connect school to local community, many adults in the community seem thrilled—and seem to sense that this work is the work that schools should be doing.

In this section three of our authors (Daniel Boster, Mary Birky Collier, and Cathie English) provide examples of their experiences with the wider community surrounding place-conscious projects. All three articulate a deep sense of community appreciation for their work. As one of our teacher research group explained, "When students actively and successfully claim public space in their communities, administrators have no choice but to be proud!"

Daniel Boster

Like most public school teachers, much of the work that I do with students is guided by an institutionalized curriculum developed by teams of teachers in my high school's English Department and then approved by the school board. In effect, then, all American literature teachers in the building teach basically the same materials and use some shared assessments. Although we vary in teaching style and may put emphasis on certain texts based on personal interest or knowledge, we all have to "get through" the "units" in about the same amount of time.

In addition, since I teach at a public school in an "accountability-driven" era focused on standardized assessment, there is pressure to prepare students to do well on these assessments. While most teachers at Ralston High School do not spend all of their time "teaching to the test," we do spend a lot of time delivering instruction that is designed to help students on Nebraska Department of Education assessments as well as college entrance exams such as the ACT.

However, I have also found that there is actually a great deal of support within my school district for a teacher to develop nontraditional learning activities with, and for, students. During my years at Ralston High School, I have done all I can to create authentic learning experiences for my students. As I teacher, I have been given the freedom to do things like the Columbus project reported in this book because I have fostered cooperative relationships with building and district administrators. I engage them in conversations to make sure they understand that I am advocating for students and am conscious of their desire to make sure that students are learning and are being prepared for assessment even while engaged in unorthodox learning activities.

In fact, during the project I write about in my chapter, I interviewed Dr. Kristi Gibbs, Ralston Public Schools superintendent of curriculum and learning, and asked her about the value of such projects. Even considering her responsibility to make sure Ralston students are prepared for assessments, Dr. Gibbs believes in such projects because they "foster collaboration" and "allow students to develop skills rather than simply the ability to recall content." She believes that projects like this one actually allow for more "authentic literacy experiences" that will "undoubtedly help them on assessments." Dr. Gibbs also expressed an appreciation for the fact that this project allowed the community, through local media coverage, to see teachers and students working together in a way that could become "a model for our community." She especially valued that the community was able to see teenagers "acting out community values of collaboration and communication."

Moreover, in addition to this project with students and teachers in my district, I have been able to recruit the help of people in the larger Omaha community to work with my students. In addition to this project, I have also collaborated with teachers at other schools to develop poetry festivals and a community social justice reading group that involved students from six high schools. I mention these activities to make the point that they have involved the voluntary efforts of many local activists, writers, and artists. I am always amazed by how willing people are to work with high school students. I have been able to find many allies who are willing to engage with high school students and encourage their desire to do something outside of the walls of their classrooms.

Mary Birky Collier

One of the most rewarding aspects of our place-conscious work was and is the "real" impact students see their writing having, as well as the ways their writing—and ultimately what happens in the often unseen school classroom—was valued by community stakeholders. One student's poem was selected for recognition in our statewide Poetry of Place Celebration, which then led to his reading for the district school board. One of the school board members, also a well-known local minister, used the poem in his sermon, giving even further exposure to student writing about our suburban place. Our local newspaper also quickly snatched up two letters to the editor written in our place-conscious work, and other students received quick responses from community stakeholders such as the city mayor's office and the superintendent of schools for our entire district.

Yearly, students continue to be selected for the annual Poetry of Place Celebration, which includes publication on the Poetry of Place website (n.d.). More students have their work published in literary magazines at the local and national levels.

Rather than leaning on test scores published in the local newspapers as ways of informing the public, making real-student thinking and writing visible and available—not only for information but also for celebration—seems a much more accurate way of informing our stakeholders about the significant work that goes on in our public schools.

Three years into our place-conscious project, my teaching assignment changed. Although I continue to teach the AP/Dual Enrollment course where I maintain significant teaching freedom, my Creative Writing course was replaced with the English 11—American Literature course required for all juniors at our school. As is the case for many public school teachers, my teaching for that course is driven by "common assessments"—teaching to them, assessing student performance, reporting assessment scores to stakeholders, analyzing those scores, and revising our teaching strategies accordingly. All of it seems particularly ironic in light of "American literature" as an obvious place to do significant place-conscious work.

In addition, I am repeatedly struck by the contrasts in level of student engagement between my AP and English 11 courses. In AP Literature, where we are freer to use critical approaches to literature like place-based inquiry, students write simply *more*, along with more intensity and engagement with their work and its clear connections to their lives. In contrast, a sort of resigned lethargy from English 11 students accompanies most of the work we do toward completing assessments.

This contrast is also reflected at the school-district administration level in terms of professional development philosophy. About ten years ago, before the full-on pressure of assessment scores, district-level administrators brought in the Nebraska Writing Project Institutes, where teachers yearly focused on their own development as writers and, in turn, their development as teachers of writing. Statewide writing scores improved, and numerous teachers evaluated the Nebraska Writing Project Institutes as providing the most significant professional development in their teaching careers. However, with the almost singular focus on assessment scores, professional development is now mostly narrowly focused toward improving assessment scores.

However, it is my work with place-conscious education that has shone a brighter light on the deficits of assessment-driven curriculum and has given me the tools to act, one step at a time, in the midst of assessment frenzy, to find small ways to help students slow down, notice, reflect, question, and shape our suburban place.

Cathie English

One of the greatest opportunities that arose through our class investigation of the dominant work in Aurora, Nebraska, was the connection we made with community members. In our work with local farmers, we received several letters from farmers expressing their gratitude for an opportunity to share their stories, including Ardean Andersen, who wrote, "Thanks to you and your students for the privilege of being included in your class project. . . . [I]t must have been quite a challenge for young people to come out to interview total strangers about their perceptions of what our life is really about." Others noted this same sense of privilege about working with students, noting that it was valuable to bring students into adults' lives and vocations. Adult workers also wanted students to see them as friends, mentors, and "people" like themselves. Many of them noted that they loved to communicate with young people and were willing to help out in any way.

My students' work in Aurora became a matter of community pride. After our work ethnographies and oral histories (and subsequent digital stories), I was contacted by other farmers who wanted to have their stories preserved. Additionally, I was asked if my students would conduct interviews with several local business owners, including sisters who had begun their own business many years ago and had several employees who had interesting stories to tell. The most recent investigation my students made into the poverty and hunger of Hamilton County elicited responses from many of the community's nonprofit organizations that were grateful to us for promoting their organizations (and a community need) through our investigation and subsequent creation of promotional videos.

Our administration was very supportive of our work ethnographies and digital storytelling project. Students attended school board meetings to present their work and to explain what they had learned from the experiences. We were supported quite well by our technology director, who created a space on our school district website for the many digital stories we created over the years. The school district also supported my classroom with the technological tools necessary for successful digital products, including tape recorders, cameras, and software. Other instructors were also supportive when students needed the hallway or a quiet classroom to complete their work. All in all, many community members were involved in the success of our students' learning.

The Common Core State Standards Initiative (2014) expects teachers to use a common set of teaching strategies and methods to understand the process of writing certain types of texts: argument, information, and narrative. Place-based writing can be aligned to the Common Core standards in writing because the investigation of local place through inquiry may elicit texts that may argue, inform, or tell a story. Using my own example of investigating the dominant work of a community, students first asked that essential inquiry question, "How has the nature of work changed in our locale?" They needed to know how it had changed by constructing questions and then conducting interviews so they could write multigenerational narratives about their own and family members' occupations. Once they had written the work ethnographies, they sought information from one adult worker to gather information about what his or her work actually looked like and wrote an explanatory (informational) text from their research gathering. Finally, students were able to analyze the data we collected over the multiple generations to make an argument or claim about the nature of work based upon the evidence in their data.

If the Common Core State Standards are written as broad interpretations, then teachers should be able to include place-conscious writing into their curriculum with ease. If students need practice in these forms of writing to pass a statewide test, then place-conscious inquiry and writing is the ultimate model in several genres. Currently, at Missouri State University where I teach English education, we are a part of the US Department of Education's i3 grant, Investing in Innovation, which is subcontracted through the National Writing Project as the College Ready Writers Program. Teachers in two rural districts, Monett and Laquey, Missouri, utilize our Ozarks Writing Project library that includes Gretchen Bernabei (2005), Jeff Anderson (2005), Jim Burke (2010), Kelly Gallagher (2011), George Hillocks Jr. (2011), and Harvey Daniels and Nancy Steineke (2011)—all teachers of writing who understand how to align the Common Core State Standards to a writing curriculum. Recently, after a visit for a professional development session at Laquey, a teacher asked for a copy of *Rural Voices* (Brooke 2003) so she could investigate ways to conduct place-conscious inquiry that would elicit student writing that aligns with the Common Core standards. Teachers in both schools have participated in graduate courses or workshops where they have developed place-conscious units around ecological issues (Missouri waterways and state parks) or developing arguments based upon a local historical event (the closing of the Springfield, Missouri, Zenith television factory).

The Activist Place-Conscious Agenda: Meeting and Exceeding State and National Standards

It is all well and good to indicate, as we have, that place-conscious education provides an alternative to the standardized assessment movement and that community adults actually value place-conscious projects. Even so, many teachers face in their schools the looming reality of standardized assessment. In our work with kindergarten through college educators through the Nebraska Writing Project, we regularly hear stories of administrators so frightened of low test scores that they ask whole departments to teach to the test. We also hear stories of departments where a standardized curriculum aimed narrowly at test preparation is presented to teachers as something that must be followed. We know that teachers at all levels need strategies for speaking back to these concerns.

In our work developing place-conscious units for our classes, we have routinely drawn on three strategies for managing the reality of state standards and their tests.

- We have connected our place-conscious units to the state and national standards that they meet, so we can show administrators which state goals the project is addressing.
- We have also connected our place-conscious units to additional alternative standards proposed by our appropriate professional organizations (National Council of the Teachers of English 2013; Conference on College Composition and Communication 2009; National Council of the Teachers of English/International Reading Association 2009; International Society of Technology Educators 2014). This work shows administrators how the project is "exceeding" the state's standards.
- We have also devoted some class time to direct and active "teaching to the test," such as Nebraska's Statewide Writing Assessment, so

> that our students know what to expect, are prepared, and are likely to succeed.

Using these three strategies, we have been able to make the case for place-conscious projects across the grade levels.

For example, consider Daniel Boster's eleventh grade Columbus teaching project. In that project, students read textbook material from Columbus's journal and an excerpt from Howard Zinn's *A People's History of the United States, 1492–Present* (1980). They conversed with each other, with the curriculum specialist at Ralston, and with the sixth grade teacher. They developed a set of teaching items, ranging from discussion prompts to a reworked version of the game of Life, for the sixth graders. They taught. They reflected.

The Nebraska Department of Education has just this year published new language-arts standards (2014). Nebraska is not a Common Core state, opting for local control of its standards. As part of the political process of opting out of Common Core, our state has had two outside agencies run a comparison of our standards to the Common Core. These agencies have found the Nebraska standards "equally rigorous and in some cases more rigorous" than Common Core.

Boster's class project does not address all the grade 11–12 language-arts standards—no single project would—but the student work does connect with several of the most demanding reading, writing, speaking, and reciprocal communication tasks. Here are a few that map on to the project:

LA 12.1.6.k (Reading)—Select text for a particular purpose, citing evidence to support analysis, reflection, or research.

LA 12.1.6.n (Reading)—Formulate and justify inferences with text evidence while previewing, reading, and analyzing literary and informational text in various formats.

LA 12.2.1.g (Writing)—Adjust writing processes to persevere in short and long term writing tasks of increasing length and complexity.

LA 12.2.2.a (Writing)—Communicate information and ideas effectively in analytic, descriptive, informative, narrative, poetic, and reflective modes to multiple audiences using a variety of media and formats.

LA12.2.2.e (Writing)—Analyze various mentor texts and/or exemplars in order to create a similar piece.

LA 12.3.1.f (Speaking)—Anticipate and address alternative or opposing perspectives when appropriate to the mode of speaking.

LA 12.3.3.e (Reciprocal Communication)—Collaboratively converse with peers and adults on grade-appropriate topics and texts, building on other's ideas to clearly and persuasively express one's own views while respecting diverse perspectives.

As this exercise makes clear, place-conscious projects like Boster's Columbus project often do connect with the most challenging state standards. A bit of work on the teacher's part (or by the students, if given access to the standards) can articulate these connections in a way that most fair-minded administrators, school board members, and parents will appreciate.

At the same time, Boster's project can be shown to connect with professional standards for education, developed by established groups of professionals. Indicating the way a given project "exceeds" state standards by connecting with professional standards is another way of showing the value of the project. Such articulation also allows administrators, school board members, and parents the information they need to do their own critical thinking about the scope of national or statewide standards.

For example, Boster's project connects directly with four of the eleven "Standards for the Assessment of Reading and Writing, Revised Addition" published by the National Council of the Teachers of English in conjunction with the International Reading Association in 2009:

1. The interests of the student are paramount in assessment. . . .
4. Assessment must reflect and allow critical inquiry into curriculum and instruction.
5. Assessment must recognize and reflect the intellectually and socially complex nature of reading and writing and the important roles of school, home, and society in literacy development. . . .

9. Assessment must be based in the local school learning community, including the active and essential participation of families and community members.

Boster's project developed from "student interest" and from "critical inquiry into curriculum." It involved the students working with an array of adults, teachers, and administrators across several schools in Ralston. Afterward, the students and school officials "reflected on the intellectually and socially complex" nature of the literacy events they tried out with the sixth graders. Using these additional professional standards, thus, could allow Mr. Boster to make the case that the project exceeds state standards and provides a potentially better and richer model of student achievement.

Similar connections between this project and more robust standards for education can be made using any of several standards offered by professional societies. Here in Nebraska we have listed several of the most important professional societies' standards for teachers of writing in our "Position Statement on Standards and Assessment," located on our Nebraska Writing Project website (2012). Our hope is that, through such "standard-mapping" activities, teachers can help to educate the many community stakeholders who have a voice in school policy.

Beyond the exercise of connecting standards to place-conscious projects, of course, looms the thorny and important issue of how individual states will test for their state standards. Here in Nebraska, our Nebraska Writing Project teachers and leaders are engaged in discussion, and some lobbying, with the state officials whose job it is to determine the tests. And, as Boster made clear in the last section, we have a responsibility to prepare our students for these tests, whatever they are, and to devote some class time to this task.

What we are advocating for in this afterword, however, is an approach to the work of teaching that recognizes the limited purpose and perspective of the national assessment industry. We are in a strange moment, historically, for teaching. In this age of assessment, we face two teaching tasks: preparing our students, the young people in our classrooms, for the difficult civic work they will face as citizens of their communities and regions, in an ever more complicated world, and helping to educate our community's adults, the many individuals who have a stake and a presence in and around education, about the complex mission we face. Functionally, we are asked to teach at two levels. Place-conscious education provides a mechanism for effective teaching at both levels. For our students, place-conscious education provides a way of connecting them to the civic issues, local publics, and rhetorical action they will need as active citizens, now and in the future. For our community adults, place-conscious education provides an opening for the hard, necessary discussions we need to have, as a culture, about the purpose of education, the purpose of assessment, and the kind of future communities our schools will help create.

Works Cited

Contributors

Works Cited

Ackerman, John, and David Coogan, eds. 2010. *The Public Work of Rhetoric: Citizen-Scholars and Civic Engagement*. Columbia: South Carolina Univ. Press.

Adler-Kassner, Linda, Robert Crooks, and Anne Watters, eds. 1997. *Writing the Community: Concepts and Models for Service-Learning in Composition*. Washington, DC: American Association for Higher Education.

Anderson, Jeff. 2005. *Mechanically Inclined: Building Grammar, Usage, and Style into Writer's Workshop*. Portland, ME: Stenhouse.

"Annual Estimates of Resident Population, Ralston, Nebraska, April 1, 2010 to July 1, 2012." http://factfinder2.census.gov.

Anzaldúa, Gloria. 1999. *Borderlands/La Frontera*. 2nd ed. San Francisco: Aunt Lute.

Au, Wayne. 2014. "Seeing Students as Humans, Not Products: Why Public Schools Should Not Be Run Like Private Businesses." In *The Big Lies of School Reform: Finding Better Solutions for the Future of Public Education*, edited by Paul Gorski and Kristien Zenkov, 143–52. New York: Routledge.

Bailey, Jon M., and Kim Preston. 2011. "Census Brief 1: Population Changes on the Great Plains." Center for Rural Affairs. http://files.cfra.org/pdf/census-brief1-population.pdf.

Battle for Whiteclay. 2013. http://battleforwhiteclay.org.

Beauregard, Robert. 2006. *When America Became Suburban*. Minneapolis: Univ. of Minnesota Press.

Berdan, Kristina, Ian Boulton, Elyse Eidman-Aadahl, Jennie Fleming, Launie Garner, Iana Rogers, and Asali Solomon. 2006. *Writing for a Change: Boosting Literacy and Learning through Social Action*. Somerset, NJ: Jossey-Bass.

Bernabei, Gretchen. 2005. *Reviving the Essay: How to Teach Structure without Formula*. Shoreham, VT: Discover Writing Press.

Berry, Wendell. 1977. *The Unsettling of America: Culture and Agriculture*. San Francisco: Sierra Club Books.

———. 1981. "Solving for Pattern." In *The Gift of Good Land: Further Essays Cultural and Agricultural*, 134–45. San Francisco: North Point Press.

———. 2003a. *The Citizenship Papers*. Washington, DC: Shoemaker and Hoard.

———. 2003b. "Going to Work." In *The Citizenship Papers*, 33–42. Washington, DC: Shoemaker and Hoard.

Bishop, Sharon. 2004. "The Power of Place." *English Journal* 93, no. 6: 65–69.

Bluestein, Adam. 2009. "Best Places to Live." In *Money*. http://money.cnn.com/magazines/moneymag/bplive/2009/top100.

Brand, Stewart. 1996. "About: The Clock and Library Projects." Long Now Foundation. http://longnow.org/about/.

Brooke, Robert, ed. 2003. *Rural Voices: Place-Conscious Education and the Teaching of Writing*. New York and Berkeley, CA: Teachers College Press and National Writing Project.

———. 2006. "Migratory and Regional Identity." In *Identity Papers: Literacy and Power in Higher Education*, edited by Bronwyn Williams, 141–45. Logan: Utah State Univ. Press.

Brooke, Robert, and Jason McIntosh. 2007. "Deep Maps: Teaching Rhetorical Engagement through Place-Conscious Education." In *The Locations of Composition*, edited by Christopher J. Keller and Christian R. Weisser, 131–49. Albany: State Univ. of New York Press.

Bruce, Heather. 2008. "Peace-Building in Indian Country: 'Indian Education for All.'" *Reflections: Writing, Service-Learning, and Community Literacy* 8, no. 1: 214–58.

Burke, Jim. 2010. *What's the Big Idea? Question-Driven Units to Motivate Reading, Writing, and Thinking*. Portsmouth, NH: Heinemann.

Cantrell, Randy. 2006. "Labor Force Implications of Population Decline in Nonmetropolitan Nebraska." *Business in Nebraska* (UNL Bureau of Business Research) 61, no. 684: 1–5.

Carlson, Steve, Hannah Hartman, and Eric Thompson. 2008. "Brain Drain in Nebraska: What Do the Data Show?" *Business in Nebraska* (UNL Bureau of Business Research) 63, no. 692: 1–7.

Carr, Patrick J., and Maria J. Kefalas. 2009. *Hollowing Out the Middle: The Rural Brain Drain and What It Means for America*. Boston: Beacon Press.

Christensen, Linda. 2009a. "Into the World." In *Teaching for Joy and Justice: Re-imagining the Language Arts Classroom*, 259–61. Milwaukee, WI: Rethinking Schools.

———. 2009b. *Teaching for Joy and Justice: Re-imagining the Language Arts Classroom*. Milwaukee, WI: Rethinking Schools.

Cody, Anthony. 2014. "The Common Core: Engine of Inequity." In *The Big Lies of School Reform: Finding Better Solutions for the Future of Public Education*, edited by Paul Gorski and Kristien Zenkov, 31–41. New York: Routledge.

Columbus, Christopher. 2006. "Voices from the Times: The Log of Christopher Columbus." In *The Language of Literature: American Literature*, edited by Arthur Applebee, 67–68. Boston: McDougal Little.

Common Core State Standards Initiative. 2014. http://www.corestandards.org/.

Conference on College Composition and Communication. 2009. "Writing Assessment: A Position Statement." http://www.ncte.org/cccc/resources/positions/writingassessment.

Congress for New Urbanism. "Canons of Sustainable Architecture and Urbanism." http://www.cnu.org/canons.

Conservation International. 2013. http://www.conservation.org/Pages/default.aspx.

Cushman, Ellen. 2006. "Towards a Praxis of New Media." *Reflections* 5, nos. 1–2: 111–32.

Daniels, Harvey, and Nancy Steineke. 2011. *Texts and Lessons for Content-Area Reading: With More than 75 Articles from the "New York Times," "Rolling Stone," the "Washington Post," "Car and Driver," "Chicago Tribune," and Many Others*. Portsmouth, NH: Heinemann.

Deans, Thomas. 2000. *Writing Partnerships: Service-Learning in Composition*. Urbana, IL: National Council of the Teachers of English.

Deloria, Vine. 1999. "Indians Today, the Real and Unreal." In *Native American Literature: An Anthology*, edited by Linda Trout, 7–15. Chicago: National Textbook.

Dewey, John. 1963 [1938]. *Experience and Education*. New York: Collier/Macmillan.

Duany, Andres, Elizabeth Plater-Zyberk, and Jeff Speck. 2000. *Suburban Nation: The Rise of Sprawl and the Decline of the American Dream*. New York: North Point.

Durning, Allen Thein. 1999. "This Place on Earth: Home and the Practice of Permanence." In *At Home on the Earth: Becoming Native to Our Place*, edited by David Landis Barnhill, 256–65. Berkeley: Univ. of California Press.

Eiseley, Loren. 1957. *The Immense Journey*. New York: Random House.

Epp, Roger. 2001. "The Political De-skilling of Rural Communities." In *Writing Off the Rural West: Globalization, Governments and the Transformation of Rural Communities*, edited by Roger Epp and Dave Whitson, 301–24. Edmonton: Univ. of Alberta Press.

FairTest: The National Center for Fair and Open Testing. 2014. "Opting Out." http://www.fairtest.org/get-involved/opting-out.

Farrell, James J. 2010. *The Nature of College: How a New Understanding of Campus Life Can Change the World*. Minneapolis: Milkweed.

Flanagan, Dan. Untitled sermon, presented at Saint Paul's United Methodist Church, Papillion, NE, May 25, 2008.

Flower, Linda. 2003. Foreword to *City Comp: Identities, Spaces, Practices*, edited by Bruce McComiskey and Cynthia Ryan, ix–xii. Albany: State Univ. of New York Press.

———. 2008. *Community Literacy and the Rhetoric of Public Engagement*. Carbondale: Southern Illinois Univ. Press.

Flower, Linda, Elenore Long, and Lorraine Higgins. 2000. *Learning to Rival: A Literate Practice for Intercultural Inquiry*. Hillsdale, NJ: Erlbaum.

Fowler, Eric. 2007a. "The Great Water Debate." *NEBRASKAland*: 16–25.

———. 2007b. "Tapped Out." *NEBRASKAland*: 32–41.

Freire, Paulo. 2000. *Pedagogy of the Oppressed*. Translated by Myra Bergman Ramos. New York: Continuum.

Gallagher, Kelly. 2011. *Write Like This: Teaching Real-World Writing through Modeling and Mentor Texts*. Portland, ME: Stenhouse.

Garreau, Joel. 1991. *Edge City: Life on the New Frontier*. New York: Anchor Books.

Goddard, Joseph. 2012. *Being American on the Edge: Penurbia and the Metropolitan Mind, 1945–2010*. New York: Palgrave Macmillan.

Goldberg, Natalie. 1986. *Writing Down the Bones: Freeing the Writer Within*. Boston: Shambhala.

Gorski, Paul. 2014. "Poverty, Economic Inequality, and the Impossible Promise of School Reform." In *The Big Lies of School Reform: Finding Better Solutions for the Future of Public Education*, edited by Paul Gorski and Kristien Zenkov, 129–41. New York: Routledge.

Gorski, Paul, and Kristien Zenkov, eds. 2014. *The Big Lies of School Reform: Finding Better Solutions for the Future of Public Education*. New York: Routledge.

Great Platte River Road Archway Monument. n.d. http://www.archway.org/.

Greenwood, David A. 2011. “Why Place Matters.” In *Handbook of Research in the Social Foundations of Education*, edited by Steven Tozer et al., 632. New York: Routledge.

Groves, Robert. 2011. “Rural and Suburban America: When One Definition Is Not Enough.” *United States Census Bureau Director's Blog, 8/2/2011.* http://directorsblog.blogs.census.gov/2011/08/02/rural-andsuburban-america-when-one-definition-is-not-enough/.

Gruchow, Paul. 1995. *Grassroots: The Universe of Home*. Minneapolis: Milkweed.

Gruenewald, David A. 2003. “The Best of Both Worlds: A Critical Pedagogy of Place.” *Educational Researcher* 32, no. 4: 3–12. doi: 10.3102/0013189X032004003.

Gruenewald, David A., and Gregory A. Smith, eds. 2008. *Place-Based Education in the Global Age: Local Diversity*. New York: Lawrence Erlbaum Associates, Taylor & Francis Group.

Haas, Toni, and Paul Nachtigal. 1998. *Place Value: An Educator's Guide to Good Literature on Rural Lifeways, Environments, and Purposes of Education*. Charleston, WV: ERIC Clearinghouse on Rural Education and Small Schools.

Hansen, Twyla. 1992. “Scars.” In *How to Live in the Heartland*, 25. Lincoln, NE: Flatwater.

———. 2003. *Potato Soup*. Omaha, NE: Backwaters Press.

Hayduk, Ronald. 2003. “Race and Suburban Sprawl: Regionalism and Structural Racism.” In *Suburban Sprawl: Culture, Theory, and Politics*, edited by Matthew Lindstrom and Hugh Bartling, 137–70. Lanham, MD: Rowman and Littlefield.

Heath, Shirley Brice, and Milbrey McLaughlin, eds. 1993. *Identity and Inner-City Youth: Beyond Ethnicity and Gender*. New York: Teachers College Press.

Heath, Shirley Brice, and Laura Smyth. 1999. *ArtShow: Youth and Community Development*. Washington, DC: Partners for Livable Communities.

Higgins, Lorraine, and Lisa Brush. 2006. “Personal Experience Narrative and Public Debate: Writing the Wrongs of Welfare.” *College Composition and Communication* 57, no. 4: 694–729.

Hillocks, George, Jr. 2011. *Teaching Argument Writing, Grades 6–12: Supporting Claims with Relevant Evidence and Clear Reasoning*. Portsmouth, NH: Heinemann.

Hothem, Thomas. 2009. “Suburban Studies and College Writing: Applying Ecocomposition.” *Pedagogy* 9, no. 1: 35–59.

Hull, Glynda, and Michael James. 2007. "Geographies of Hope: A Study of Urban Landscape and a University-Community Collaborative." In *Blurring Boundaries: Developing Writers, Researchers, and Teachers; A Tribute to William L. Smith*, edited by Peggy O'Neill, 255–89. Cresskill, NJ: Hampton.

Hursh, David. 2007. "Assessing 'No Child Left Behind' and the Rise of Neoliberal Education Policies." *American Educational Research Journal* 44, no. 3: 493–518.

International Society of Technology Educators. 2014. "Standards for Students." http://www.iste.org/standards/standards-for-students.

Jackson, Wes. 2010. *Consulting the Genius of the Place: An Ecological Approach to a New Agriculture*. Berkeley, CA: Counterpoint.

Johnsgard, Paul. 1986. *Those of the Grey Wind: The Sandhill Cranes*. Lincoln: Univ. of Nebraska Press.

Johnson, Kurt. 2011a. "Aurora 'Proactive' in Growing Non-farm Jobs." *Aurora (NE) News Register*, Apr. 13.

———. 2011b. "Economic Data Often an 'Eye-Opener.'" *Aurora (NE) News Register*, Mar. 9.

———. 2011c. "Long-Term Growth Strategy Paying Off." *Aurora (NE) News Register*, Apr. 27.

———. 2011d. "What Do Economic Trends Say about Life in Hamilton County?" *Aurora (NE) News Register*, Mar. 2.

Journey for Justice Alliance. 2014. http://www.j4jalliance.com/.

Juneau, Denise, and Mandy S. Broaddus. 2006. "And Still the Waters Flow: the Legacy of Indian Education in Montana." *Phi Delta Kappan* 88, no. 3: 193–97.

Kilborn, Peter. 2009. *Next Stop, Reloville: Life Inside America's New Rootless Professional Class*. New York: Times Books.

Knopp, Lisa. 1996. *Field of Vision*. Iowa City: Univ. of Iowa Press.

Kooser, Ted. 2005. *Flying at Night: Poems, 1965–1985*. Pittsburgh: Univ. of Pittsburgh Press.

Kunstler, James Howard. 1993. *The Geography of Nowhere: The Rise and Decline of America's Manmade Landscapes*. New York: Touchstone.

———. 2001. *The City in Mind: Notes on the Urban Condition*. New York: Free Press.

Kuzelka, Robert, and Charles Flowerday. 1993. *Flat Water: A History of Nebraska and Its Water*. Lincoln: Univ. of Nebraska Press.

Lane-Zucker, Laurie. 2004. Foreword to *Place-Based Education: Connecting Classrooms and Communities*, by David Sobel, i–iv. Great Barrington, MA: Orion Society.

Lang, Robert. 2003. *Edgeless Cities: Exploring the Elusive Metropolis.* Washington, DC: Brookings Institution Press.

Langdon, Philip. 1994. *A Better Place to Live: Reshaping the American Suburb.* Amherst: Univ. of Massachusetts Press.

La Vista, Nebraska. n.d. http://www.cityoflavista.org/.

Learning Community of Douglas and Sarpy Counties. n.d. http://www.learningcommunityds.org/about.

Leopold, Aldo. 1949. *A Sand County Almanac and Sketches Here and There.* New York: Oxford Univ. Press.

———. 1992. *The River of the Mother of God, and Other Essays.* Madison: Univ. of Wisconsin Press.

Leopold Education Center. n.d. http://www.aldoleopold.org/.

Leopold Education Project. n.d. http://www.aldoleopold.org/programs/lep.shtml.

Lindstrom, Matthew, and Hugh Bartling. 2003. *Suburban Sprawl: Culture, Theory, and Politics.* Lanham, MD: Rowman and Littlefield.

Long Now Foundation. 1996. "About." http://longnow.org/about/.

Louth, Richard. 2011. "The New Orleans Writing Marathon." In *The Writing Marathon: "In Good Company Revealed,"* edited by Richard Louth, 1–13. Hammond: Southeastern Louisiana Writing Project.

Louv, Richard. 2008. *Last Child in the Woods: Saving Our Children from Nature-Deficit Disorder.* Chapel Hill, NC: Algonquin Books.

Lucy, William, and David Phillips. 2000. *Confronting Suburban Decline: Strategic Planning for Metropolitan Renewal.* Washington, DC: Island Press.

Manley, Robert. 1993. "Land and Water in 19th Century Nebraska." In *Flat Water: A History of Nebraska and Its Water,* edited by Robert Kuzelka and Charles Flowerday, 9–31. Lincoln: Univ. of Nebraska Press.

Mathieu, Paula. 2005. *Tactics of Hope: The Public Turn in English Composition.* Portsmouth, NH: Boynton/Cook.

McComiskey, Bruce, and Cynthia Ryan, eds. 2003. *City Comp: Identities, Spaces, Practices.* Albany: State Univ. of New York Press.

McKibben, Bill. 2010. *Eaarth: Making a Life on a Tough New Planet.* New York: Times Books.

National Audubon Society. 2013. "Crane Viewing at Iain Nicolson Audubon Center at Rowe Sanctuary." http://rowe.audubon.org/.

National Council of the Teachers of English. 2013. "NCTE Framework for 21st Century Curriculum and Assessment." http://www.ncte.org/positions/statements/21stcentframework.

National Council of the Teachers of English/International Reading Association. 2009. "Standards for the Assessment of Reading and Writing, Revised Edition." http://www.ncte.org/standards/assessmentstandards.

National Park Service. 2013. "Murdoch Site/Mormon Pioneer Trail." http://www.nps.gov/mopi/planyourvisit/site6.htm.

National Writing Project. 2003. *Because Writing Matters.* San Francisco: Jossey-Bass.

Nebraska Department of Education. 2014. "English/Language Arts Standards." http://www.education.ne.gov/read/PDF/2014_Updated_ELA_Standards_Vertical_Version_k_12.pdf.

Nebraska Educational Television. 2012 [2007]. "The Price of Water." http://www.netnebraska.org/basic-page/television/price-water.

Nebraska Natural Resources District. n.d. http://www.nrdnet.org/.

Nebraska State Board of Education. 2009. "Nebraska Language Arts Standards." http://nlcs1.nlc.state.ne.us/epubs/E2000/R059-2009.pdf.

Nebraska Statewide Arboretum. 2013. "Sustainable Landscapes for Healthy Homes and Communities." http://arboretum.unl.edu/.

Nebraska Writing Project. 2012. "Nebraska Writing Project Advisory Board Position Statement on Standards and Assessment." http://www.unl.edu/newp/policy-statement-standards-and-assessment.

Ngozi Adichie, Chimamanda. 2009. "The Danger of a Single Story." TED Talk. http://www.ted.com/talks/chimamanda_adichie_the_danger_of_a_single_story?language=en.

Nowacek, Rebecca S. 2011. *Agents of Integration: Understanding Transfer as a Rhetorical Act.* Carbondale: Southern Illinois Univ. Press.

Overhue, Jenny. 2010. *Economic and Demographic Trends: Aurora, Hamilton County and the Surrounding Area.* Columbus: Nebraska Public Power District.

Owens, Derek. 2001. *Composition and Sustainability: Teaching for a Threatened Generation.* Urbana, IL: National Council of Teachers of English.

Papillion, Nebraska. n.d. http://www.papillion.org/.

Pheasants Forever. n.d. http://pheasantsforever.org/.

Pipher, Mary. 2007. *Writing to Change the World.* New York: Berkeley/Penguin.

"Poetry of Place." n.d. Nebraska Writing Project. http://www.unl.edu/newp/poetry-place.

Powell, Douglas Reicheart, and John Paul Tassoni, eds. 2009. *Composing Other Spaces.* Cresskill, NJ: Hampton.

Pratt, Mary Louise. 1991. "Arts of the Contact Zone." *Profession* 91: 33–40.

Ravitch, Diane. 2013. *Reign of Error: The Hoax of the Privatization Movement and the Danger to America's Public Schools.* New York: Alfred A. Knopf.

Renée, Michelle, and Tina Trujillo. 2014. "The Trouble with Federal Turnaround Policies and Their Impact on Low-Scoring Schools." In *The Big Lies of School Reform: Finding Better Solutions for the Future of Public Education*, edited by Paul Gorski and Kristien Zenkov, 153–68. New York: Routledge.

Reynolds, Nedra. 2004. *Geographies of Writing: Inhabiting Places and Encountering Difference.* Carbondale: Southern Illinois Univ. Press.

Rich, Adrienne. 1972. "Teaching Language in Open Admissions." In *On Lies, Secrets, and Silence: Selected Prose, 1966–78*, 51–68. New York: W. W. Norton.

Robbins, Sarah, and Mimi Dyer, eds. 2005. *Writing America: Classroom Literacy and Public Engagement.* New York: Teachers College Press.

Robinson, Jay. 1990. *Conversations on the Written Word.* Portsmouth, NH: Boynton/Cook.

Rose, Shirley, and Irwin Weiser, eds. 2010. *Going Public: What Writing Programs Learn from Engagement.* Logan: Utah State Univ. Press.

Ross, Carolyn. 1995. *Writing Nature: An Ecological Reader for Writers.* New York: St. Martin's.

Rousculp, Tiffany. 2006. "When the Community Writes: Reenvisioning the SLCC DiverseCity Writing Series." *Reflections* 5: 67–88.

Rural School and Community Trust. n.d. "Place Based Forum." http://www.cmi.ruraledu.org/place-based-forum.

Sanders, Scott Russell. 1994. *Staying Put: Making a Home in a Restless World.* Boston: Beacon.

Savage, Lydia, and Mark Lapping. 2003. "Sprawl and Its Discontents: The Rural Dimension." In *Suburban Sprawl: Culture, Theory, and Politics*, edited by Matthew Lindstrom and Hugh Bartling, 5–17. Lanham, MD: Rowan and Littlefield.

Seitz, David. 2004. *Who Can Afford Critical Consciousness? Practicing a Pedagogy of Humility.* Cresskill, NJ: Hampton Press.

Silko, Leslie M. 1986. *Ceremony.* New York: Penguin Books.

Sinor, Jennifer. 2011. "Writing Place." In *Placing the Academy: Essays on Landscape, Work, and Identity*, edited by Jennifer Sinor and Rona Kaufman, 3–24. Logan: Utah State Univ. Press.

Smart Growth Network. 2013. "Smart Growth Online." http://www.smartgrowth.org.

Sobel, David. 2004. *Place-Based Education: Connecting Classrooms and Communities*. Great Barrington, MA: Orion Society.

Somerville, Margaret, Kerith Power, and Phoenix de Carteret. 2009. *Landscapes and Learning: Place Studies for a Global World*. Rotterdam: Sense.

Starnes, Bobby Ann, Angela Carone, and Cynthia Paris. 1999. *From Thinking to Doing: Constructing a Framework to Teach Mandates through Experience-Based Learning*. Mountain City, GA: Foxfire Fund.

Stone, Michael K. 2010. "A Schooling for Sustainability Framework." *Teacher Education Quarterly* 37, no. 4: 33–46.

Stuhr Museum. n.d. Stuhr Museum of the Prairie Pioneer. http://www.stuhrmuseum.org/.

Teaford, Jon. 2006. *The Metropolitan Revolution: The Rise of Post-urban America*. New York: Columbia Univ. Press.

———. 2008. *The American Suburb: The Basics*. New York: Routledge.

Theobald, Paul. 1997. *Teaching the Commons: Place, Pride, and the Renewal of Community*. Boulder, CO: Westview.

Tolbert, Linda, and Paul Theobald. 2005. "Finding Their Place in the Community: Urban Education Outside the Classroom." *Childhood Education* 82, no. 5: 271.

Trout, Lawana. 1999. *Native American Literature: An Anthology*. Lincolnwood, IL: NTC.

Tuan, Yi-Fu. 1977. *Space and Place: The Perspective of Experience*. Minneapolis: Univ. of Minnesota Press.

US Census Bureau. 2012. "State and County QuickFacts." http://quickfacts.census.gov/qfd/index.html.

Van Camp, Richard. 2004. *The Lesser Blessed*. Vancouver, BC: Douglas and Molntyre.

Vivian, Robert. 2007. "Hereafter in Fields." In *The Big Empty: Contemporary Nebraska Nonfiction Writers*, edited by Ladette Randolph and Nina Shevchuk-Murray, 56–61. Lincoln: Univ. of Nebraska Press.

Wardle, Elizabeth. 2007. "Understanding 'Transfer' from FYC: Preliminary Results of a Longitudinal Study." *WPA: Writing Program Administration* 31, nos. 1–2: 65–85. http://wpacouncil.org/archives/31n1-2/31n1-2wardle.pdf.

Watershed Information Network/Environmental Protection Agency. 2013. http://www.franklinccd.org/EPA%20%20Watershed%20Information%20Network%20Homepage.htm. Watershed questions redirected Aug. 14, 2013, to the

EPA's Watershed Academy, http://water.epa.gov/learn/training/wacademy/index.cfm.

Weisser, Christian, and Sidney Dobrin. 2001. *Ecocomposition: Theoretical and Pedagogical Approaches.* Albany: State Univ. of New York Press.

Welch, Don. 1992. *The Platte River: Poems.* Kearney, NE: Welch Kearney Press.

Welch, Nancy. 2005. "Living Room: Teaching Public Writing in a Post-publicity Era." *College Composition and Communication* 56, no. 3: 470–92.

———. 2008. *Living Room: Teaching Public Writing in a Privatized World.* Portsmouth, NH: Boynton/Cook.

Winter, Dave, and Sarah Robbins. 2005. *Writing Our Communities: Local Learning and Public Culture.* Urbana, IL: National Council of Teachers of English.

Woodward, Ashley. 2005. "Jean-François Lyotard (1924–1998)." In *Internet Encyclopedia of Philosophy,* edited by J. Fieser and B. Dowden. http://www.iep.utm.edu/lyotard.htm.

Zencey, Eric. 1996. "The Rootless Professors." In *Rooted in the Land: Essays on Community and Place,* edited by William Vitek and Wes Jackson, 15–19. New Haven, CT: Yale Univ. Press.

Zenkov, Kristien. 2014. "Lying about Teachers and Their Training." In *The Big Lies of School Reform: Finding Better Solutions for the Future of Public Education,* edited by Paul Gorski and Kristien Zenkov, 79–92. New York: Routledge.

Zinn, Howard. 1980. *A People's History of the United States, 1492–Present.* New York: HarperCollins.

Zukin, Sharon. 2010. *Naked City: The Death and Life of Authentic Urban Spaces.* New York: Oxford Univ. Press.

Contributors

Mary Birky Collier teaches English at Papillion–La Vista High School in suburban Omaha, Nebraska. She has also taught as an adjunct instructor at Nebraska Wesleyan University, Grace University, Doane College, and Metropolitan Community College. She has worked with the Nebraska Writing Project since 2004, serving as high school facilitator for Embedded Institutes, on the Advisory Board, and as codirector.

Sharon Bishop recently retired after more than thirty years of high school teaching at Heartland Community Schools: Henderson/Bradshaw. She has received a Kiewit Excellence in Education Award and a Foxfire Exemplary Classroom Award and was inducted into the Nebraska Language Arts Educators Hall of Fame in 2012. She has published articles on her teaching in *English Journal*, *Rural Voices*, and *Literacy Teaching and Learning in Rural Communities*. She has been a leader in the Nebraska Writing Project since 1997, serving as Rural Institute facilitator, as codirector, and as invited speaker at several National Writing Project events. She currently serves on the Nebraska Writing Project Advisory Board.

Daniel Boster is an English teacher and instructional coach at Ralston High School. He has a BA from the University of Texas and an MA from the University of Wisconsin–Eau Claire, and he recently completed a PhD in rhetoric and composition at the University of Nebraska–Lincoln. He has served in leadership positions and facilitated institutes for the Nebraska Writing Project since 2007. He is the editor of *What Teaching Means: Stories from America's Classrooms* (2012).

Robert E. Brooke is a professor of English at the University of Nebraska–Lincoln. He has served as the director of the Nebraska Writing Project since 1984. He has published five books and more than fifty articles on the teaching of writing, including *Rural Voices: Place-Conscious Education and the Teaching of Writing* and the Braddock Award article "Underlife and Writing Instruction."

Cathie English is an assistant professor of English and codirector of the Ozarks Writing Project at Missouri State University. She teaches secondary and middle school English methods courses and graduate courses focused upon teacher leadership, literacy, and place-conscious pedagogy. She also coordinates professional development efforts in rural schools related to the teaching of argument writing. She has served in several capacities for the National Writing Project, including leadership roles in technology, new sites, and professional writing. She formerly taught secondary education for twenty-one years in rural Nebraska, where she was also associated with the work of the Nebraska Writing Project.

Jeff Lacey teaches English at Ralston High School in Omaha, Nebraska, where he sponsors the environmental club and is the codirector of the Metro Area High School Poetry Festival. He is the official deadline poet for the *Bellevue Leader*, and his poetry has been published in the *Hiram Review*, *Measures*, *Great Plains Quarterly*, and, most recently, *Voices for Equity and Diversity in Education: A Literary Anthology*.

Susan Martens is an assistant professor of English and director of the Prairie Lands Writing Project at Missouri Western State University. Before earning her PhD, she taught high school English for twelve years in Arlington, Nebraska. Her work has appeared in *College Composition and Communication*, *Louisiana Literature*, *English Journal*, and in the Rogue Faculty Press collection *What Teaching Means: Stories from America's Classrooms*.

Bernice Olivas is a graduate teaching assistant at the University of Nebraska–Lincoln. She received her MA in 2012. She works as a writing consultant for the Boise State McNair Scholars program and is part of the Writing Lincoln Initiative.

Aubrey Streit Krug is a graduate teaching assistant at the University of Nebraska–Lincoln, where she is pursuing her PhD in English. Her research focuses on literature and the environment, especially on the Great Plains, and she is a graduate fellow at UNL's Center for Great Plains Studies. She has also served as an associate coordinator of composition for UNL's English Department. Her essays have been published in the *Journal of Ecocriticism*, *Writing on the Edge*, and the collection *Plants and Literature*.

Left to right as pictured: Aubrey Streit Krug, Robert E. Brooke, Susan Martens, Sharon Bishop, Mary Birky Collier, Cathie English, Bernice Olivas, and Daniel Boster. *Not pictured*: Jeff Lacey. Photograph courtesy of Kate Brooke.